MEXICO'S RESILIENT
JOURNALISTS

REUTERS INSTITUTE GLOBAL JOURNALISM SERIES

REUTERS INSTITUTE GLOBAL JOURNALISM SERIES

Series Editors: Rasmus Kleis Nielsen and the Reuters Institute for the Study of Journalism

Reuters Institute for the Study of Journalism, Steering Committee
Alan Rusbridger, editor, *Prospect Magazine*
Prof. Wale Adebanwi, Presidential Penn Compact Professor of Africana Studies, University of Pennsylvania
Sir Michael Dixon, principal, Green Templeton College, Oxford
Dr. Richard Fletcher, director of research, RISJ, Oxford
Prof. Timothy Garton Ash, professor of European studies, St Antony's College, Oxford
Prof. Jane Green, professor of political science and British politics, Nuffield College, Oxford
Kate Hanneford-Smith, director of operations, RISJ, Oxford
Helen Lewis, journalist, *The Atlantic*
Geert Linnebank, trustee of the Thomson Reuters Foundation
Mitali Mukherjee, director, Journalist Programmes, RISJ, Oxford
Prof. Gina Neff, executive director of the Minderoo Centre for Technology and Democracy, University of Cambridge, and professor of technology and society, Oxford
Prof. Rasmus Kleis Nielsen, director, RISJ, and professor of political communication, Oxford
Prof. Nicholas Owen, joint head of the Department of Politics and International Relations, Oxford
Prof. Kate O'Regan, director, Bonavero Institute of Human Rights, Faculty of Law, Oxford
John Pullman, global head, video and pictures, Reuters
Eduardo Suárez, head of editorial, RISJ, Oxford
Nina Tomlin, head of administration and finance, Department of Politics and International Relations, Oxford
Antonio Zappulla, CEO, Thomson Reuters Foundation

Matthew Powers, *NGOs as Newsmakers: The Changing Landscape of International News*
Thomas Hanitzsch, Arnold S. de Beer, Folker Hanusch, and Jyotika Ramaprasad, *Worlds of Journalism: Journalistic Cultures Around the Globe*
Benjamin Toff, Ruth Palmer, and Rasmus Kleis Nielsen, *Avoiding the News: Reluctant Audiences for Journalism*

For a complete list of books in this series, see the Columbia University Press website.

JULIETA BRAMBILA

MEXICO'S RESILIENT JOURNALISTS

How Reporters Manage Risk
and Cope with Violence

Columbia University Press / *New York*

Columbia University Press
Publishers Since 1893
New York   Chichester, West Sussex
cup.columbia.edu
Copyright © 2024 Columbia University Press
All rights reserved

Library of Congress Cataloging-in-Publication Data
Names: Brambila, Julieta, 1986– author.
Title: Mexico's resilient journalists : how reporters manage risk and cope with violence / Julieta Brambila.
Description: New York : Columbia University Press, 2024. | Series: Reuters Institute global journalism series | Includes bibliographical references and index.
Identifiers: LCCN 2024009414 | ISBN 9780231201308 (hardback) | ISBN 9780231201315 (trade paperback) | ISBN 9780231554039 (ebook)
Subjects: LCSH: Journalists—Violence against—Mexico. | Journalists—Crimes against—Mexico. | Reporters and reporting—Mexico. | Journalism—Mexico.
Classification: LCC PN4974.V56 B73 2024 | DDC 079.72—dc23/eng/20240306

Cover design: Noah Arlow
Cover image: Shutterstock (pen)

*To my parents,
Alejandra and Francisco,
for your light, love,
and encouragement*

CONTENTS

Preface ix

Acknowledgments xi

Introduction: "Outrage Brought Us Together"   1

PART I
WHAT'S GOING ON HERE?

1 Why Has It Become So Easy to Kill Journalists?   31

2 The Wave of Violence Against the Press   61

3 Violent Censors   91

CONTENTS

PART II
HOW DO JOURNALISTS PERSEVERE?

4 Strategies for Autonomous Safety 115

5 Strategies for Resistance 149

Conclusion 187

Appendix I. Glossary of Translated Terms 215

Appendix II. Study Design 221

Appendix III. List of Interviews 227

Appendix IV. Time Line 233

Notes 235

Bibliography 267

Index 285

PREFACE

Public humiliation, online harassment, political intimidation, dismissal, surveillance, imprisonment, and murder: these are all aspects of the recent massive assault on press freedom and journalistic autonomy around the world. Yet even within this trend, Mexico stands out in the Western Hemisphere as the most dangerous country for journalists. However, although the work of Mexican journalists has become more visible, precarious, and dangerous, so too has it become more necessary. Consider the words of crime-beat journalist from *El Diario de Juárez* in Ciudad Juarez, Chihuahua, whose friend, an experienced crime-beat reporter, was shot dead outside his own home seven years ago: "Of course we're all afraid, of course we're all frightened, but we have always felt that quitting journalism is the worst thing that can happen to you, and that includes the death of your colleagues."

This journalist's adamant refusal to back down shows that Mexico's historic rise in bloodshed is not the whole story. What this book reveals is that the violence of the last two decades was responded to—just as the reporter explained—by a major reconfiguration within the field of journalism. A small, strategic, and influential group of critical journalists whom I classify as resilient newsmakers has driven this transformation.

Resilient newsmakers have innovated strategies and mechanisms in response to this adverse environment. They have done so while continuing to report and publish the most relevant and challenging stories: those involving corruption, abuse of power, public security, and human rights. But they have also done so to protest—often shoulder to shoulder with other civic allies—the arbitrary violence, assaults, and censorship they face. This new role for journalists, of course, has not been a smooth transition, but rather a process of pain, learning, self-awareness, and empathy. Yet all of these hardships have allowed resilient newsmakers to form coalitions with like-minded colleagues and civic allies by redefining their professional values and practices, rethinking their surroundings, including their own newsrooms, and reassessing their role as one of public service.

Hence, this book must explore the state of violence and risk in which these journalists live and work. But, even more importantly, it must also reveal the ways these strategic journalists have succeeded in navigating the turbulent waters from which it is their duty to report.

ACKNOWLEDGMENTS

I would like to express my deepest gratitude to my loved ones, especially my parents, Alejandra and Francisco, and my brother, Juan Carlos, who have granted me their unconditional love, comprehension, and support during each of my personal and professional adventures. This book, as well as all that I have achieved, has been because of this and thanks to them. Thank you for so much, thank you for everything. Likewise, the strength to finish this book was enhanced by the encouragement, love, and happiness provided by my dear Fer, who accompanied me and endowed me with comfort and strength whenever this project and its vicissitudes made me doubt that it would ever come to pass. Thank you for encouraging me and for always being by my side, my love. Friendship and companion play no less role than love and caring in life. I would also like to thank my dearest friend, Liz, who has been a source of inspiration and support thought the making process of this book. Thank you, Liz, for listening to me and advising me in all phases of this project. I am very lucky: you are the best friend everyone dreams of having.

That said, my greatest debt is to the more than seventy-nine persons who generously granted me their time and attention to discuss the challenges

ACKNOWLEDGMENTS

of their profession. I am especially grateful to those newsmakers who reopened their wounds and shared their memories, impressions, and fears with the sole objective of relating in the first person what it means to practice journalism in the wilder regions of Mexico. Their testimonials have not only enlightened my work but have also taught me so much about adversity, resistance, and perseverance. Their voices and testimonies guided every page of this book. Thank you always, for what you have already given and for what your work continues to contribute to our society.

Over the years, my research has greatly benefited from the support, advice, and guidance of a network of colleagues who have backed my endeavors. I am grateful to Professor Sallie Hughes of the University of Miami for her continued and decisive support throughout my professional career. Since I began to read her work over fifteen years ago, Sallie has been a source of inspiration for conducting rigorous research that helped spearhead the academic conversation without lessening the social impact of its agenda. In recent years, I have had the good fortune to be able to rely on her advice and friendship while collaborating with her and, indeed, continuing to learn from one of the greatest scholars of contemporary journalism.

The idea for this book emerged in 2017, when Professor Rasmus Klein Nielsen invited me to send a manuscript to Columbia University Press after I completed a research seminar at the Reuters Institute for the Study of Journalism at Oxford University. What seemed at first a rather adventurous and overwhelming idea became one of the greatest challenges and satisfactions of my professional career. His confidence and inspiration, as well as his support during the more challenging moments, have helped make this book possible.

The book's design was outlined under the guidance of Professor Barbie Zelizer during a research residence in 2018 at the Center for Media at Risk of the Annenberg School for Communication at the University of Pennsylvania. Thank you, Barbie, for taking me in that summer, for your generosity and advice, and for helping me build the foundations of this book.

At Columbia University Press, I am grateful for the patience, follow-up, and commitment of my editor, Philip Leventhal, who, since the summer

ACKNOWLEDGMENTS

of 2020, has provided continuity to this project and always, with immense dedication, brought its publication to safe harbor. I would also like to thank the entire CUP team that made *Mexico's Resilient Journalists* possible. You're the best.

I would also like to thank those who contributed their knowledge and dedication to this project: Tanya Huntington, for her determination in maintaining the fidelity of this work beyond all language barriers, for her sagacious translation, and for enriching in diverse ways the manuscript and its style; Benjamin Platt, for getting the best out of the text and honing a more direct, powerful, and persuasive prose; Violeta Santiago, for her devotion, rigorousness, and creativity in attending to the words and details of this book; and Carlos Morales, for his help, dedication, and engagement with this project.

The main arguments and ideas presented here were nourished by generous and ongoing exchanges with brilliant people such as Professor Dan Hallin of the University of San Diego, Professor John Nerone of the University of Chicago, and Professor Sergio Aguayo of El Colegio de México. They kindly read my manuscript and offered enriching comments and enlightening suggestions that, together with their wisdom and patience, provided this book with great substance and clarity. My thanks to each and every one of you. You have inspired me in different ways and stimulated my academic career over all these years.

The feedback of an anonymous reviewer at Columbia University Press also enriched my manuscript. I would like to thank that individual for their time and effort and the interest taken in my work, as well as for their detailed commentary, which strengthened this book. Additionally, I benefited from the advice, attentive ear, and feedback of extraordinary scholars like Matthew Powers, Benjamin Smith, Mireya Márquez, and Mariana Sánchez. Of course, this book also owes much to the many investigations conducted and published in Mexico and elsewhere over the past decade regarding the resistance of journalism in adverse, repressive, and even violent surroundings. My thanks to the authors of these works.

This book began as a doctoral dissertation at the universities of Sheffield and Leeds in the United Kingdom, sponsored by a grant from

ACKNOWLEDGMENTS

Mexico's Consejo Nacional de Ciencia y Tecnología. Upon my arrival in northern England in fall 2013, Professor Jairo Lugo-Ocando guided me fluidly and affectionately through the waters of British academia, as well as my own research and path in life. At the University of Leeds, the advice and inspiration of Professor Katrin Voltmer played a decisive role in ensuring the clarity and explicative power of my work. *Mexico's Resilient Journalists* would not exist without their support, for which I am immensely grateful.

I am also grateful for the warmth and encouragement of Professor Jackie Harrison at the University of Sheffield. She invited me to participate in a research project that turned out to be critical to defining my research agenda and, of course, had a determining influence on the focus of this book. In the distant heavens, I am grateful to the late Professor Jay Blumler at the University of Leeds, with whom I had the weekly privilege of sharing the ideas that sustain this book, and who always gave me sage advice seasoned with good humor. Thanks to Jay, I was able to finally find my own strategy of resistance and dodge many adversities.

Books like this one represent a collective effort, comprising dozens of testimonials, memories, and interpretations, not to mention research and imagination, as well as passion, dedication, reflection, and feedback that transcend time and space. They are born of the solitude of reflection, enriched by conversation, and finally assembled through self-awareness and criticism. Nonetheless, no matter how collective, the responsibility for articulating an honest and persuasive narrative fall solely on the author's shoulders, as do any simplifications or omissions.

INTRODUCTION

"Outrage Brought Us Together"

On February 15, 2014, a group of sixteen resilient newsmakers—journalists and activists who defend freedom of expression—left Mexico City on a quest. Their mission was so dangerous it bordered on recklessness: they sought to unravel what really happened to Gregorio Jiménez de la Cruz, a 43-year-old crime-beat journalist who had been abducted and murdered just ten days earlier.

Their destination was equally dangerous: Villa Allende, five hundred kilometers southeast of the nation's capital, in the city of Coatzacoalcos in Veracruz State. The third most populated state in the country, Veracruz, was governed at the time by a politician who abused his power, Javier Duarte, who was allegedly in collusion with criminal organizations. In Veracruz, abductions, extortions, robberies, disappearances, and violent confrontations became commonplace from 2009 to 2014, exacerbated by confrontations between corrupt local government forces and multiple organized crime cells. During Duarte's tenure as governor (2010–2016), an astonishing nineteen journalists disappeared or were murdered, far more than any other state of Mexico.

INTRODUCTION

"On our way to Coatzacoalcos, we had an argument: 'Why were we going there?'" recalled a member of this special mission, long-form journalist Emiliano Ruiz Parra (aged 38). "We decided to split into several teams and make as much headway as possible in a limited amount of time: We spoke to sixty communicators, people from Gregorio's family, and the district attorney assigned to the case. We also gained access to the file.... The team could cover all of these activities within a seventy-two-hour period."[1] As another eagle-eyed investigative reporter told me, "We were determined to piece together what had happened."[2]

Stocky and with a well-groomed mustache, Jiménez de la Cruz got his start in journalism through his passion for photography, an art he first practiced by documenting social events such as weddings and baptisms. Later, after local media recruited him, Jiménez de la Cruz used his camera to document disturbances and disputes, as well as violent, bloody incidents in his community. Next, he learned to write news articles empirically as a contributor reporting from Villa Allende for media such as *Liberal del Sur*, *En la Red*, and *Notisur*.

Like most local journalists in Mexico, Jiménez de la Cruz practiced his trade despite acute job insecurity. His earnings of US$175 a month were only slightly higher than the average minimum wage. Like many other hyperlocal journalists, such financial hardship pushed him to embrace a perverse logic of morbidity and risk. He covered the bloodiest news because it was the best paid. But he did so without the benefit of a fixed salary and health care, much less the training to carry out high-risk news coverage.

Jiménez de la Cruz was overwhelmed by how crime had consumed Villa Allende in recent years. And so, in response, the journalist dedicated himself to documenting the community's increasingly violent robberies, score settling between criminal cells and local businesspeople or union leaders, and thriving kidnapping industry.[3] He confronted this task by practicing a journalism in which, all too frequently, the borders between news and opinion were erased. And although he sometimes used a pseudonym—"El Pantera" (The Panther)—many of Jiménez de la Cruz's articles carried his byline. In a community of just twenty thousand, identifying himself made the journalist an easy target. Daniela Pastrana—an investigative journalist

INTRODUCTION

and author specializing in human rights, cofounder of the collective Periodistas de a Pie, and one of the principal backers of the special mission to Villa Allende following Jiménez de la Cruz's murder—told me, "His death was convenient to a lot of people."[4]

On the morning of February 5, five heavily armed men entered Jiménez de la Cruz's home. There was no question that he was the one they were after nor why he was their target: upon entering the house, the men shouted, "He's the photographer!"[5]

That same day, news of the journalist's kidnapping broke on local journalism chat groups. At first, there was hope that Jiménez de la Cruz could be found alive, and so, initially, the kidnapping galvanized the local, regional, and national journalism trade as never before. Groups of civic-minded journalists broke their silence to demand justice, both on the streets—marching in cities like Coatzacoalcos and Xalapa, the state capital of Veracruz, as well as Mexico City—and on social networks, using hashtags like #QueremosaGoyoVivo (#WeWantGoyoAlive), #LoQueremosVivo (#WeWantHimAlive), and #DóndeEstáGoyo (#WhereIsGregorio).

As noted in the preface, this unprecedented reaction did not occur in a void. The arrival of the new millennium saw a disproportionate spike in attacks on the press, but this, in turn, generated several years of mobilization cycles and protests to end such violence. Several national networks, including the collective Periodistas de a Pie, emerged from this period. As Pastrana explained, female investigative reporters founded the collective to train and support local journalists. The collective also acted as a mechanism of group support, boosting resilience among journalists whose work political and criminal violence had disrupted. Thanks to the collective's conviction, protesting—when Jiménez de la Cruz was kidnapped, for example—had become synonymous not only with resistance but hope as well.

Pastrana, who maintained her generous, maternal demeanor as she recalled this painful episode, told me, "Our excitement at thinking that they might set him free was great. But when [the newspaper] *Reforma* broke the story that he was dead, it was terrible, it was sad. I even believe it hit us as though he'd been a relative. It was too much."[6]

INTRODUCTION

That same night the death of Jiménez de la Cruz was announced, two dozen journalists and activists met in Mexico City to decide what to do. "Outrage brought us together . . . because it wasn't just an attack on one person, family, or career, but an attack on the entire profession," Ruiz Parra recalled. Those who showed up were united by anger but unable to come to a consensus on what to do. Some believed it was not their role as journalists to take to the streets; others, more politicized, suggested that the general public be invited to participate in a massive nationwide mobilization. The most courageous among them believed it was their turn to take to the streets. They backed a show of total solidarity with their colleagues from Veracruz.

Ultimately, these two dozen mourners decided to create a collective, which they baptized "Prensa, no disparen," or "Press, Don't Shoot!" Comprising investigative journalists, *cronistas* (authors of news chronicles), and activists, the collective had two fundamental goals. First, they planned to organize a meeting at the symbolic Angel of Independence monument in Mexico City and demand the resignation of the governor of Veracruz. This meeting ultimately took place on February 24, 2014, garnering widespread participation among journalists and local support from many press networks and collectives from major cities nationwide. However, as on other occasions, public support was lukewarm—indeed, almost nonexistent—and there was very little coverage in major media outlets. Some outlets even went so far as to prohibit staff members from participating in the protest.

The collective's second objective was far more dangerous: to go to Coatzacoalcos, where its mission—which opened this introduction—would document and report on what had occurred. If the murderers wanted to silence the press, the collective would, instead, give them as much publicity as possible. In addition to nationally renowned journalists, the mission was composed of members of organizations that defend freedom of expression, such as Reporters Without Borders (RSF), Sociedad Interamericana de Prensa (SIP), and Artículo 19 Mexico. While in Coatzacoalcos, the Prensa, no disparen mission spoke to communicators and relatives who—despite knowing that government operatives and organized crime lookouts were spying on them—risked their lives by talking to them.[7]

INTRODUCTION

"Gregorio, asesinado por informar al público" (Gregorio: Murdered for Keeping the Public Informed) was published one month later. This comprehensive investigative reporting documented the incivility and criminality that reigned in Coatzacoalcos. Moreover, the report sought to rescue Jiménez de la Cruz's case from the climate of systemic oblivion that allows most crimes to go unsolved. The report poked holes in the official version, which argued that he had been murdered as a result of a dispute with his neighbors. From a journalistic standpoint, at least, by investigating and exposing Jiménez de la Cruz's assassination, some measure of justice was achieved.

All of these responses to the murder of Jiménez de la Cruz were unique. But the most important aspect, according to Ruiz Parra, was how the situation endowed journalists with a political conscience:

> The journalism trade took on a greater political and professional awareness . . . upon realizing that as a profession, they had to mobilize to defend themselves and that also, defending the press as a trade implied another kind of defense: the right to information, which forms part of the democratic agenda of a country and is perhaps even the most valuable aspect. And, well, that much still remains to be done.[8]

For Ruiz Parra, the horrific murder and remarkable response exemplify the changing fate of journalism in Mexico: they illustrate the deadly stakes as well as some of the new strategies journalists learned to protect themselves. Moreover, they did so guided by outrage, as well as by their political and professional conscience.

In this, Ruiz Parra is assuredly correct. But a closer analysis of the Prensa, no disparen mission to Coatzacoalcos reveals so much more. This story shows what lies beneath the facade of democratic normalcy: a maelstrom of criminal and political repression that has shaken so much of Mexico's territory. Journalists—as witnesses and first responders—have been unable to escape its turbulence. Jiménez de la Cruz's demise exemplifies the precariousness and risk in which many journalists in Mexico live and work, especially those who find themselves somewhere along the professional and

INTRODUCTION

economic margins or are obliged to become war correspondents in their own homes.

And yet, Jiménez de la Cruz's story also demonstrates how profoundly the field of journalism has been reconfigured in recent years. It shows how groups of independent, civic-minded journalists, relying on their life experiences, organizational resources, and networks of empathy and trust, led this sea change. They went on reporting and publishing no matter what the cost. In this case, the mission to Coatzacoalcos was explicitly created to protest the disappearance of Jiménez de la Cruz and demand justice for his murder. Yet the mission was also designed to continue their murdered colleague's work and to tie up some of the loose ends he left behind.

This book describes a variety of reasons why journalists like Jiménez de la Cruz have been attacked or murdered more and more frequently over the past twenty years across Mexico. Even more importantly, it tells the story of engaged and independent newsmakers who have acquired a political and professional conscience, like Jiménez de la Cruz himself, who challenged a pact of silence, or like the members of the Prensa, no disparen mission.

Among journalists nationwide, there is a sense of fear, pain, and growing outrage. Yet despite—and, indeed, because of—these obstacles, brave, resilient journalists have found meaning and direction, as well as new ways of living and working through this dark era. Unexpectedly, such obstacles have only strengthened these newsmakers' most cherished conviction: silence is not an option.

THE PARADOX OF JOURNALISM IN MEXICO

The era of greatest threat to journalism is also that of its greatest vigor.[9]

—DIEGO OSORNO, LONG-FORM JOURNALIST AND CRONISTA

México bronco, or "wild Mexico," refers to a longstanding political culture that employs violence to resolve differences.[10] By the start of the new millennium, however, indices of violence and criminal activity had exploded, far surpassing those of even Mexico's civil wars.

This dangerous change began at the start of the new millennium, just after the federal government launched a direct campaign of aggression, employing both police and military forces, which destabilized the existing balance among large, organized crime syndicates, all three levels of government, and armed groups of citizens (known as *autodefensas*, or "self-defense groups"). This campaign, known as the Mexico Drug War, was carried out in collaboration with, and under the auspices of, the U.S. government through the Mérida Initiative and other bilateral agreements. Obeying a logic of political polarization, the campaign, led since 2006 by former president Felipe Calderón, was implemented by institutions—dedicated to national politics, local politics, public security, and criminal justice—that were already weak and, in some cases, corrupt and authoritarian.

Ultimately, the government campaign caused the already debilitated social pact to break down completely, generating a series of human rights crises. This resulted in chilling statistics from 2006 to 2018, including 250,000 drug-related homicides, 60,000 missing persons, and 20,000 displaced persons. Perhaps most alarming were the extremely high rates of impunity: 95 percent of all criminal activity went unsolved and unpunished. This, predictably, left a broad wake of resentment, pain, and fear throughout the country.

Journalists had to live through this barbarity while documenting and reporting it. And for this double duty, the press (just like other groups vital to society, such as activists) paid a very high price. Hence, from 2000 to July 2023, the total number of murdered and missing journalists stood at 157, more than any other country in the hemisphere. Beyond these lethal figures, in 2022 alone, Artículo 19 Mexico documented 696 attacks against the press; of these, over half are intimidations and threats, while the rest are a mixed bag of physical attacks, digital aggressions, and other, more extreme forms of violence, such as abductions and torture. In 2022, Mexico ranked among countries with the worst levels of freedom of expression on the continent (128th out of 180 countries, according to Reporters without

INTRODUCTION

Borders) and, worst of all, among nations with the highest level of impunity in Latin America for murders of journalists.

Additionally, the critical press experienced unprecedented turmoil. The growing commercialization and extravagance of news, the Great Recession of 2009, and, from 2020 onward, the economic crises caused by COVID-19, the lack of job opportunities, and the social media boom have all undermined journalism. Increasingly, citizens turn to social networks for social contact, entertainment, information, and news. Consequently, major traditional news organizations have experienced an economic debacle, further compromising their anemic independence from political power. At the same time, broad sectors of the press have suffered from economic struggles. This economic turbulence, when exacerbated by criminal violence, leaves entire communities uninformed simply because they no longer receive regular, reliable journalistic information.

Fortunately, journalism has not come to an end. But it has undergone a process of transformation. Given the situation, some strategic sectors of the press have been reconfigured. Their goal is to expose and report the many vices of the political system and its institutional deficits. And also, therefore, to investigate and document the causes and consequences of the rising crime while, at the same time, giving a voice to the victims of violence.

This generation of critical reporters—whom I refer to as resilient newsmakers—are defined by their commitment and capacity for adaptation to multiple adversities. They share a common belief that practicing journalism is more important now than ever. Enriched by different experiences and reflecting diverse values, resilient newsmakers have emerged both in traditional forms of media and digital endeavors and professional collectives. Moreover, they have been recognized in many parts of the country for their goal of continuing to practice journalism and, even more importantly, for showing how—through their work—they have managed to confront a violent reality.

These strategic groups of journalists have realized that to practice journalism is to face violence and abuse of power head-on. This is a civic vocation and a public service in a country like Mexico. In doing so, they have shown themselves capable of inventing and sharing creative strategies—on

INTRODUCTION

a personal, organizational, and social level—that seek to mitigate the risks inherent to their work while continuing to report with cautious but determined autonomy to expose the climate of hostility in which they live.

Major shake-ups can, sometimes, engender new and challenging ways of practicing critical journalism. As such, this book explores how the "inferno," as Javier Valdez, who won international awards for his coverage of criminal violence, put it, they've had to live through, may have been what finally spawned this cadre of resilient newsmakers.

Because journalism in Mexico must cope with a paradox. Right now, there is greater freedom of expression than during the authoritarian regime of the Partido Revolucionario Institucional, or PRI (1929–2000). At the same time, more threats are assailing the press, with more extraordinary cruelty and constancy than ever. Now that groups of civic-minded journalists scattered across the country practice a kind of hybrid, public-service journalism—one that is autonomous, pluralist, and collaborative—not a single day goes by in which a set of intolerant and powerful actors fails to attack them with total impunity. "In contemporary Mexico," cronista Diego Enrique Osorno told me, "there's loads of censorship, loads of intimidation, and widespread job insecurity; at the same time, there is so much vitality, creativity, and rigor, not to mention plenty of dissidents in the news media."[11]

Journalists are showing greater daring and courage than ever; however, they also face a level of barbarity previously unknown. And yet, the more the powers try to silence these resilient newsmakers, the louder their outcries.

Based on seventy-nine interviews with newsmakers (including editorial directors, managers, editors, journalists, and digital journalists) and activists, as well as numerous documentary sources, this book explores the main forces limiting journalistic autonomy (the freedom to practice their profession). Most of these interviews took place between 2014 and 2018 and reference facts, stories, and experiences that almost always began in the 2000s. It also examines the personal, organizational, and social resources these resilient newsmakers can employ in generating new strategies and mechanisms to report and expose arbitrary acts committed against them. It shows

INTRODUCTION

how resilient newsmakers (both as professionals and as individuals) find themselves considerably limited by forces of action that meddle and attempt to control their journalistic duties. Still, even this has only led them to adapt further.

Within an environment that asphyxiates the practice of journalism (especially on a local level), this book empirically shows that not all reporters react the same way to these adversities. Although they may at times fall silent, they do so only as an extreme survival mechanism while awaiting the right time to break that silence.

More importantly, as a working hypothesis, the book suggests that some critical journalists—those who are devoted to their work as a public duty and also possess ample resources, both symbolic and material—have generated strategies at a personal, organizational, or collective level to continue reporting and publishing. These strategies are driven by the value ascribed to journalism as a watchdog of justice and a transformer of reality. But for this laudable status to be viable and effective requires more than heroism or blind determination. Instead, what truly defines journalism's special status and power is how journalistic ideals are backed up by resources: for example, the rich breadth of journalists' own life experiences, the commitment and disposition of their media organizations to keep the presses running despite censorship, and their empathy and ability to connect and generate reliable, durable relationships with their peers and journalistic sources.

This book, therefore, has two objectives. First, it explores why attacking the press has become so common and feasible. Second, it illuminates how the press has adapted to this atmosphere while continuing to function.

Academia, the mass media, and public opinion refer frequently to violence against the press in Mexico. But it is seldom successfully unpacked in all its complexity. This book seeks to understand the principal phenomena that feed into this violence, including factors within the journalism field (such as job insecurity, high digital visibility, and a lack of support from media moguls). It also scrutinizes the logic followed by this violence, considering its spatial and temporal patterns and the perverse goals pursued by a variety of censors.

INTRODUCTION

On the other hand, this book also seeks to learn more about the incentives that push strategic segments of the press to continue to carry out their professional duties despite the atmosphere of repression. We know very little about how the press operates in a context like contemporary Mexico, where democratic rules do not apply equally to all citizens and where de facto powers and corrupt authorities rule unchecked across national territory. This even though the press has been one of the primary vehicles allowing us to become aware of, unravel, and react indignantly to the most terrible and scandalous events that have assailed our nation. Therefore, my investigation has as its objective the interrogation of what allows these journalists to continue to work under clearly adverse conditions, delving into not only why they do it but how they do it.

INSECURE DEMOCRACY, ANTI-PRESS VIOLENCE, AND A VULNERABLE PROFESSION

Although violence, in general, has been omnipresent, the forms that violence takes come and go, corresponding to rising and falling levels of general violence within and between societies (with war being the classic example) as well as changes in the social and political roles of the news media and developing norms for journalism.[12]

—JOHN NERONE, *VIOLENCE AGAINST THE PRESS: POLICING THE PUBLIC SPHERE IN U.S. HISTORY*

The news has always been a source of conflict regarding information, and violence against the press has been an ongoing presence in the history of journalism. In this book, such violence is defined as physical, verbal, or digital attacks that coerce journalists in their professional practice.[13] This is very similar to political violence, according to political analyst Stathis Kalyvas: violence against the press seeks not to exterminate its victims but rather to control them.[14] This could be direct control, for example, when a

INTRODUCTION

reporter is murdered, as in the case of the abduction and decapitation of Jiménez de la Cruz. But it can also be through indirect control, by spreading fear: "I'm next!" exclaimed a colleague of Jiménez de la Cruz covering the crime beat, upon learning of the findings of the Prensa, no disparen collective.[15]

As a social phenomenon, the varying degrees and forms of violence against the press change over time. They take on the shape and frequency of our sociopolitical and economic surroundings, as is rightly indicated in the above epigraph by media historian John Nerone from his magnificent study on violence against the press throughout U.S. history.[16] This violence—which is the most extreme form of coercion of the press and represents a public health issue—leaves behind clues regarding the limits public speech may encounter within a specific context. In Mexico (as I will explore in detail in chapter 4), speech is de facto limited, thanks to intolerance among the politically powerful and their need for secrecy to cover up abuse, illegal actions, and atrocities, along with the growing need to instill fear through narco-terrorist attacks.

In the United States, according to Nerone, such direct and indirect control diminished during the twentieth century with the establishment of contemporary democratic institutions. However, in Mexico—as in many other fledgling democracies—this trend has slowed or even reversed, as the scholar Silvio Waisbord mentioned in his groundbreaking article on this topic.[17] In the case of Mexico, violence against the press has been exacerbated in ways never before seen.

"Yes, there used to be aggressions. I'm a veteran reporter, and yes, we were getting roughed up every now and then in the '70s and '80s," a reporter told me, with the self-confidence that comes only with a lifetime of experience covering politics and social movements in a country rife with upheaval.[18] And while this is true, it has not generally been the focus of attention among those who study media. In recent years, revisionist analyses, such as those of the historian Benjamin Smith, have demonstrated that violent coercion played an important role in the repertoire of censorship during the authoritarian period, especially from 1940 to 1960, and above all in strategic regions of Mexico, where more subtle forms of control were

INTRODUCTION

inoperable. However, as I describe in chapter 3, acts of violence against the press in the 1990s pale in comparison to the skyrocketing numbers and sadism seen in the 2000s.

Any increase in violence against the press, as studied by researchers Anita Gohdes and Sabine Carey, indicates the degree of social decomposition and denotes a human rights crisis.[19] As a journalist from Michoacán put it, "When they kill a journalist, it's because the degree of violence and impunity is very high, as is the gravity of the issues at hand."[20]

The "gravity of the issues" this journalist referred to may be summarized as what academic Sallie Hughes and her colleagues call insecure democracy.[21] Such a society is characterized by democratic deficiencies, combined with strong authoritarian practices and corruption, elevated levels of criminal violence, overwhelmed or broken institutions of public safety and justice, economic stagnation and concentration of wealth, myriad social inequities, informality, and high indices of poverty.

Insecure democracies like Mexico are characteristically risky for journalists in particular. This is because there is a democratic facade that backs critical journalism, yet one that fails to guarantee the lives and safety of reporters. These are countries where freedom of the press exists but is fragmented. That is, such freedom is intermittently available for some journalists (for instance, in big metropolises like Mexico City) but often shut down, above all among those who work with the more delicate issues in their communities (for instance, in rural areas). Mexico is, perhaps, one of the most extreme examples of this kind of democracy, a regime that has incubated more barbarity, murder, trauma, and fear than almost any other in the region, including the military dictatorships of the twentieth century and populist regimes of the twenty-first century. And yet, as some have shown, this insecure democracy paradoxically offers better conditions than any authoritarian regime for the practice of critical journalism serving the public interest.[22]

Moreover, in Mexico, journalists must not only navigate the quicksand that living in an insecure democracy implies but do so from the even more vulnerable position of journalism as a profession. While in Mexico, much like anywhere else, some media outlets and journalists still enjoy a certain

INTRODUCTION

reputation and considerable influence, as a trade, journalism has become more susceptible. This vulnerability underlies the risks that threaten the profession. It is not by chance that, at a time when this profession is in a state of constant flux and reconfiguration around the world, more people than ever have died practicing journalism. And this has occurred mostly in places like Mexico, which are not cataloged as conventional war zones.

As a sphere of action, journalism acts to provide us with greater certainties. And yet, it is journalism itself that finds itself under attack and immersed in doubt.

These are uncertain times for journalism, according to Barbie Zelizer, and various global trends help explain this: the press is being intimidated by officials who from top to bottom weaponize their power; the business model of journalism is broken and has been unable to come up with entirely sustainable alternatives; younger audiences increasingly consume information from social media instead of journalistic institutions; and public confidence in the press as an institution has been undermined overall insofar as its historic role as a dispassionate reporter of the news is concerned.[23] In Mexico, of course, these trends have been even more exacerbated. There is an elevated historic dependency of journalism on government funds to subsist. Moreover, there is a lack of concern among owners of media outlets for journalists, widespread job insecurity, and a lack of social appreciation, accompanied by a general state of mistrust and fragmentation in the trade.

This helps to explain why there are significant gaps—perhaps out of deliberate connivance, perhaps out of a lack of skill—in major media outlets' coverage of some of the most important stories of their time, including those that touch on abuse of power, corruption, and crime. In most of these cases, outlets, especially at a local level, are reduced to passive journalistic routines, reproducing official discourse, surviving without readership, and opportunistically pleasing the powers that be while maintaining a convenient or even deathly silence.

Like other historic phases such as the 1990s, in contemporary Mexico, groups of renegade journalists in various regions are breaking these silences, giving rise to new spaces where the powerful prefer to keep to the shadows. These groups of newsmakers were pushed to do so by the extreme times

INTRODUCTION

in which they lived. They were also driven by the idea that the struggle to practice journalism is necessary, now more than ever. One has to adapt, but one must never surrender.

RESILIENT NEWSMAKERS

Despite everything we've lived through, we have never refrained from continuing to do our jobs. . . . Of course we're all afraid, we're all frightened, but we have always felt that quitting journalism is the worst thing that can happen to you, and that includes the death of your colleagues.[24]

—POLITICAL BEAT JOURNALIST IN CIUDAD JUÁREZ, CHIHUAHUA, DECEMBER 11, 2015

The reporter who gave the above testimonial is a resilient newsmaker. Since 1992, she has covered public security issues and the police beat in Ciudad Juárez, a border city historically linked to the traffic of narcotics and human beings where violence increased sevenfold between 2008 and 2010. For more than two decades, she has worked for *El Diario de Juárez* newspaper, for which—during the moments of greatest tension—it fell to her to cover up to twenty homicides from 7:00 a.m. to 3:00 p.m. on a single day.

This reporter, age 48, also had to cover the murders of her colleagues Armando Rodríguez in 2008 and Luis Carlos Santiago in 2010, both from the same newspaper, the city's most important legacy periodical. Practicing journalism, she says, allows her to continue to research and expose the murders of her colleagues. Continuing to report, as she has done, also means learning to survive in quicksand: digging deeper even while dodging criminal gangs, the government, and police forces.

In a calm yet determined voice, she described the protocols she follows when covering public-security stories: "[I] contact my boss. I carry a telephone with a pager so they can locate me, reach me on the telephone. We go out there as a press pool to cover homicides. We work in close contact with other colleagues." Self-aware, she knows that in this trade, one never

INTRODUCTION

stops learning. She believes that in terms of public-security journalism, it makes a difference knowing who—and how many—have fallen in an era marked by violence.

"The only way to shield ourselves," she told me, "was to do, or try to do, a more professional job as journalists." And so, after confronting "totally perverse scenarios," she and a group of five colleagues in 2011 formed the Red de Periodistas de Juárez: a collective endeavor for active journalists dedicated to providing training on how to report while at the same time privileging one's own physical and mental well-being.

Resilient newsmakers like her form part of a heterogeneous generation of journalists. They constituted a tiny portion of the more than thirty-six thousand full-time journalists and communication professionals in Mexico by 2020. Resilient newsmakers represent different realities and different professional models that are sometimes contradictory. *Resiliencia*, according to the Real Academia Española (RAE), is "the capacity for adaptation of a living being in the face of a disturbing agent or an adverse state or situation." This concept has been revisited by psychology. It refers to our capacity for adaptation with favorable results despite adverse circumstances, depending on an array of individual, family, social, and cultural factors. Thus, if we apply the concept to journalists, they may be defined as resilient actors under certain circumstances. In this vein, resilient newsmakers have also developed a significant capacity for adaptation to continue to practice civic-minded journalism through cautious tactics despite a prevailing atmosphere of repression and violence.

The significant capacity for adaptation I identify here is derived from the work of Rosemary Novak and Sarah Davidson.[25] They are among the first investigators to find that journalists, having gone through traumatic situations, subsequently encounter strategies through their professional duties that help them come out ahead, both personally and collectively.[26] Civic-minded journalism, according to Sallie Hughes, is an "autonomous, proactive and politically diverse" form of journalism, which became ingrained in Mexican journalism just as the country transitioned toward a more pluralistic and democratic political regime in the late 1990s.[27] This is very similar to the concept of critical journalists developed by María

INTRODUCTION

Repnikova in China and Russia, joined together by "their pursuit of social justice and their quest to push the envelope of permissible reporting."[28] Cautious journalism, according to a groundbreaking investigation completed by Frida Rodelo in Sinaloa, "is characterized by approaching delicate subject matter and is defined by the surrounding economic and safety conditions."[29]

All three of these phenomena are encompassed in resilient newsmakers. The term, however, is an empirical category and does not constitute a type of journalism. Instead, the phrase *resilient newsmakers* describes how a subset of professional journalists commit to adapting and continuing to do their jobs.

These professionals form part of what the sociologist Pierre Bourdieu called the field of journalism; that is, they are actors who follow similar rules of the game in a nation-state, characterized by producing journalistic stories and news items.[30] And, as actors in the field of journalism, they also share how their resources are used to conceptualize, share, and execute cautious mechanisms and strategies in the face of adversity. By no means do they constitute a majority within the field of national journalism. Instead, they form a very small but influential and critical group indispensable to the health of public life in their communities. They practice journalism by writing exposés of the powerful, denouncing an arbitrary justice system, or giving voice to the victims of violence and inequality.

They do not share a coherent set of professional goals and ideals. Instead, resilient newsmakers share a sense of purpose they ascribe to the kind of civic-minded journalism that they carry out. Indeed, when asked why attacks against the press are relevant, they explain very different kinds of virtues.[31]

Vigilance: "Because we are the pebble in the shoe, because that way, their path to doing and undoing is not as clear" (national correspondent in Oaxaca).[32]

Agents of change: "The function journalists fulfill is important to the development of cities and communities; at the end of the day, it is an important activity. The moment you stop the free flow of information or obstruct information to the press, you are basically putting the brakes on the development of an entire community" (deputy director in Ciudad Juárez).[33]

Dissemination: "This is relevant because attacks on freedom of expression and informative practice undermine our right as humans to information and freedom of expression. Which is also relevant because it impedes the enjoyment of these rights and hampers the social objective of the press to inform, to act as a channel, and to serve society" (freelance journalist from Monterrey).[34]

Although they comprise a minority of journalists in Mexico, resilient newsmakers articulate aspirations for journalism that many share. The vast majority of Mexico's journalists—according to a poll led by researchers Mireya Márquez and Sallie Hughes—recognized themselves as part "of a more proactive journalism, aware of the socio-political challenges of the country and committed to their immediate surroundings and social transformation."[35] However, commitment to their ideals and the goal of social transformation does not necessarily result in the change they seek.

However, resilient newsmakers have persevered and learned to develop creative and prudent strategies and mechanisms. In so doing, they have been able to transcend their limitations and practice a kind of social-value journalism by informing, reporting, and by informing and communicating to the public key concerns about where they live and work.

To do so, these resilient newsmakers—independently, and for diverse reasons—practice different forms of journalism, especially daily, investigative, reportage, and long-form. Moreover, as shown by some of the cases described in this book, resilient newsmakers constantly jump from one genre to another or even between formats (from paper to radio to digital, among others). Sometimes, this is practical; for example, they continue covering daily news required by their workplace even while working longer-term on investigative projects. Other times, their disenchantment with the daily news compels them to seek other genres (such as long-form or documentary journalism) better suited to capturing the complexities they wish to report.

INTRODUCTION

Even so, resilient newsmakers do produce certain kinds of daily news coverage. And daily coverage such as the police beat and public safety topics continues to fulfill—as shown by the stories of Jiménez de la Cruz—a social function. This function is something anthropologist Pablo Piccato termed "criminal literacy" in his description of police beat coverage in mid-twentieth-century Mexico.[36] No doubt it is necessary to recognize the negative social and moral consequences that yellow, sensational journalism may have.[37] Even so, such everyday journalism can make life bearable in truly dangerous urban areas, for example, by reporting on which areas or routes are the most dangerous, and how to avoid them.

To make life bearable is also the goal of a great many investigative journalists, but they do so by exposing what the powerful wish to hide. Instead of newspapers, their broad investigations take the shape of long-form articles or even books.[38] Unlike those who publish in dailies, investigative journalists—who may act as national correspondents or as newspaper representatives—are better positioned in the field of journalism since they often have the backing of major media outlets (whether local or national). Not only do they have more time to develop their stories, but they also have access to better sources, more refined journalism practices, and national and international contacts. Rarely do major media outlets in radio and television accommodate this kind of reporter because they tend to generate major tensions with the politically powerful. Many of them contribute to a variety of media or specialized media like the influential national magazine *Proceso*. By revealing what is almost always kept hidden, investigative journalists can acquire a reputation and considerable influence.

In addition to daily journalists and investigative journalists are chroniclers, another category of resilient newsmakers. Over the past two decades, a new generation of long-form journalists emerged in Mexico that were dedicated to literary journalism. More importantly, these chroniclers were convinced that neither daily newspapers nor investigative journalism were able to encompass the complexity of the devastating reality the country was experiencing, especially the pain, suffering, and fortitude of all the victims this vortex of violence has left behind.[39] Some of these chroniclers—who are reminiscent of both the cronistas among Latin American modernists and New

INTRODUCTION

Journalism in the United States—arrived at this genre out of disenchantment with the daily news and investigative journalism; some of them, like Diego Enrique Osorno,[40] are convinced that literary resources can lend greater honesty, texture, depth, and perspective to their stories.[41] Like investigative journalists, chroniclers often position themselves among the most privileged strata of journalism (one that enjoys more visibility and influence than beat reporters). However, the formats they typically resort to (long-form articles, reportages, or books) lead them to the freelance world. Chroniclers acquire higher prestige not only in the field of journalism but also in literature because of the quality of their journalistic oeuvre.

All these kinds of resilient newsmakers tend to collaborate. In the trying times they report on, they share work with those whom they trust, empathize with, and with whom they have professional affinity. Since exclusives are no longer at the center of the profession, and since no one covers the barbarities of any country in solitude, they have become collaborative journalists out of both necessity and conviction.

Like other damaged social groups, such as women in Ciudad Juárez or the relatives of the missing, resilient newsmakers have channeled their strengths into collaborative reporting initiatives: they are aware that their voices become louder and carry farther in a chorus. This has led them to create initiatives such as the collective Prensa, no disparen, which investigated the murder of Jiménez de la Cruz, or far more institutionalized and ambitious mechanisms, such as the Red de Periodistas de Juárez, referred to by the reporter in the above testimonial. As we shall see further on, the origin, existence, and trajectory of these initiatives are highly varied and contingent on the objectives of the participants, as well as the resources (both material and symbolic) they have access to. Their collaborative and solidary spirit has developed against the grain, conquering entrenched barriers of mistrust and competition that persist in the field.

In the process, resilient newsmakers have also taken on greater political and group awareness, as Ruiz Parra put it. Political consciousness—as part of a vibrant social group constantly under pressure—has led them to hold fast to their journalistic ideals, so as to bounce back and denounce the arbitrary acts committed against them. Moreover, these journalistic ideals

INTRODUCTION

have been far more than just a safety factor (as commonly believed). In territories like Mexico, where it is a day-to-day struggle to have one's rights respected, journalists have become rebels in their trade and activists who seek freedom of the press. Naturally, their exposés tend to be directed against the state, although they may also focus on less visible actors who are equally responsible for their many vulnerabilities while on the job, such as the owners of media outlets.

This process (as demonstrated by the case of the collective Prensa, no disparen) has not been exempt from vocational tensions. Such a political approach challenges the conventions of English-language journalism by suggesting that, even while carrying out high-quality, civic-minded journalism, sides may be taken.

Resilient newsmakers are professionally close to—and even may form part of—the generation of journalists Sallie Hughes described almost twenty years ago in *Newsrooms in Conflict* as civic-minded journalism, Mexican style. The main elements and values of such journalism are plurality, assertiveness, and independence. Major tensions that gave rise to this generation—such as economic and political liberalization—were synthesized and catapulted from the copy desks of the nation's most influential newspapers.

Unlike the civic-minded, resilient newsmakers have found tensions not only in newsrooms; they have also faced multiple threats in their immediate surroundings. Conflict is all around them since they have essentially become war correspondents in their own communities. Moreover, most do not share the same enthusiasm for democracy they felt twenty years ago. Like most Mexicans, journalists are disenchanted with the governments that, beneath a facade of political alternance, have continued to perpetuate the same practices of corruption and abuse of power.

Therefore, the main catalyst of resilient newsmakers has not been the democratic struggle, as it was twenty years ago among adherents of civic-minded journalism. Instead, resilient newsmakers emerged from their courage to continue to work and report the overwhelming climate of intolerance and violence they live in. The former were driven by the mirage of democracy; the latter were joined together by outrage.

INTRODUCTION

AGENCY, CAPITAL, AND STRATEGIES

> *The social world is accumulated history, and if it is not to be reduced to a discontinuous series of instantaneous mechanical equilibria between agents who are treated as interchangeable particles, one must reintroduce into it the notion of capital and with it, accumulation and all its effects. Capital is accumulated labor (in its materialized form or its "incorporated," embodied form) which, when appropriated on a private, i.e., exclusive, basis by agents or groups of agents, enables them to appropriate social energy in the form of reified or living labor. It is a vis insita, a force inscribed in objective or subjective structures, but it is also a lex insita, the principal underlying the immanent regularities of the social world. It is what makes the games of society—not least, the economic game—something other than simple games of chance offering at every moment the possibility of a miracle.*[42]
>
> —PIERRE BOURDIEU, THE FORMS OF CAPITAL

Consider the reporter from *El Diario de Juárez*, who, in the epigraph of the last section, explained her belief that nothing was worse than no longer practicing journalism, not even being forced to cover the death of a colleague. It is difficult to comprehend just what compelled her, and so many other journalists, to reach that conclusion. It may be even harder to understand how she transformed that conviction into actual practice.

Why do resilient newsmakers like her generate and implement certain journalistic strategies at an organizational level (constant monitoring by their bosses) or a collective level (covering stories as a pool or forming a professional network) instead of choosing other alternatives? What material and personal resources do they need to possess to successfully implement these strategies? How does reporting complement them? And how similar or different are they from the strategies of other journalists who face similar situations?

These kinds of questions constitute what scholar Julie Battilana calls the paradox of embedded agency: why do some actors select one strategy while others opt for another?[43] To escape this paradox, she proposes that we analyze social phenomena using the powerful concept of capital, as developed by sociologist Pierre Bourdieu in his influential field theory. The concept of capital has not been examined very often among those who study the press. Even so, some investigations show that capital can explain how journalists react differently to similar contexts, whether they are covering the conflict in Syria,[44] or creating online news startups in France and the United States.[45]

Capital, according to Bourdieu, is accumulated work, a force of stored inertia that permits and outlines social action. The volume and forms of capital available to the actors allow them to compete but also to collaborate within a determined sphere of action. Capital is formed by material and symbolic resources possessed, for example, by journalists in their profession. According to Bourdieu, capital is developed in three fundamental ways: economically, culturally, and socially. As a whole, these forms of capital "make the rules of society."

In the case of individual journalists, these kinds of capital include their professional training, the kind of media they work for, and their networks of contacts. As a whole, these forms of capital endow journalists with greater symbolic capital (that is, prestige and influence).[46] Indeed, symbolic capital is the most prized resource in the field. According to Bourdieu, in all fields of action, actors seek to accumulate the greatest possible capital. Greater forms of capital endow actors with additional capacities to operate in their sphere of action. Capital also endows journalists with wider margins of professional autonomy. As Michael Schudson comments, greater levels of capital allow them to negotiate better terms and extend their margins of professional independence, for example, with regards to their editors in newsrooms or externally, from pressures originating in the government or market.[47] In this book, greater levels of capital will grant greater resources to help navigate and resist the environment of repression and intimidation in which journalists operate.

For the purposes of this book, the concept of cultural capital refers to the training, life experiences, knowledge, skills, and techniques that are important to journalists as they perform their jobs. Such traits are almost

INTRODUCTION

always acquired during their academic training and empirical professionalization and from the complex situations the practice of their trade can lead to, including experiences of risk, trauma, or violence.

Organizational capital refers to resources that emanate from journalists' affiliation with one or several journalistic companies.[48] This includes, in a very basic sense, their income and job security, as well as the kind of media they work for: a prestigious national political magazine like *Proceso*, for example, or a digital endeavor of more recent creation such as *Espejo* magazine in Sinaloa. They include material and institutional tools, as well as the support and confidence journalists need to complete their jobs, such as backing from their editors and media owners when they cover sensitive stories.

Finally, the concept of social capital refers to the strength and consistency of one's social networks, particularly among journalist colleagues. As a sector, this kind of capital is very similar to professional solidarity; that is, the value that procures mutual and horizontal collaboration among journalists. This trade solidarity—which often may include only a handful of like-minded journalists—allows them to develop collective strategies of reporting and publication. On a secondary level, social capital may also include other networks of social and civic allies that are relevant not as journalistic sources but by forming broader social coalitions with specific demands, as is the case of the collective Prensa, no disparen. These social movements are very similar to what scholars Soledad Segura and Silvio Waisbord call media movements or what Mexican scholar Grisel Salazar labeled strategic allies.[49]

The division between forms of capital is, of course, an artificial one. After all, in the daily practice of journalism, some forms of capital complement and overlap others. But this division helps us understand what resources journalists may rely on to practice their profession under frankly adverse conditions.

The capacity to convert one form of capital (symbolic capital in the form of prestige) into another (the capacity to work with better journalistic sources) is key for Bourdieu. Given that all forms of capital are "accumulated work," this convertibility follows the equivalent of the "principle of

INTRODUCTION

the conservation of energy, where profits in one area are necessarily paid for by costs in another." For example, national correspondents (who enjoy prestige and organizational support) may often receive sensitive information from other local colleagues who cannot publish, given that they do not enjoy the advantages of prestige or a strong media outlet to back them.

Where newsmakers stand in the field of journalism is determined by what kinds of capital they have at their disposal and at what amount. And, as will be shown further on, those who possess greater capital are better equipped to confront adverse surroundings. This is why throughout this book (especially from chapter 4 onward) we will analyze how resilient newsmakers with greater degrees of capital are more capable of practicing their profession under extreme conditions. Even in high-risk situations, these resilient newsmakers have been able to endure by employing some of the central resources within their reach, whether personal (their life experience and training), organizational (in the case of those who belong to a media outlet committed to public service), or collective (by forming professional networks and broader civic coalitions). By drawing on such capital, these journalists have been able to invent and share creative strategies to mitigate the risks inherent to their practice. Moreover, they have been able to continue reporting with cautious yet determined autonomy, even while denouncing the climate of hostility in which they live.

Resilient newsmakers who display higher degrees of forms of capital also possess a greater capacity to develop strategic actions that allow them to confront the fears they are exposed to while at the same time practicing civic-minded journalism with a critical purpose. To this end, I have labeled "strategies for safety autonomy" as the set of tactics aimed at developing a brand of cautious journalism, operational tactics, and collective actions allowing the investigation and publication of some of the most dangerous stories in their communities. These strategies refer to the capacity to expand journalists' degree of professional autonomy while reducing work-related risks. They include reportage and investigative precautions, strategic editorial policies, and the generation of collective coverage and publication initiatives. By scrutinizing the mechanisms that led them to learn from their context and integrate what they have learned into their daily routines, this

INTRODUCTION

chapter explains how different kinds of resilient newsmakers exploit their resources—cultural, organizational, and social—to generate strategies that expand their degrees of journalistic autonomy.

Likewise, resilient newsmakers also deploy what I call strategies for resistance, tactical maneuvers that critical journalists implement to adapt to, resist, or even confront a challenge. In this sense, I consider resistance a state of mind, a professional spirit, or a public vocation. Therefore, the forms of capital analyzed in this book catalyze actions of confrontation and denunciation on a personal, organizational, and collective level. By exploiting their cultural capital, journalists have found in their professional values the mechanisms of protection and resilience they need to persevere. Journalistic organizations that are civically engaged and economically strong, on the other hand, have undergone a process of adaptation that has allowed them not only to better protect their journalists but also confront the powerful and denounce the crimes committed against them. After suffering aggression against one of their members, groups of resilient newsmakers have collectively found empathy and solidarity among like-minded colleagues and developed networks of indignation and denunciation to protest the attacks and crimes committed against them.

As a sagacious observer, a journalist may channel abilities into experiences to develop an eye-opening story or survive a challenge. In these cases, the capital on which each journalist can rely—personal, organizational, and social resources—catalyzes their actions. In other words, journalists create initiatives to act based not only on who they are and what happens to them but also on what happens to their colleagues. What this means is that the strategic decisions journalists make do not emerge solely on an individual level but rather function collectively.

Strategies of safety, autonomy, and resistance, whether on an individual, organizational, or collective level, share similar patterns and characteristics. On all three levels of analysis, actions of resilience and resistance are commonly unleashed after an affront is suffered, such as an attack on a journalist or news organization. Moreover, on an individual, organizational, and collective level, actors undergo a reflexive process during which the importance of their professional labor proves crucial to moving forward. In

INTRODUCTION

this process, trust also plays a vital role—trust in oneself as well as organizational or collective trust. Additionally, on all three levels of analysis, actors develop a contextual sensitivity, which they often refine with the passage of time, that gives rise to the development of a repertoire of actions of resilience, resistance, and combat.

Many narratives on anti-press violence have been limited to approaching journalists as victims of censorship and fear. My intention in this book is to challenge this notion by presenting journalists as actors with a capacity for political action, as self-aware subjects.

This book is divided into two parts: Part 1 examines the politics of violence against the press and attempts to answer in three chapters the famous question posed by sociologist Erving Goffman: What's going on here?

Part 2 unravels how cultural, organizational, and social capital is used by a group of resilient newsmakers. It also shows how such capital is deployed by resilient newsmakers to mitigate the risks inherent to their work while creating mechanisms and strategies to confront their fear, resist, and develop a more cautious, civic-minded journalism.

PART I

WHAT'S GOING ON HERE?

1
WHY HAS IT BECOME SO EASY TO KILL JOURNALISTS?

Unfortunately, journalism is a high-risk profession because we are the messengers. We are the connection between society and what is really going on, and we are responsible for communicating that reality.[1]

—FRANCISCO CASTELLANOS, INVESTIGATIVE JOURNALIST FROM MORELIA, MICHOACÁN

Mexican journalism finds itself amid a perfect storm driven by far-reaching political and social transformations over the last three decades. These include the end of the electoral authoritarian system that governed the country for seventy years, the rise of autocratic subnational governors, and the threat of powerful organized crime syndicates. But the storm also arose out of disruptive transnational economic and labor trends: the boom in digital technologies, accelerated job insecurity, and a growing mistrust of the media, both in terms of the news and its coverage. All these factors came together to strike at the extreme vulnerability of professional journalism.[2]

Hence, in this chapter, I assess internal and external factors in journalism that fuel this perfect storm now assailing the press. External factors include political, economic, and criminal changes that decisively reshaped the discipline, encouraging the present climate of violence, intimidation, and risk. Factors internal to the field of journalism include power relations and dynamics that have increased the danger to which reporters are exposed, ranging from the boundaries of and extent to which they exercise freedom of the press to the routines and vices of journalistic practice.

Through interviews with newsmakers and available data, this chapter will look into what constitutes intimidation and attacks on the press from a historical and sociological perspective. Therefore, the question that guides this chapter is, what factors explain the perfect storm of intimidation and fear that the press faces in Mexico?

FACTORS OUTSIDE THE PROFESSION: AN INSECURE DEMOCRACY, AUTHORITARIAN GOVERNORS, AND CRIMINAL CIVIL WARFARE

In the final decades of the twentieth century, Mexico underwent a transformation. Although they arose outside the field of journalism, these recent political and economic shifts have all too frequently shaped journalism as well. That's because they have determined the distribution of political power, the emergence of authoritarianism at a local level, and the boom in criminal civil warfare, along with other major social transformations (like the strengthening of value chains involving Mexico and North America or the rise of digital technologies).

Politically, over the last few decades, Mexico left behind its earlier hegemonic party rule under the PRI (a phenomenon the political analyst Andreas Schedler called electoral authoritarianism). The new, twenty-first-century political regime offers far greater political plurality. It is presumably more democratic, yet it has failed in terms of social justice, equality, freedom of expression, and public security.

At the same time, since the 1980s, Mexico has become embedded in a global market economy, particularly regarding exchange rates and value chains throughout North America. In the process, it became a country dominated by "crony capitalism" with a high concentration of wealth among the few. As of 2018, 41 percent of the population remained mired in some level of poverty.

From 2000 to 2018, the transition to political plurality and public life focused on guaranteeing egalitarian electoral competition. But it set aside necessary social and fiscal redistribution reforms, the fight against inequality and corruption, public security, access to justice, and human rights safeguards. This explains why the Mexican path to political plurality left considerable democratic, social, and organizational deficits in its wake. Moreover, these have been exacerbated in a country that is starkly unequal in terms of economics and institutional capacities, both culturally and geographically. The country also suffers, in this case, from its federal political composition—i.e., states are legally and politically autonomous but depend economically on the federation. In some communities, the presence of the rule of law has waned because of the predominance of criminals who often work in collusion with corrupt government officials.

These democratic deficits have produced complex phenomena (political, social, and criminal). These, taken together, have increased the lethal risk to which journalists are exposed, especially given that, now more than ever, there are cultural and institutional incentives to criticize the powerful.

MEXICO: AN UNSAFE DEMOCRACY

(Starting in 2000), sensitive issues such as corruption, human rights, impunity, public security, and topics previously considered confidential regarding the party in power were no longer taboo. Apparently, a realm of greater freedom opened up, but it was also one of greater fear among those in public office of being caught in certain acts of corruption.[3]

—BALBINA FLORES, ACTIVIST

Democratic countries are not necessarily any safer for journalists than dictatorial regimes. At first glance, this may seem contradictory. In fact, such unsafe democracies are a growing concern around the world.[4]

This phenomenon was correctly perceived by Balbina Flores, a correspondent at Reporters Without Borders (RSF) for the past twenty years. A journalist and activist since the late 1980s, Flores has taken the side of journalists under attack, often performing fieldwork during major political-economic and criminal transformations in Mexico, including the slow collapse between 1980 and 2000 of electoral authoritarianism (1929–2000) and the consolidation of the market economy.

While speaking with me, Flores sits surrounded by files documenting attacks against journalists and posters on the wall demanding justice for these crimes. She explains how the relationship between the press and power was reconfigured in the mid-1990s. The outcome of this change was the rise, in influential press sectors, of a new journalism that was not just economically and editorially independent but more critical, autonomous, and pluralistic. This brand of journalism, it must be noted, has never been hegemonic in media culture in Mexico—primarily due to the prevalence of passive, acritical journalistic practices complacent with power.[5] Still, Flores explains, the start of this century saw a flourishing in journalistic values and norms, which transformed the critical press of major cities into proactive vehicles of civil discontent and catalyzers of political change, a phenomenon scholar Sallie Hughes baptized as civic journalism, Mexican style.[6]

And yet, electoral democracy, Flores notes, also opened a Pandora's box of risks for the practice of critical journalism. While political forces from the opposition occupied the presidency and Congress, the country underwent a complex reconfiguration in power distribution. In some sense, it was the worst of both worlds: those groups already entrenched in authoritarianism (such as governors) maintained their privilege; new actors, meanwhile, were empowered (such as drug traffickers, businesspeople, the clergy, and civic society) and gained a great deal of momentum.[7]

Such a profound reconfiguration of power significantly impacted the boom in violence against the press. This was explained to me by political analyst Sergio Aguayo, one of those most knowledgeable of the period. This new order has been "definitive" in producing violence for journalists, he explained,

> because bastions of the old authoritarianism survive [such as] governors, municipal presidents, and even some official agencies. And blocs of power have emerged that are interested in modulating or silencing what the press has to say. I am thinking here of legal or illegal entrepreneurs: the

most well-known hail from organized crime, but there are also some legitimate businesspeople trying to put the brakes on what's said. They've had success in a great many states because their media are founded not to inform but rather to cover other areas of business. This is because the journalism trade is very debilitated, atomized, poorly paid, and, therefore, relatively defenseless because state organisms in charge of protecting them don't do their jobs properly.[8]

Indeed, as associations that defend freedom of expression have documented, the principal group of aggressors against the press comprises this range of empowered figures Aguayo mentions. They include government agents on different levels, especially powerful governors and their political groups; public security forces, notably municipal police and the armed forces that carry out police work; organized crime, self-defense groups, and violent civic organizations (such as teachers' unions); *caciques* (local political bosses); and, to a lesser degree, business associations. Indeed, as Aguayo notes, the current attacks on the press can be understood only through the empowerment of these groups. They shun any form of public scrutiny and have no qualms about using their influence against their critics. After all, they act under the assumption they are untouchable (given the poor track record of criminal justice in Mexico).

During the same period, this new power distribution also provided journalism with greater margins of autonomy, as pointed out by activist Balbina Flores in her testimonial. Media outlets gained greater economic and political preeminence within an environment of greater party competence and a boom in political marketing and media coverage of the public sphere. On the one hand, they became legitimate agents of change by exposing corruption scandals. On the other, they acted as skillful businesspeople who garnered more sizable political niches and editorial business opportunities (such as market-guided journalism), nearly always exploiting their proximity to and complicity with the political elite.[9] Thus, the onset of electoral democracy opened the possibility of a journalism that differed from previous practices, whether better distanced from the agendas of political power or of a more critical, proactive, and diverse slant.

However, at the same time, this new journalism was something of a trap. The state, after all, failed to guarantee a civic practice of journalism, free of repression and attacks. Unsafe democracies do not favor journalism. Thus, democratic openness was a poisoned apple for the critical press. This may seem counterintuitive since the liberal theory of democracy assumes an almost causal relationship between democratic political regimes and a critical press. Even so, that is not the case in Mexico.

And Mexico is not the exception. The disproportionate increase in attacks against journalists in post-authoritarian Mexico forms part of a global pattern among countries transitioning from an authoritarian regime to a more plural one. This is especially true of countries that have also experienced elevated levels of violence and possess political institutions deficient in security and justice. The political transition in Mexico was insufficient as it centered on only minimal procedures to ensure free and competitive elections. Moreover, even with significant advances in transparency and accountability, more ambitious reforms—in terms of economic inequality, progressive taxation, access to justice, and safeguarding human rights— have been hamstrung.

Conceptually, Mexico possesses a hybrid political regime, the most dangerous kind for the practice of journalism. Hybrid regimes boast democratic political institutions, such as free elections, yet suffer from authoritarian inertia and maintain strong institutions plagued by opacity, abuse of power, and corruption.[10] In particular, hybrid regimes display a strong antiliberal component, given that despite their democratic facade, they cannot democratically strengthen the rule of law. Unlike classic authoritarian regimes, such as Mexico's electoral authoritarianism, hybrid political regimes offer significant economic, political, cultural, and legal incentives for the press to exercise a more civic journalism. However, unlike consolidated democratic regimes, they provide the critical press with few guarantees of safety and access to justice—or none at all.

Different global comparative studies reflect these hybrid regimes' unique danger. In a study of murders of journalists around the globe, German researchers Christian Bjørnskov and Andreas Freytag found that such murders are more likely in countries that possess high levels of freedom of the press alongside corruption and a weak rule of law, such as Mexico.[11] Something similar was found by Víctor Asal and his colleagues in a study analyzing the murders of journalists worldwide between 1992 and 2008: journalists in democratic countries with political conflicts and low levels of governance are at a greater risk of being murdered than in authoritarian countries.[12]

Taking these studies into account, Sallie Hughes and Yulia Vorobyeva found that the most dangerous kinds of hybrid regimes are those, like Mexico, in which there are unequal minimal rights and guarantees across the country.[13] Such subnational authoritarianisms are booming nationwide, which, the authors note, explains violence against the press. This phenomenon, specifically in Mexico, is analyzed in the following section.

AUTHORITARIAN GOVERNORS

> *There is no way to escape these processes, [and] in general terms, state governments establish very perverse, tricky mechanisms to ensure that the media are always subjected to these negotiations.*[14]
>
> —JULIO HERNÁNDEZ LÓPEZ, COLUMNIST

Within regional journalism, governors are one of the primary sources of control and censorship. Following the fall of national *priismo* (PRI dictatorship) during the 1990s, state governors benefited from unparalleled political autonomy and became local political bosses.[15] Moreover, various reforms endowed them with considerable prerogatives in terms of security, justice, education, and greater federal fiscal resources. Along with this power, they acquired the capacity to control different arenas such as Congress, the courts, elections, budgets, and the media. All this has meant state governors can commonly build alliances with other local powers, including businesspeople and even drug traffickers.

Cocooned in local regimes with marked authoritarian tendencies, these regional leaders operate with significant autonomy, operational capacity, and resource management. In fact, their local authority is so broad that they control most aspects of public life in a state—elections, public finances, access to justice, and, of course, the media—without any counterbalance whatsoever. Indeed, in popular imagery, these powerful figures of the Mexican political system are commonly depicted as colonial viceroys.[16] In the past three decades, these local powers have become political figures with a marked national influence: since political alternance began, three out of four presidents have been ex-governors.

Consider the local newspaper directed by Julio Hernández (the epigraph at the start of this section is attributed to him). Not only a director, Hernández López is also a nationally renowned progressive political columnist. In 2005, the newspaper suffered blowback from a governor with conservative political affinities, who was annoyed by the publication's editorial stance. "The state governor said that not only would our periodical have its advertising suspended," explained Hernández López, "but he also launched an information boycott, failing to provide us with information or supply us with information generated by governmental activities that, of course, are of public interest."[17] He explained to me in great detail the "very perverse, very tricky" arrangements used by governors to punish critics or reward those who praise and flatter the powerful. Cases like these are constantly replicated across the country.

When they cannot control the press, regional leaders co-opt it. They do so by offering juicy, opaque clientelist arrangements. Sometimes, to avoid violent repercussions, journalists opt to maintain "obligatory understandings." But such arrangements, of course, are highly pernicious to a critical, independent press. "[The discretional use of official advertising] is quite common. It's something structurally embedded that takes place nationwide, on every government level, and across party lines," said Justine Dupuy, a senior analyst at an independent research center.[18] In Mexico—where local advertising markets are not as buoyant and periodicals find it hard to survive on readership—these opaque, clientelist arrangements constitute a shocking 70 percent of the advertising income for local media.

Such harmful clientelist practices are long-standing in Mexico.[19] However, they were exacerbated by the boom in viceroy-governors, especially in a political environment where they had gained a capacity for political and financial resources and power as never before.

In this, Mexico is like other federative countries that transitioned from an authoritarian regime on a national scale, such as some Latin American or former Soviet bloc countries. In such countries, the onset of political plurality nationwide did not automatically translate into adopting deep-rooted democratic practices and institutions on a local level.[20] Following Mexico's national political alternance, so-called subnational authoritarianisms emerged. These subnational units are embedded in national regimes that are presumably democratic but where fundamental rights are violated in a recurring fashion (electoral fraud, political violence, and serious human rights violations) and where discretional, opaque practices prevail within local government.[21]

During the same period, investigations into corruption became common: in 2017, seventeen former governors were investigated for corruption.[22] One inside witness of this change is Rafael Rodríguez Castañeda, who was general editorial director of the influential magazine *Proceso* for over twenty years (1999–2020). When we met at the magazine's headquarters, he related the following: "[Vicente] Fox washed his hands of relations with [the governors].... He said, 'Here, everyone is free to do as they please,' and so the governors became actual caciques with singular independence in every state.... Therefore, they have money and local clout, and they no longer have to answer to the chief executive in office."[23]

To maintain control and contain political scandals, explains political analyst Edward Gibson, these powerful governors implement "border control" strategies designed to maximize political dominion, avoiding the intervention of external forces by stemming and controlling information flows.[24] Governors and their political groups also employ these strategies to control the media in general and the practice of critical journalism in particular.[25]

To achieve this control—which has never been and can never be absolute—governors resort to a "media manipulation menu" that seeks to coerce the practice of journalism.[26] The application of this menu does not take place in a historic vacuum but, rather, to a large degree, follows certain patterns of the past (especially that of the machinery of institutionalized political manipulation in operation since the 1950s and 1960s), given that it consists of a broad range of cultural, administrative, legal, and economic resources, in addition to violence.[27] Among the control strategies used by governors, the following four are the most popular:

1. The local propaganda apparatus, including discretional access to information, documents, and government sources.
2. The political use of defamation and libel laws to intimidate critical journalism (above all, to reduce the publication of corruption scandals).[28]
3. The use of material, economic, and financial incentives to reward allies and punish critical journalists. These incentives may take on many forms: they may involve direct payments to journalists and, on a business level, advertising agreements, contracts that are almost always directly adjudicated and may extend for multiple years.
4. The use of violent aggression against independent and critical media and journalists, ranging from intimidating or aggressive phone calls to public disqualifications, threats, beatings, and other attacks up to and including homicide.

The application of this manipulation menu, as researcher Grisel Salazar indicates, is not homogenous among subnational governments.[29] Rather, state governors face the dilemma of choice: the decision of when to use one strategy versus another.

Taking into consideration other regional studies, Salazar proposes that this choice, especially between economic incentives and violence, is determined by the balance governors strike between the cost of repression and the material and political resources they possess.[30] Thus, when they have no economic restrictions, governors opt for financial incentives, given that they wield control over the local Congress and possess greater margins of discretional use of the state budget. By contrast, when governing subnational entities with harsher socioeconomic conditions, they opt for violence. In their provocative study, researchers Sallie Hughes and Mireya Márquez found that violence against the press is less common and more attenuated

WHY HAS IT BECOME SO EASY TO KILL JOURNALISTS?

in those places where the use of economic resources with clientelist objectives and coercion of the media are highly effective.[31]

Finally, as Salazar also points out, although the media manipulation menu used by contemporary governors may be very similar to that of the past, there are some important differences. First, the boom in digital technologies makes it practically impossible to control the production and dissemination of political content within a determined local jurisdiction. Second, institutional limitations on maintaining a democratic facade on a subnational level to avoid national attention—as a strategy to prolong the governors' political careers—or that of the international community. Third, in states with a well-developed political culture and strong political opposition, the manipulative actions of governors may be limited because of local counterbalances such as congresses, courts, and political opposition.

As I will explore further on, the governors' control of information is also limited by journalists. Specifically, it is determined by the strategies that critical journalists and their independent allies implement to continue investigating and exposing corruption despite blowback.

THE BOOM IN CIVIL CRIMINAL WARFARE

We keep talking about drug trafficking, but no one investigates drug trafficking. We run the news items that come from agencies, arrests, and facts that are already public knowledge, but there is no further investigation to avoid risks . . . once the situation gets complicated. There were definitely attacks because, well, two colleagues were killed, a reporter and a photographer, and there were direct threats. As deputy director, I received various threatening calls in which they said that we should take down publications from our website, or that they knew we were working on some story and warned us not to go public, or not to publish certain things that they knew we had covered. Like when the question of hanging banners or graffiti on walls became very popular, either with messages for opposing gangs or the government. All of which did in fact motivate our previous investigation, which was subsequently buried.[32]

—DEPUTY DIRECTOR, *EL DIARIO DE JUÁREZ*

WHAT'S GOING ON HERE?

In 2008, in Ciudad Juárez, the government launched Joint Operation Chihuahua, a military campaign involving over ten thousand military troops that sought to quell the age-old but renewed battle between the cartels of Juárez and Sinaloa and their respective armed factions for control over routes, profits, and illegal markets. From 2008 to 2010, violence increased in the city sevenfold, and as a result, between 2008 and 2010, the practice of journalism was also dramatically subverted in Ciudad Juárez. This was due to the eruption of a criminal insurgency and the heavy-handed, abusive reaction of the state, as indicated by the above testimonial the deputy director of *El Diario de Juárez*, the most relevant legacy newspaper in terms of civic vocation in the state of Chihuahua.

The criminal insurgency has left in its wake a turbulent legacy of fear, death, and abuse not only toward journalists but the civilian population as well. Both journalists and academics have found this conflict difficult to catalog. "I realized from the start that it is a strange phenomenon because it is a nontraditional armed conflict with nontraditional actors," said Ioan Grillo, an influential British investigative journalist who has resided in Mexico since 2000.[33] Austrian political analyst Andreas Schedler audaciously calls it a "civil criminal war,"[34] given that he finds it similar to the influential "new wars" concept developed by British scholar Mary Kaldor.[35] These "new wars," according to Kaldor, are unlike other conflicts where an ideological banner is waved. Instead, they follow a purely economic logic in which combatants try to maximize their gains. Rather than waged between sovereign nations, these "new wars" are armed conflicts between public forces and armed militias within nation-states.

However, this Hobbesian scenario was not always the norm. Drug trafficking has a very long history in Mexico.[36] But except for very specific episodes—for example, Operation Condor in the 1970s—high levels of violence have not always accompanied Mexican trafficking.

In fact, the electoral authoritarian regime coexisted with a Pax Mafiosa during the second half of the twentieth century.[37] The balance in this arrangement was maintained by the conformation of a hegemonic criminal organization that received security from the regime—on a municipal level at first, then state, and finally, federal—in exchange for sharing economic gains. This arrangement was reconfigured in the late 1980s because of realignments in the criminal world and economic liberalization among its corrupt political allies and the reconfiguration of the cocaine market in the United States. From that moment on, this presumably peaceful equilibrium gradually broke down, and a fragmentary dynamic became the norm among criminal organizations.

Incentives to coexist peacefully were fractured pari passu with the fragmentation of political power nationwide. One of the central causes of exacerbated contemporary criminal violence, according to researchers Guillermo Trejo and Sandra Ley, was the breakdown,[38] starting with the political liberalization of the 1980s, of government-run criminal protection networks.[39]

Party alternance advanced on a local scale starting in 1989. But this, according to researchers, created a rupture in the criminal arena that, to subsist, had to create new networks of protection by arming powerful private militias. These new networks settled into the gray areas of the state where criminals intersect with security officials and corrupt justice distribution. Given the situation, these criminal insurgent militias took on a major military force capacity and rapidly entered into an expansionist phase to conquer new routes and territories. An agent of change during this process was Los Zetas, the armed branch of the Cartel del Golfo, composed of former elite military officers from the Mexican army. Their military strategy and brutality allowed them to reconfigure protection networks by extending them first to other criminal organizations and afterward to the civilian population.

This environment of criminal expansionism and uncertainty intensified in 2006. That year, after winning the presidency in a highly questionable election, President Felipe Calderón (2006–2012) declared a full-on battle against organized crime. By that time, gangs possessed growing militias broadly supplied with arms from the United States that controlled multiple activities beyond the transportation of narcotics, including extractive industries among the civilian population and a buoyant domestic consumption of illegal drugs.[40] Within this context, the government deployed hundreds of thousands of military officers and police officers in places with a major criminal presence, including the previously mentioned 2008 Joint Operation Chihuahua in Ciudad Juárez.

This strategy of military confrontation, as Trejo and Ley have argued, was implemented following a partisan logic. In areas governed by party identities similar to those of the president, they opted to contain criminal violence through cooperation and empowerment of local government. In contrast, in areas characterized by political fragmentation—primarily, where left-wing administrations were in office—political conflict prevailed. This meant the national government failed to cooperate with these local governments, which, in turn, enabled the strengthening of criminal cells and the continued expansion of their criminal influence. Such institutional weakness was exacerbated in election years and most of all at the level of municipal government.

This was a window of opportunity for organized crime cartels. According to Trejo and Ley, they engaged in territorial wars, seeking to ensnare local profits and to control structures within the government that would provide them with greater protection and influence. Importantly, these criminal cells sought not only political but territorial control. Consequently, "regimes of criminal governance" were configured: "territories where, de facto, criminal gangs control different dimensions of local organization such as the political, economic, and social life of communities and districts in urban areas."

In these territories, the cartels also controlled forms of public expression, including journalism. "It is dangerous, for example, to go to certain towns in a state where there is a very strong presence and influence of drug traffickers," commented a journalist from the political section of a major newspaper in Jalisco. "It's dangerous because, from the moment you arrive, you realize that they are already starting to follow you. Sometimes they actually stop you and ask, 'Who are you? Where are you going? What are you going to do? What are you going to write about?'"[41]

The acceleration of violence was not only due to bellicose party politics and the boom of "criminal governance regimes." Even victories over the cartels—specifically, "decapitations," where their leaders were captured or assassinated—only gave rise to additional major local crises and more bloodshed. And these local crises, in turn, infected other states. In 2009, criminal violence was present in only six states: Baja California, Chihuahua, Durango, Guerrero, Michoacán, and Sinaloa. Little by little, others joined them. In 2010, Nuevo León, Tamaulipas, and Nayarit followed. In 2011, Veracruz.[42] This geographic expansion was fueled by the fragmentation of criminal gangs.

In 2006, there were just six cartels. Various internal divisions and reaccommodations forced them to become eight in 2009, and then eleven in 2010. These major cartels, in turn, clashed with local, atomized criminal cells; by 2010, these smaller units had reached an estimated total of 114.[43]

Thus, the main consequence of the state's decapitation strategy was the fragmentation of criminal territories, and its consequence was utter chaos. "The terms of understanding between the state and the criminal mafia were broken once the war started," said a top executive of *Reforma*, one of the nation's most influential daily newspapers, "triggering a lack of control and causing the cartels to reconfigure, generating gang disputes that were far more violent."[44]

Indeed, from 2007 to 2012, homicidal violence increased fivefold. It increased significantly in certain regions like the Gulf of Mexico and northeastern, western, and southeastern Mexico. High rates of homicide occurred in towns used for the transportation of narcotics, either as consumer markets or as zones of territorial dispute between drug cartel cells.

Other crimes increased alongside the rise in homicides, including abductions, extortion, and robbery. The increase in violence overwhelmed a country with unreliable and inefficient institutions of public security and distribution of justice. Indeed, by 2016, only 0.0006 percent of cases of willful homicide related to this war (perpetrated between 2006 and 2015) were solved.[45] Hence, across the nation, it became easier to kill not only journalists but anyone.

The bellicose strategy of Fox and Calderón against criminal organizations was effectively continued by the PRI administration of President Enrique Peña Nieto between 2012 and 2018. The only exception was the new administration's public silence regarding the situation. The continuation exacerbated several problems. First, though there had been a marked decrease in homicides linked to organized crime, starting in 2014, lethal criminal violence increased and expanded territorially. And it rose even in states that until then had remained relatively on the sidelines, such as Baja California Sur, Puebla, and Quintana Roo. In this context, just a few notable cases, like the southeastern state of Yucatán, have remained a peaceful exception to burgeoning criminal violence; researchers explained that this is due to multiple factors, including interagency cooperation and coordination between authorities from different parties.[46]

Second, the atomization of criminal gangs continued. The 114 criminal organizations operating in 2010 had practically doubled by 2016. In some areas of the country, this triggered widespread mayhem.

Third, the growing atomization of cartels caused them to branch out into other business sectors. These included legal enterprises, like mining in Michoacán, but also new kinds of illegality, such as robbery, extortion, and abduction.[47]

Finally, given the circumstances, regimes of criminal governance multiplied. Simultaneously, other parallel orders of governance emerged—such as self-defense groups—that entered into disputes with organized crime cells and the state.

A different sort of consequence emerged outside the criminal gangs: the rise of violence perpetuated by police officers and the military. During the presidential administrations of Felipe Calderón (2006–2012) and Enrique Peña Nieto (2012–2018), these were presented as a consequence of the "War on Drugs." Yet such acts, committed by police officers and the military, included cases of abduction, human trafficking, clandestine mass graves, homicides in the streets, and illegal arrests. All of these, though perpetrated by officers of the state against alleged criminals, are considered serious human rights violations.

In the war to control the narrative, this crossfire between government officials and criminal elements left the press between a rock and a hard place. At first, the media, except for a handful of national and local exceptions, fell in line with the official discourse without putting up a fight. This widespread use of government information as "news," as I was told by the deputy director of *El Diario de Juárez*, was not purchased with sweetheart deals and bags of money, nor did it stem from the journalists' lack of skill. Instead, embracing the official narrative, he maintained, was simply an extreme version of self-censorship. (Moreover, as this deputy director also stated in the above testimonial, drug-trafficking cells increased their counter-communications repertoire to attract or influence journalistic endeavors.) In the end, silence nearly always prevailed, with only a few bits of superficial information released.

"We keep talking about drug trafficking," he said, "but no one investigates drug trafficking." In a handful of cases, above all in major cities, to practice public-minded journalism with a certain degree of autonomy, journalists and their allies opted to implement journalistic and editorial strategies that were both personal and collective. Even so, a top social research center, in a documented joint study with the magazine *Vice*, found that only 45 percent of the bloody events registered nationwide were published in the media.[48]

FACTORS INTERNAL TO THE FIELD: JOB INSECURITY, LOW RISK AWARENESS, AND A LACK OF SOLIDARITY

Over the first two decades of the twenty-first century, Mexican journalism has experienced an ongoing transformation, even beyond the dramatic impact of the rise in criminal violence. The omnipresent influence of the digital world, such as the boom in digital platforms, has overwhelmed journalistic autonomy, as have forces of renewal that originated in civil society (on a local, national, and international level), the market economy, and political pluralism. And, like other professional areas, Mexican journalism has also followed historical patterns that have prevailed since its formation in the early twentieth century, such as profound centralism, urban concentration, precariousness, pernicious proximity to political power, and distancing from the public.

Moreover, Mexican journalism cultivates only a limited professionalism, which is deeply atomized. This means that different journalists in different regions or publications possess differentiated or heterogeneous journalistic values. For example, during much of the twentieth century, the dominant model of journalism during electoral authoritarianism was servile, passive, and complacent.

But today, that is changing. In recent decades, broad, influential, and strategic journalism segments in traditional national and local media, as well as among digital startups or freelance journalists, have operated under hybrid formats and mental structures. These include civic, militant, and collective models, as well as media with a strong commitment to society and victims of the criminal civil war. Lamentably, these hybrid journalisms, whose vocation is to serve the public interest, tend to be more profitable civically and socially than economically.

Thus, journalists run too many risks, increasing their exposure to violence and their likelihood of coming under attack or suffering intimidation. The following section explores the underlying factors: job insecurity, low-risk awareness, and a lack of social support or solidarity.

JOB INSECURITY

> *More and more often, news organizations fail to provide benefits . . . which is a contradiction in terms when you consider the fact that our jobs involve a lot of risk. . . . So what you should have, the very least you ought to be able to count on, would be social security, and there isn't any.*[49]
>
> —JOURNALIST IN MAZATLÁN, SINALOA

Widespread job insecurity elevates the material vulnerability that journalists suffer. Such insecurity also degrades their work's quality and professional autonomy[50] and catalyzes physical and psychological risks.[51] The above testimonial from a Mazatlán, Sinaloa, journalist describes how meager salaries and a lack of health services form a widespread pattern in many media outlets she has worked for over the past twenty years. I heard similar testimonials from other journalists I spoke to. Indeed, "barring violence," poor working conditions are one of the main risks in their profession.[52]

Job insecurity describes an uncertain, unpredictable, high-risk type of employment.[53] Not unique to the press in Mexico, such insecurity has been a major global trend since the 1970s. In the world of creative industries, some experts sounded the alarm more than a decade ago regarding the accelerated job insecurity of media professionals, including journalists.[54] They indicated continuous global economic crises, especially the 2008 financial crisis; major transformations in labor organization caused by growing flexibility in labor conditions; and digital disruptions, including the crisis of traditional journalism's business model, have catapulted this process.

While the business and labor relations crisis in journalism forms part of a global pattern, various factors exacerbate it even further in Mexico. Most importantly, the country's pauperization of labor, which is not exclusive to the press sector, contributes to economic stagnation. Mexico has experienced low levels of economic growth (2.6 percent from 1990 to 2017), extremely high levels of informal employment (57 percent by 2018), and high poverty rates (43 percent of the population by 2017), together with extremely low minimum wage levels. Even before the 2008 crisis, workers were already working for severely diminished salaries and were exploited at jobs where their future employment was uncertain.

This discouraging economic environment has devastated the journalism industry, which remains distanced from its readership and still mainly depends on official advertising to subsist. The havoc wrought by the 2008 financial crisis, in addition to the boom in digital platforms and changes in labor organization, was particularly notable in the news industry, which suffered closures of media outlets and mass firings. For example, Televisa, Mexico's most important television network, embarked on a financial restructuring because of the global financial crisis. Moreover, journalists have no regional or national unions that will fight for their rights owing to historic corporatist mistrust and business sector opposition.

I conducted most of the interviews for this book from 2014 to 2016. At that time, the average salary of a local reporter with a signed, fixed contract—eight out of ten have one—was around US$250 to US$300 per month. These contracts, moreover, feed into a news factory complex in which journalists need to work more than eight hours a day while manufacturing dozens of news items per week.

Many, however, lack even a fixed contract. Indeed, over the past few years, the ranks of traditional and digital media newsmakers without a fixed salary or benefits or who simultaneously produce content for various platforms and different media outlets have swollen. This often obliges journalists to charge piecemeal, say, US$15 to US$50 per published article, depending on relevance. This is a widespread practice in Mexico, brought on by popular illegal subcontracting strategies that allow businesspeople to evade taxes. According to a national poll, journalists, to supplement meager salaries, on average, produce news items for more than two media outlets, which often appear on three or four platforms.[55] This same poll shows that nearly two out of ten journalists work part-time and almost always do so without a formal contract. The actual figure, however, is doubtless several times higher.

This growing "flexibilization" of journalism has caused many reporters to migrate to digital entrepreneurship formats. With very few exceptions, these, unfortunately, rarely result in profitable journalistic projects, economically or socially speaking. One journalist, aged fifty, who covers general news stories for a local television station in Morelia, Michoacán, commented, "[Michoacán] is a state with a lot of economic issues, so if a media outlet doesn't pay you, it's very difficult for you to finish the job. Then you are sidelined from that outlet and practically starve. You must dedicate your time to doing something else and perform journalism without earning any money."[56]

Moreover, illegal subcontracting schemes leave journalists, including those who cover political, public safety, and police-related beats, with no social security system, deprived of even the minimum benefits required by law. Besides being illegal, that leaves journalists helpless, especially those who cover areas involving a certain level of risk. "If something happens to

WHY HAS IT BECOME SO EASY TO KILL JOURNALISTS?

you, if they kill you, the company washes their hands because you aren't under contract," a regional police reporter who covers Estado de México explained to me.[57] Even journalists find it difficult to compensate for these shortcomings with their own resources. Like many others, investigative journalist Anabel Hernández has stated that private insurers refuse to provide her with coverage because of her profession.

Job insecurity leads to burned-out reporters and, ultimately, perniciously degrades the practice of journalism itself. A journalist covering the political beat in Jalisco (aged 37) summarized: "[Job insecurity] forces you to be mediocre and fail to inform. You end up compiling information provided by government agencies; you end up reproducing bulletins. . . . Here, anyone who wants to be a reporter, anyone who really wants to be one, has to scratch their own back because the company probably won't defend you and won't provide the necessary conditions for you to do a good job as a journalist."[58]

LACK OF RISK AWARENESS AND PROTECTION

> *Safety protocols for journalists usually have been adapted from coverage scenarios in war-torn nations. And what we are experiencing in Mexico is an irregular war with no fronts and no rear guard, where you don't know the enemy. So, international protocols used for the coverage of armed conflicts don't apply to this new situation Mexico is going through.*[59]
>
> —INVESTIGATIVE JOURNALIST FROM MONTERREY, NUEVO LEÓN

Journalists, like the general populace, were taken by surprise when criminal civil war broke out in Mexico. The above testimonial is from an investigative reporter who covers the country's northeastern region (Coahuila, Nuevo León, and Tamaulipas) for an influential national magazine. In his line of work, he reported on terrible events linked to criminal violence, including civilian massacres perpetrated by powerful criminal organizations, such as the fearsome Los Zetas, that almost always operate under the protection of corrupt public security forces. Like the vast majority of journalists in the region, his own experience helped him devise security strategies that he implemented to provide this coverage. As he notes above, the most common safety protocols for journalists worldwide were not designed for a conflict like the one in Mexico but rather to cover regular warfare.

A critical catalyst of risk is the lack of specialized training to cover areas like public safety, justice, and politics. One investigative reporter (aged 55) I interviewed specializes in subjects of public safety and corruption. But she described the lack of awareness among some local journalists regarding the minefield that many cities and towns across the nation have become:

> The leap local journalists have taken has been unconscious: from covering the news of the day [where] there were accidents, a car bomb here, a drowning there, a crash involving multiple vehicles. . . . They went to shootouts, dead men found tossed by the side of the road with their throats cut, bearing messages. . . . And so, the news of the day started to involve regional or even national security issues, and they were unprepared. How could they not be vulnerable?[60]

More knowledgeable than most regarding Mexico's regional complexities, she has formed part of the Sociedad Interamericana de Prensa (SIP) for over a decade. This association brings together media entrepreneurs in Mexico. A watershed organization from the early 2000s, the SIP has backed different risk-training programs on an organizational level. However, these joint initiatives have had little impact on corporate culture nationwide, above all because newspapers in northern Mexico have led them.

Most journalists I interviewed explained to me that their editorial boards rarely offer them security training. "There isn't a single company in Veracruz that is concerned about this," said one young reporter from Veracruz.[61] In the few cases where training has taken place, protocols are usually implemented in reaction to a direct attack on colleagues or media outlets. Since media outlet business owners have done little to protect helpless journalists, international civil organizations have shouldered the burden and introduced initiatives to enhance training in high-risk situations.[62]

Journalists have also started training one another. Motivated to address the shortcomings in Mexican journalism, a group of journalists founded the association Periodistas de a Pie in 2007. One of the founders of this collective, journalist Daniela Pastrana, explained to me how dozens of training programs showed local journalists how to cover the treacherous and complex realities they found themselves in. Early on, Periodistas de a Pie realized their program would have to differ from the training some international organizations offer. Their training was not just about providing reporters with personal or digital security training but also teaching them how to read the political context so they would be more sensitive and perceptive to changes in power and the local criminal environment.[63]

The need for such political training became evident in the 2014 murder of local journalist Gregorio Jiménez in Veracruz. The special mission to clarify his murder, discussed in the introduction, included Daniela Pastrana. She explained to me that their investigation revealed that, in all likelihood, Jiménez could not tell where the fatal blow would come from. "If anything's clear to me, it's that he never even knew why they killed him," she said. "He never understood how to make a connection between the cases he published. He never saw what one had to do with the other. . . . It was convenient for a lot of people to have him killed because five or six articles he had published were related, but he was not aware of this."[64]

Since then, dozens of civil organizations defending freedom of expression, along with networks and collectives of independent journalists, have started to provide different kinds of training on personal security for journalists. Such education almost always operates under the premise that additional training is necessary to report what they are experiencing. However, for sharp observers like an investigative journalist and editor, this endeavor has fallen short. Ultimately, we still have not succeeded in developing a deep-rooted culture of awareness and risk prevention in Mexico.

LACK OF SOCIAL SUPPORT AND PROFESSIONAL SOLIDARITY

When Eliseo [Barrón] was gunned down, I was the one who actively sought out the solidarity of colleagues, asking them to sign a full-page insert published the day after his murder. I'm the one who organized the protest where we took to the streets for the first time. I'm the one who goes around talking to colleagues in person to learn what it is we have to do, what it is we can do. I'm that guy, but I really felt frustrated at times because we haven't been able to make that leap of charity, of solidarity, of fraternity, of truly acting as colleagues in this trade, in our profession.[65]

—JOURNALIST AND COLUMNIST FROM DURANGO

Once this perfect storm had gathered over the field of Mexican journalism, reporters found themselves atomized not only within their own profession but standing alone before a society that perceived them as distant or foreign. This solitude may be ascribed to a lack of support and solidarity that journalists all too often display toward crimes against the press, as described in the above testimonial from a journalist whose friend and colleague was murdered.

On May 26, 2008, the corpse of Eliseo Barrón was found bearing signs of torture. He was a reporter specializing in public security and narcopolitics for the newspaper *Milenio Torreón*. Barrón had exposed how Gómez Palacios, Durango, had turned into a minefield. And he did so by reporting events that had become everyday, such as criminal infiltration of the municipal police or the settling of accounts between government forces and the Sinaloa and Los Zetas cartels, which were disputing the territory at the time.

Due in good measure to the fact that Barrón's paper formed part of a major chain of newspapers, the murder of Eliseo Barrón set off a wave of local, national, and international indignation. On a local level, marches replete with journalists—accompanied by a few members of the civilian population—were organized under the slogans "We are all Eliseo!" "This war is not ours!" "Not one reporter less!" However, as demonstrated in the above testimonial by a journalist who was very close to Barrón, in the beginning, it was not easy to gain the solidarity and support of local colleagues. It was also hard to keep up sustained pressure and cohesion over time. Eventually, the movement fell apart.

WHY HAS IT BECOME SO EASY TO KILL JOURNALISTS?

In the long run, the lively support of the marches faded because, according to this journalist, unjustified jealousy and envy always prevail. "We are a fairly vulnerable sector," he said. "We are responsible for that."[66]

Owing to the competitive nature of their jobs, journalists operate in environments that make professional solidarity difficult to achieve. Even in surroundings where there may be journalistic and editorial cooperation, competition tends to prevail as reporters seek to gain exclusives and publish scoops. In those countries where journalism has evolved with structural professional limitations, it is even more challenging to attain strong solidarity and mutual support among journalists. Mexico belongs to this category.

During my fieldwork for this book, I observed, time and again, a lack of solidarity among peers. When I asked my interviewees, How would you describe the response of the journalism trade to aggressions against the press? The vast majority reacted with words like *apathy, lack of support, indifference,* and *indolence*. One freelance journalist from Sinaloa summed up this fragmentation and atomization as follows: "In general, we are disjointed, mistrustful, apathetic, very individualist."[67] Strikingly, this is not a new phenomenon.

Solidarity among journalists in Mexico has historically been lacking. Various factors can help to explain this. First, the lack of unity comes from a natural competitiveness among journalists. "There is a very special envy that circulates in journalism, where rather than support one another, they set up obstacles and barriers—natural forms of envy, publication envy," as a television journalist from Michoacán put it.[68] Such envy, by the way, is often nourished by the news organizations themselves. For example, the influential newspaper *Reforma* prohibits its contributors from inviting other colleagues to cooperate, a practice repeated even by the newspaper's small, local editorial staff.

Second, there is a well-defined class division between elite journalists and all the rest, not to mention the broad inequality of a majority of street reporters subordinated to elite boards of directors, who possess considerably superior resources.

The third element that exerts a negative influence is the blurry, heterogeneous norms and values upheld by members of the trade. A poll taken in

2015 found that journalists have myriad or even conflicting conceptions of journalistic responsibility. There are also high levels of mistrust among them, especially those who operate regionally under the control of authoritarian political actors or criminal gangs, who, in turn, tend to infiltrate the profession to control it.

In addition, another counterproductive factor is the persistence of clientelist relations between the press and political power. This was a kind of corporatist organization consolidated during the period of electoral authoritarianism (1929–2000) that was clientelist and corporate in nature. These classic embedded associations—characterized in a comparative investigation by researchers Hallin and Papathanassopoulos—tend to weaken the bonds of solidarity and unity in the profession, given that political interests weaken professional autonomy.[69] The Sindicato Nacional de Redactores de la Prensa—which dates back to 1923—is an example of associations that, for decades, had a *charra* (a government-backed union leader) distanced from the interests of journalists. Labor unions of this kind exist in rural Mexico, where political connections help them adapt to changes in administration.

In fact, over the past few years, such relations have also been forged between journalists and the criminal underworld.[70] These clientelist relations between political patrons and journalists, as the researcher Daniel Hallin and his colleagues have correctly indicated, have substantially weakened professional trust.[71] "There is this historically justified fear that once a journalist reaches a position where they may represent their colleagues, it becomes easier for them to enter into personal negotiations with power. To represent, endorse, and justify. And that is an ongoing debate that for starters, erodes our efforts to organize," columnist Julio Hernández López told me.[72] Guillermo Osorno, one of the organizers of Agenda de Periodistas, commented to me in an interview that, despite a strong demand among the participants to create a national labor union, journalists avoid associating with such groups at all costs, which is why the Agenda de Periodistas prefers to refer to themselves as a national coordinator.[73] One co-founder of Red de Periodistas de Juárez stressed that the members of the network are not a guild and that they "have no relationship of rapport with the government whatsoever."[74] The fears described by these newsmakers continue to be justified; corporatist organizations exist through which political figures exert influence over broad swaths of local journalism.

Professional solidarity is even more difficult to attain within a context of criminal violence, of the kind described at the beginning of this section. As shown by Andreas Schedler, trust tends to diminish in scenarios of criminal civil warfare.[75] In the case of the press, this is particularly important. In some states—above all in places like Tamaulipas, Chihuahua, Coahuila, Michoacán, and Veracruz—the criminal element has even infiltrated copy desks by means of fear, violence, and bribery. The phantom of suspicion, as an investigative journalist from Morelia, Michoacán, told me, is one of the major barriers that still exist within the field of journalism.[76] In addition, in some cases, this lack of union and support is rooted in the imagery that aggressions against the press are narrowly focused and that pressures and attacks on sentinels of the written word will not reach them. "Mostly, the response is apathy. Colleagues tend to think, 'It won't happen to me,'" explained a political news reporter in Oaxaca.[77] A sentiment that, incidentally, echoes a general perception among most of the population that criminal violence has a narrow focus and therefore none of their business.[78]

All these factors contribute to the limited duration, in most cases, of public outrage and protest following attacks or crimes committed against the press. As indicated by theorists who study social movements, the cost of collective action (organization, clear and common objectives, resources) wears down most mobilization efforts. However, as time passes, a minimal consensus has been achieved between journalists' demands and goals. This, in turn, has meant that handfuls of independent journalists have succeeded in establishing truly autonomous associations that enhance professionalization while simultaneously allowing them to demand justice for the crimes committed against them.[79] For some of Eliseo Barrón's colleagues—including the journalist whose testimonial leads this section—this collective organization process took several years to complete.

Solidarity has been lacking not only within the field of journalism but also among the general public. Mexican society has not internalized the drama experienced by journalism because it feels far removed from it. For some who have studied this distancing—for example, in other countries with a recent authoritarian past—this has to do with a historic mistrust of the press. This is because, in Mexico, the press has almost always acted on the side of political elites, in what the legendary journalist Julio Scherer called an arranged marriage. In many of the social protests that have taken place in Mexico City recently, a habitual slogan continues to denounce the *prensa vendida*, or "sold-out press." According to several studies, trust in media and journalistic institutions has, in fact, declined in recent years, mainly because of an abundance of information and the boom in "fake news."[80] Society, simply put, still does not trust its media.

Moreover, as Schedler has also explored, solidarity with any victims of violence has been difficult to achieve. In Mexico, the general population, though it may experience violence, has no great affinity with journalists subjected to violence because of their work. For most of the populace, this internal armed conflict does not involve everyone; there are only a few who kill their own. This also can be felt in the absence of citizens and civil society in protests that clamor for an end to impunity and violence against the press. The citizenry does not stick its neck out to defend journalists, and it does not protest when they are attacked.

Violence against the press is undoubtedly exacerbated by a generalized public distrust of the news system or journalism as an institution. And this is a very common problem among otherwise established democracies today.

In Mexico, the press is left to fend for itself. And thus, the press finds itself more isolated than ever.

It is far too easy to kill journalists in Mexico. Within the profession itself, journalists confront a major transformation: job insecurity, a lack of interest among media outlet owners, professional atomization, and low levels of trust within the profession and society at large. Such internal failings are exacerbated by the crisis outside the profession resulting from the emergence of subnational hybrid regimes and criminal governance. A superior central power no longer mediates these newly empowered figureheads, who thus take on a greater capacity to exert strength and influence. The result has been, at the local and national level, a novel environment of risk and violence against the press.

WHY HAS IT BECOME SO EASY TO KILL JOURNALISTS?

Given the situation, journalists have navigated the turbulent waters Mexico's deficient democracy brought with it, and the outbreak of criminal and political violence, with a great deal of uncertainty, paying a high price in blood and terror. In the next chapter, I will delve into the logic behind this wave of violence against the press.

2

THE WAVE OF VIOLENCE AGAINST THE PRESS

VIOLENCE AGAINST THE PRESS: DIRECT OR INDIRECT?

By violence against the press, I understand everything that somehow prevents us from doing our job.... Attacks on freedom of speech, libel, ... forms of aggression, lack of protection protocols provided by businesspeople who own the media, police brutality, collusion between delinquents and the authorities, impunity, lack of training for the journalists themselves; I consider all of this to be violence.[1]

—ERICK MUÑIZ, NATIONAL NEWSPAPER CORRESPONDENT, MONTERREY, NUEVO LEON

Few agree on what constitutes violence against the press. Indeed, this was one of the first things I discovered while completing my field research for this book. The concept of violence against the press takes on specific meanings depending on personal, sociopolitical, historical, and cultural considerations, especially among journalists.

WHAT'S GOING ON HERE?

Consider the testimonial opening this chapter. The quote is from Erick Muñiz, a correspondent with eighteen years of experience who covers the political beat in Monterrey. He offers a rather broad interpretation of violence against the press. According to him, such violence transcends physical and psychological attacks and includes "everything that somehow prevents us from doing our job." This definition covers a lot of ground, from shortcomings in the justice system to political and criminal depravity to the labor conditions journalists work under.

This loose conception of violence against the press is something I encountered while interviewing journalists who have experienced situations of extreme violence. In this case, Muñiz was incarcerated unjustly for having published information considered inconvenient by a local official. This attests to the fact that even among those who have undergone the most drastic forms of physical and psychological aggression, labor and economic circumstances matter, as do social and political contexts.

With this spectrum of meanings in mind, researcher Sallie Hughes and I make a conceptual distinction between direct and indirect violence against the press.[2] Of these two types of violence, I will use the first definition in this chapter and throughout most of the book. "Direct violence," which is the kind more commonly wielded against media outlets or associations that defend freedom of speech, refers to verbal or psychological attacks perpetrated against journalists or commentators for exercising their profession. "Indirect violence," as per Galtung, refers to blurrier structural constraints, whether consisting of an economic, material, cultural, or symbolic nature reproduced under a determined dominant system. Such limitations include economic inequalities, gender or sex stigmatization or discrimination, and all kinds of hatred based on cultural or racial motives. Although I have focused here on the former, it could be argued that direct and indirect violence are intersectional. For example, indirect violence includes economic precarity, including structural, economic, or cultural aspects, that enhances the risk of direct violence. Likewise, identity and symbolic aspects shape attacks on women and gender minorities.

Moreover, indirect violence against the press is typically more diffuse. Direct violence, in contrast, is always more strategic. Its motives are specific, and its targets have first and last names. This is also true in cases of so-called mob censorship, which is the online harassment of journalists perpetrated through direct messages, blogging, website postings, and doxing. Even when a broad range of actors, including discontented citizens, may have perpetrated these attacks, the targets are always well defined and identified.[3]

Few scholars have illuminated direct violence as extensively as the media historian John Nerone. He states, with good cause, that violence against the press is rarely noise. Instead, such violence is, crucially, a message that has been encoded as fear to pursue a tactical objective: "Acts of violence against the press say something. Acts of violence have rarely been just noise—senseless explosions of passion, bestial reactions from bestial people. On the contrary, most of the acts of violence discussed here were quite strategic. Furthermore, they might all be usefully considered as statements, often in dead languages, about the commonly agreed upon properties and boundaries of public discourse."[4]

From Nerone's comments, we can infer that violence against the press is very similar to political violence, which also tends to be calculated. Like political violence, direct violence against the media follows specific patterns and structural regularities. And these, once exposed, present a panorama traced in a language of blood, silence, and fear, a language seeking to determine what can or cannot be documented or said. Indeed, the same properties of political discourse can be outlined based on aggression and fear.

In the following sections, I will explore the rationale followed by violence against the press. To that end, I will rely on documented and anecdotal information and data to amplify the voices of dozens of journalists, defenders of freedom of the press, and public officials.

THE GREAT WAVE OF VIOLENCE AGAINST THE PRESS

There was already a scenario of violence against the press characterized by threats, persecution, harassment through legal actions, and harassment

WHAT'S GOING ON HERE?

> *through discretional administration of advertising. But then, extreme violence against the press became more acute. The watershed moment was when far more extreme violence began to be expressed through homicide, ruthless murder: unprecedented forms of physical elimination of journalists that included poisoning, torturing to death, forced disappearances. None of which had previously existed in Mexico.*[5]
>
> —MARCO LARA KLAHR, SCHOLAR AND INVESTIGATIVE JOURNALIST

The spiral of political and criminal violence that encompassed the nation nearly two decades ago led to previously unimaginable scenarios. Suddenly, on a greater scale than ever, journalists became like any other group critical of society, such as political candidates for the opposition,[6] or activists.[7] During this period, critical journalists, like others, experienced unimaginable levels of extreme violence and risks for exercising their profession as witnesses and agents of change. This took the form of increasingly frequent and virulent attacks, explains Klahr, who has toured dozens of local newsrooms nationwide as a consultant on freedom of expression and high-risk news coverage. Violence against the press did already exist, he explains, and, indeed, is nothing new. However, Klahr explains that such violence was revamped in the late twentieth and early twenty-first centuries. This recent violence has been far more deadly and far more sadistic. I call this phenomenon the great wave of violence against the press. An expansive flood of attacks directed against journalists and the media started at the beginning of the twenty-first century, especially in rural Mexico. A broad array of state and extra-state actors has perpetrated these attacks. An environment of media distrust, corruption, political intolerance, criminal violence, and impunity frames them.

From 2006 to 2018, the years this book covers, 120 journalist homicides and 26 forced disappearances were registered, a figure far greater than any earlier period in national history. Such numbers are horrifying in and of themselves. Yet they offer only a rough approximation of how expansive these attacks against the press were, not to mention the sheer breadth of the ensuing fear and silence.

THE WAVE OF VIOLENCE AGAINST THE PRESS

As a result, Mexico has become one of the most hazardous places in the world to exercise journalism in recent years, a truth even more relevant from a comparative perspective. The wave of anti-press violence in Mexico is comparable to other attacks on the press similar in magnitude, such as the journalists felled during foreign invasions (Iraq from 2003 to 2011) or openly armed conflicts (Syria from 2013 to 2029). While the number of deaths may be similar, the horrifying difference is that, in Mexico, these murdered journalists are not just "collateral damage."[8] Here, as in Colombia, Russia, and Central America, murdered journalists are the chosen and targeted victims of political and criminal violence.[9] For the most part, they do not fall in the crossfire; instead, they are actively sought out at their homes or places of work, where they are intimidated, beaten, and killed, often with indescribable viciousness and cruelty.

The journalists and commentators murdered in Mexico have often succeeded in stirring up hornet's nests with their publications or images. However, many get caught up in the whirlpools of corruption and criminality that engulf their communities. The victims are local beat journalists like Salvador Olmos García in Oaxaca; investigative journalists like Francisco Javier Ortiz in Tijuana and Miroslava Breach in Chihuahua; crime beat and public safety journalists like Eliseo Barrón in Durango; and photojournalists and activists like Rubén Espinoza in Veracruz.

Because of their cultural status and the social repercussions involved, journalist homicides often receive a great deal of public attention. At the same time, even with this exposure, such attacks tend to exacerbate the already harsh climate of aggression against and intolerance of the press. Homicide represents only the tip of the iceberg: many other attacks against the press are also documented. In 2018, for example, for every murdered journalist, at least sixty attacks against the press took place, according to Artículo 19 Mexico.

So, how did we end up here? This nightmarish reality gradually emerged, concentrated among only a handful of territories and newsrooms until it metastasized. In 2003, the forced disappearance of Jesús Mejía Lechuga took place in Veracruz; this was one of the first such incidents in this wave of attacks.[10] In 2006, the building that housed a legacy newspaper in Nuevo Laredo came under attack with assault weapons and explosives, "the first armed assault against the facilities of a media outlet to use explosives since the war on drugs began."[11] From 2006 to 2016, more than fifty-seven attacks were documented against media outlets in thirteen different states,[12] including some with grenades.[13] From 2006 to 2016, more than twenty-four disappearances were documented, mainly in municipal areas with criminal governance in Tamaulipas, Veracruz, Guerrero, and Michoacán.[14] The cruelty of forced disappearance lies not only in the loss of a loved one but in the vacuum it leaves behind once they are torn away from the world.

As the taboo against harming the press gradually disappeared, the brutality increased. Threats became more virulent and frequent, occurring in person, through third parties, or via digital media. Illegal arrests and kidnappings became more common, especially in territories where the state was losing control. There were more and more cases of forced internal displacement of journalists for security reasons.[15] Fear and censorship worsened as well. In 2007, self-censorship, as a means of mitigating the risks associated with their profession, was employed by 67 percent of Mexican journalists.[16]

Post-traumatic stress and other mental disorders also increased, especially among journalists who were harassed or who covered criminal violence and its effects on society.[17] Indeed, a direct relationship was found between the risk that journalists confront and manifestations of stress,[18] as well as a greater tendency to experience symptoms of post-traumatic stress disorder, depression, or anxiety, in comparison with those who do not cover news related to violence and drug trafficking.[19] The levels are similar to those suffered by war correspondents,[20] but with a significant difference: Mexican journalists live and work in the zone where the violence takes place.[21]

In light of the increased instances and new forms of violence against the press, the following sections outline responses to these questions: What are the institutional circumstances underlying this great wave of violence? Why does journalism require a democratic state to function? Why is there an unequal distribution of the risks involved in practicing journalism? And what demographic, symbolic, material, and geographic factors catalyze that risk?

WITHOUT A DEMOCRATIC STATE, THERE CAN BE NO CRITICAL JOURNALISM

I believe that the main reasons [for violence against the press] are impunity, negligence in the procurement and administration of justice, and the general crisis that the justice system is experiencing in Mexico. This becomes a vicious cycle: no sanctions means no punishment for those who attack journalists; hence, the aggressions continue because there aren't any institutions capable of punishing the attackers.[22]

—VÍCTOR RUIZ ARRAZOLA, ATTORNEY AND ACTIVIST

Attacks against the press commonly occur in countries where the state is in crisis, explains Argentinean academic Silvio Waisbord.[23] They occur when the state is abusive, repressive, or absent, that is, where state actors (public or military officials) or extra-state sectors (political bosses or organized crime) employ violence indiscriminately, wielding brute force with impunity against personal or group targets to achieve ideological or economic goals. In this Hobbesian scenario of violence and impunity, anyone can kill a journalist. Furthermore, anyone can kill any citizen without experiencing repercussions. A reporter covering the crime beat in Veracruz who allegedly received a death threat from the governor of the state and is now in exile in Chiapas summed it up as follows: "I do not believe my colleagues are safe. We live in a lawless state."[24]

Such lawlessness reinforces the already high degree of institutional mistrust of the rule of law and meting out of justice in Mexico. Indeed, only 17 percent of those queried in a national poll of journalists trust national security agencies.[25] This wariness is also reflected in the media. "How are we going to trust in a state institution to protect us," asks Edgar Cortez, a Jesuit theologian who has, for two decades, provided legal consultation to journalist victims of serious human rights violations, "when the state itself is harassing me?"[26]

Perhaps even more disheartening is the extremely high levels of impunity (close to 100 percent in cases of journalist homicide). In cruel murders linked to organized crime, impunity has become so high that, as Schedler claims, "in practical terms, this is the equivalent of privatizing the death penalty."[27] Such levels of impunity create and exemplify severe deficiencies within the justice system, according to an activist and journalist who provides legal consultation to threatened journalists in the state of Jalisco:

> Since there is so much impunity and corruption, any public agency or ministry can be easily bribed. Evidence is easily tampered with, files easily go missing, and police officers are easily persuaded because they know that generate a justice apparatus so lax they will enjoy full impunity. Wherever there is impunity, taking steps to ensure justice will be served may seem increasingly far-fetched. I attribute the general sense that no investigation or justice can exist under this great halo of impunity.[28]

Academics, civic organizations, and journalists have amply documented the labyrinth of complicity, bureaucracy, and ineptitude described here. They portray a justice system with severe authoritarian inertia, one that is, moreover, highly bureaucratic, sluggish, and corrupt and tends to be dismissive of victims' fundamental rights. The criminal civil war greatly exacerbated this already untenable scenario. Therefore, for victims and their relatives, even gaining access to the justice system is often like entering a maze or falling into an abyss of red tape.

Weak or abusive government security and justice institutions, a lack of trust in institutions, and criminal impunity signify that citizens cannot rely on the essential elements necessary for healthy social coexistence. These deficits notably affect critical social groups, such as political opposition candidates, human rights defenders, intellectuals, and journalists, because they cannot perform their roles without fearing for their physical and psychological integrity.

Critical societies, of which the press is a fundamental element, require an efficient democratic state. Since this is unavailable to Mexican journalists, it becomes very easy to threaten and silence them. Journalists, as the academic and activist Sergio Aguayo has stated, "are a strategic group with no protection."[29] Without protection, there can be no genuinely autonomous or critical journalism.

Consequently, the international community, dedicated public officials, academics, and journalists have pressured the government to create specialized agencies to ensure nationwide security and justice in the journalistic trade for the past twenty years.[30] Two such governmental agencies are the Mecanismo de Protección para Personas Defensoras de Derechos Humanos y Periodistas, created in 2012, and the Fiscalía Especial para la Atención de Delitos Cometidos contra la Libertad de Expresión (FEADLE), created in 2006. Additionally, from 2007 to 2018, state laws that guarantee the protection and integrity of journalists in twenty states across the nation were approved.[31]

However, some specialists, activists, and journalists were crude and direct in discussing these agencies. Many defined them as merely bureaucratic institutions uncommitted to aiding victims. For example, as journalist and scholar Sergio Aguayo commented: "They consider themselves bureaucracies, and laws are passed, but then they appoint characters who have no sense of commitment to direct these bureaucracies. Also, they are bureaucracies sustained by quota-based parties, and therefore . . . created with no motivation, no understanding, no trust from the victims. . . . The agency meant to protect journalists forms part of this bureaucracy. They are void of content, paper tigers."[32]

Aguayo has backed civic institutions that defend fundamental political rights since the late 1970s. His assessment echoes across government and civic reports that say how poorly the Mecanismo and FEADLE perform their stated goal of protecting journalists.

There is still a long way to go. This was made clear in a report I wrote in 2018, commissioned by the U.S. Agency for International Development (USAID) and a local NGO. The report found—echoing my conversations with activists, public officials, and journalists —a series of deficits in these new agencies. These included a lack of institutional coordination and human and material resources, strong political and criminal pressures that have undermined operations, obstacles related to bureaucracy, and a lack of expertise among public officials, not to mention a deep-seated institutional mistrust.[33] Until we transform these inertias, these agencies will continue to be paper tigers.

It is worthwhile to point out that these agencies' poor performance is no exception to the rule in how justice is determined and meted out in Mexico. The malfunctioning of these agencies is the norm. One cannot expect institutions embedded in a system with such widespread deficiencies and vices to behave differently.

The following pages stem from an examination of the Mecanismo and FEADLE I conducted from 2010 to 2016. Unfortunately, some of these deficiencies and the inertia have continued during the administration of President Andrés Manuel López Obrador between 2018 and 2024. The federal government recognized in 2023 that a reform of the Mecanismo is necessary, given that it operates in reaction to aggressions and lacks a preventive focus, which would be more desirable. Concerning the track record of FEADLE, while it is true that there have been advances in solving some cases during this administration, it is also true that the vast majority of attacks on the press go unpunished.

A TRICKY GUARANTEE OF SECURITY

At the Secretaría de Gobernación, an experienced public official specializing in human rights explained to me the particularities, advances, and limitations of the Mecanismo de Protección para Personas Defensoras. This public official said, "The idea is to provide support for the person at the moment [of an emergency] and gradually seek ways for them to continue to develop."[34]

Once registered as someone in acute or specific danger, a journalist is theoretically offered a range of protections, services, and support. The usual protection measures include assigning police protection, monitoring, and panic buttons; less common are installing security cameras, assigning bodyguards, and even extracting the journalist from the location. By 2018, there were 339 journalists registered with this agency. However, as the official explains, they employ only thirty-odd officials to guarantee their safety. The public official recognizes that "it would be necessary to reinforce the Mecanismo with more personnel," especially, the official says, with more highly trained personnel.[35]

The public official explains that the Mecanismo was formed, much like other agencies created to defend human rights, by public officials from different areas who, unfortunately, did not possess suitable professional profiles or sensibilities. Therefore, practically since its founding, the agency has run training programs, commonly backed by international agencies such as the European Union, USAID, and Freedom House, to streamline processes and train staff, particularly in forming specialized risk assessment scenarios.[36] These agencies have also contributed to enhanced journalists' awareness of how the Mecanismo works. The Mecanismo is a legal framework run by the Secretaría de Gobernación, which, following an individual assessment process, provides journalists and human rights defenders with protection in the event of imminent danger. In 2018, at least one-third of journalists working in high-risk zones were unaware of its existence, according to a national poll.[37]

At that moment, the cornerstone of the Mecanismo was risk assessment, in which specialists and citizen representatives play a role. Through risk assessment, which in urgent cases may be completed within just a few hours, the urgency and type of protective measures are determined like "a tailor-made suit," said the public official, "with only those security mechanisms deemed necessary."[38] After a careful evaluation, the tailored suit granted by the Mecanismo commonly includes protective measures agreed on jointly with the beneficiary. Following this process, the Mecanismo acceptance rate has been high: four out of five applicants can register for it.[39]

Although many applicants do gain access, their evaluations nearly always advance at a snail's pace. This is counterproductive: following a threat, protective measures can bring peace of mind but, more importantly, can sometimes make the difference between life and death. "Initial contact is not sufficiently agile or capable of gathering enough information about the applicant," says activist Edgar Cortez, an attorney who is also a member of the Advisory Council of the Mecanismo, a citizen-led organism integrated with the government-run board.[40] A poll of Mecanismo beneficiaries found that nearly 60 percent found the response time inadequate or greater than the lapse of time established by law.[41] The national correspondent Erick Muñiz explained that, after suffering death threats and adhering to the Mecanismo, preliminary security measures arrived two weeks later, even though his risk evaluation recommended "immediate attention."[42]

Beyond this sluggishness, another recurring criticism is that the protection measures don't always align with the reality experienced by journalists. The Mecanismo recognizes that specific protective measures, such as security cameras and police vigilance, can attract too much attention. Moreover, these sorts of measures are often insufficient. "The most they come up with is to try and set up semipermanent surveillance at your house or give you a cell phone so that you can check in. But in general, they don't know what to do in a threat situation," explains an investigative journalist.[43] "Sometimes, the only final solution is not even to seek refuge in Mexico City, but to flee the country," he says.[44] This journalist left Mexico after documenting episodes of violence and serious human rights violations in some of the zones of silence in Tamaulipas and Nuevo León.

Another recurring criticism is that the protection measures do not always work. The panic buttons, for example, malfunction. These are small battery-operated devices with an integrated GPS, similar to automatic garage door openers. Once activated, they send a signal to public security officers who come to the rescue. Emilio Lugo, who was in exile because of death threats, told me that his panic button did not always work adequately.[45] When I asked about this, the public official of the Mecanismo explained that many beneficiaries prefer to keep the panic button turned off; afterward, when they want to turn it on, it doesn't work. They do this, the public official says, out of fear that their geolocator is in the hands of authorities from Secretaría de Gobernación. This agency directed political espionage in Mexico up until the 1990s.

Extracting a journalist and relocating them to a safer place is sometimes necessary. "In extreme cases, extraction of a person is necessary. They are told they must leave and can no longer continue to live there," says the public official. However, the official recognizes that this "is not that simple" because even when they know they are at risk, "they don't want to move."[46]

It is also complicated because displaced journalists are commonly asked, for their safety, to lower their professional profiles and dedicate themselves to another career to earn a living. For most journalists, this is a nightmare. They do not have the backing of the Mecanismo to continue reporting, nor are they offered any other midrange or long-term alternatives to reinsert themselves in the workforce. Emilio Lugo, who was aided by the Mecanismo, received death threats from military officials and organized crime cells. He comments, "I flatly refused to indulge the Mecanismo's whim and stop working or publishing."[47] Even while in exile, he collaborated with the Associated Press on the investigation of a civilian massacre perpetrated by the military. Constantly checking the panic button assigned to him during our interview, he told me his journalistic endeavors had elevated his risk level. He even claimed that his aggressors knew where he was taking refuge. He said they could have already come for him if they had wanted to.

And if they had followed through on their threats, it would not have been the first time a journalist under the Mecanismo's protection came under attack. The Mecanismo works to increase security and mitigate risks, but there remains the danger that something may happen. This is more common than the agency likes to admit publicly. From 2013 to 2016, a shocking 29 percent of beneficiaries protected by the Mecanismo were nonetheless subjected to some form of aggression. As the Secretaría de Gobernación public official told me, "We can't control these kinds of attacks, either."[48]

Even when appropriately deployed, then, the Mecanismo is far from perfect. Worse yet, the authorities don't always do all they can to avoid certain forms of aggression against journalists who adhere to the Mecanismo.

On July 24, 2018, on the main avenue of Playa del Carmen in Quintana Roo, Rubén Pat was murdered at close range. At the time of his killing, Pat was the director of the weekly *Playa News* and had been registered with the Mecanismo for over a year. He joined in June 2017 after being arrested, threatened, and tortured by Playa del Carmen municipal police officers whom he had denounced for allegedly colluding with criminal gangs. Two months before his murder, Pat requested that the Secretaría de Gobernación reinforce his security measures. But such reinforcement never came. "The Mexican authorities," lamented Reporters Without Borders Mexico, "failed to protect this journalist adequately."[49]

Cases like Pat's reinforce journalists' historic mistrust of the Mecanismo. "I would dare say that perhaps half, or slightly more, arrive filled with doubt," says activist Edgar Cortez.[50] Several years after its creation, the lack of confidence in the Mecanismo has not substantially subsided among journalists.

As I will explain later, the absence of government strategies that offer protection to journalists has forced them to seek other forms of protection outside the state. Over the past two decades, as discussed in chapter 5, independent networks have emerged that are characterized by their quick response, financed by national and international civic organizations that assist journalists in high-risk situations.

THE POLITICS OF IMPUNITY

"Let me tell you something: wherever I go, across the republic, practically the first question anyone ever asks me is, Why haven't you asserted jurisdiction over the Rubén affair?" a high-ranking official at the Fiscalía General de la República (FGR) confides. He refers to the murder of Rubén Espinosa, a photojournalist for *Proceso* magazine in Veracruz, who was killed along with four women in a middle-class apartment in Mexico City on July 31, 2015. In his office, he categorically states that the FGR has not claimed investigative jurisdiction because "It has not been confirmed that his death had anything to do with freedom of expression."

The murder of Rubén, an activist and journalist who caused the local administration discomfort, ought to have been investigated by the Fiscalía, according to national organizations that defend freedom of expression.[51] However, no case file has been opened to date.

"[There is cause for concern] over the extremely arbitrary and unclear exercise of the faculty of jurisdiction [of FEADLE]," Artículo 19 Mexico stated in a press bulletin regarding the Espinoza case.[52] In this same bulletin, the NGO argues that the Fiscalía should assert its jurisdiction over cases tracked by the agency since 2013; in other words, Artículo 19 is asking that the federal government assert its authority, at a local level, over crimes committed against freedom of expression nationwide. Such a federal step is crucial in a country like Mexico, where the courts almost always face political pressure from state governors. This legal attribute of the Fiscalía is a means of breaking through the well-oiled mechanisms of control that governors employ in their territories.[53]

In the journalistic profession, however, according to Balbina Flores, the Mexican representative for Reporters Without Borders, there is a widespread perception that the Fiscalía is lukewarm, choosing not to claim jurisdiction to avoid confrontations with state and local governments.[54] In cases with an ongoing investigation, the Fiscalía almost always declines to assert jurisdiction.

The ability to assert jurisprudence, also known as federalization, was one of the demands made over fifteen years ago by a substantial group of media outlets, journalists, and national and international organizations that defend freedom of expression to shed light on the disappearance of crime-beat reporter Alfredo Jiménez Mota in 2005, in Hermosillo, Sonora.[55] Indeed, the government's response to this was the creation of the Fiscalía. However, to date, both the disappearance of Mota and the murder of Espinosa, as well as dozens of similar cases, remain unsolved.

As in other countries with anti-press violence, impunity in crimes against journalists is exceptionally high; only in 4.4 percent of cases are any judicial provisions filed. Impunity, on the other hand, is not limited to this trade. Nationwide, only five of every hundred crimes are solved.[56] Hence, for many journalists, the Fiscalía is a paper tiger, just as Sergio Aguayo claimed.

So, the Fiscalía faces the daunting task of solving crimes against freedom of expression in a country with extremely high levels of impunity. But it also has to do so at a moment of profound transformation in the press and journalism industry sectors, where the lines that distinguish who is or is not a journalist have been blurred.

This practically epistemological distinction between who is a journalist and who isn't also has repercussions regarding the administration of justice. "Much of the debate involves whether someone was a journalist or not," says the high-ranking official from PGR.[57]

On January 25, 2015, twenty-two days after at least six heavily armed people had abducted him from his home, the body of Moisés Sánchez Cerezo was found. He ran the weekly newspaper *La Unión*, a community media outlet dedicated to covering public life in Medellín de Bravo, Veracruz, including deteriorating social conditions and lack of public security. However, "according to the criteria of the Fiscalía, Moisés Sánchez did not practice journalism, and that is why the case fell beyond jurisprudence," comments Víctor Ruiz Arrazola, journalist and attorney for the Casa de los Derechos de Periodistas.[58] At first, he says, the case was not opened for two reasons: Sánchez did not make a living from journalism—he drove a cab—and did not publish in traditional media but in a small, printed daily or on blogs and social networks.

Soon afterward, following an appeal promoted by Artículo 19 Mexico, the Fiscalía reversed its decision and opened a case file. Today, we know that the mastermind behind this crime was the mayor of Medellín de Bravo, who is currently at large; we also know that the ones who committed the murder were municipal police officers, who were jailed in 2018 and are presently serving a twenty-five-year prison sentence.[59]

On top of all this, another major problem for the Fiscalía and other judicial agencies is that they almost always assume up front that crimes against journalists are not motivated by the victims' professional careers but are crimes of passion, petty crimes, or gang violence. Regarding the photojournalist Rubén Espinosa's murder, Mexico City officials who leaked part of the investigation to local media said at first that the crime was not linked to his journalism. Espinosa's "number was up," according to the authorities, while other journalists shared the same fate because they were allegedly involved in messy love affairs.

Therefore, there is a widespread perception that the Fiscalía lacks the political willpower to investigate these cases. Consequently, there were multiple public demands that journalism be included as a line of investigation among independent organisms. During an interview at the central offices of the Comisión Nacional de los Derechos Humanos (CNDH), someone from the program to defend journalists told me, "The CNDH has emphatically declared through press bulletins that the line of investigation that has to do with the person's journalistic profession is the one that must be exhausted. It is fundamental to clearly indicate whether the aggression had anything to do with their work as a journalist."[60]

However, such demands have been of little avail. More than half of the journalist homicides registered by the CNDH are not currently under investigation by the Fiscalía. This is because journalism is still not considered to be the main motive behind these murders.

Furthermore, journalism as a primary line of investigation is almost always disqualified with the complicity of government-affiliated media. "What the Procaduría always does is choose a handful of journalists and leak information to them to discredit the victims," says analyst Lara Klahr.[61] Journalists, he continues, become victims of their "parallel tribunals."

Another limitation of the Fiscalía is a lack of qualified personnel. In 2016, the Fiscalía had only nine public ministers to attend to a backlog of dozens of cases. Despite this, official figures show that the Fiscalía investigated 1,140 cases in 2018. However, a large caseload does not necessarily translate into an abundance of justice. Of those cases, by 2019, only 186 were granted jurisdiction, and guilty sentences were obtained in only 10, that is, 0.86 percent of the total number.[62]

Given this desolate landscape, many journalists are understandably reluctant to report crimes committed against them and greatly mistrust the Fiscalía's efficiency in combatting impunity. A national poll among journalists who work in violent surroundings found that, after having been subject to aggression, only 20 percent filed a report;[63] the vast majority didn't report out of distrust or because they felt that doing so was a waste of time.[64] A journalist from Monterrey, Nuevo León, who heads an association of local journalists, spoke of the lack of a culture of complaint among her colleagues: "It is unlikely that my coworkers will present a complaint, which is why we can't speak of hard-data statistics."[65]

WHAT'S GOING ON HERE?

Few democratic countries worldwide possess a legal code for protecting journalists as robust as Mexico's. This legal framework, which includes the Mecanismo and the Fiscalía, was created ad hoc as the government responded to the epidemic of attacks against journalists. However, it has done little to stop this great wave of violence. Killing and harassing journalists continues to be dirt cheap. Even with the help and supervision of national and international organizations, these agencies notably fail to perform adequately. They will get out of this rut and elevate their trustworthiness only if they procure better results, such as more robust sentencing against those guilty of attacks against journalists.

Indeed, as I have indicated till now, a pattern that has presented itself across Mexico is that no matter where they report from, journalists operate amid great uncertainty concerning security and justice. On many occasions, public officials and authorities have proven incapable of protecting them; in contrast, they are all too willing to attack them, especially if this is deemed convenient to their corrupt interests or criminal ties. Moreover, journalists are unequally exposed to the risk of attack, a theory that leaped out at me from the start of my investigation.

Demographic characteristics of the journalists themselves can catalyze or mitigate this risk through professional, organizational, and social resources at their disposal, as well as the locations where they live and work. The following and final section of this chapter will describe these risk-determination factors.

UNEQUAL RISK DISTRIBUTION: DEMOGRAPHICS, RESOURCES, AND GEOGRAPHY

Once I agree that the regional journalist, the regional reporter, or photographer is far more exposed, it follows that a series of rules of the game need to be followed, such as what to say and what not to say in response to pressure from different factors, for example, the state government in

THE WAVE OF VIOLENCE AGAINST THE PRESS

office, the municipal government in charge and, obviously, the formidable powers that be that are the drug traffickers.[66]

—RAFAEL RODRÍGUEZ CASTAÑEDA, GENERAL DIRECTOR OF *PROCESO* MAGAZINE

During our conversation at the main offices of *Proceso*, one of Mexico's most influential political magazines, Rafael Rodríguez Castañeda, who served as general director from 1999 to 2020, discussed the many risks journalists are exposed to here. He is exceptionally well versed regarding the relationship between the press and power. In 1993, he published a book that became a classic, *Prensa vendida* (Media for Sale), regarding the love affair between presidentialism and political journalism. He commented that outside Mexico City, local journalists still face plenty of risks and limitations while doing their jobs because they need to obey the rules of the game established by local power brokers. He recognizes that in many states, the reality of journalistic coverage is far more complex, filled with obstacles like authoritarian political enclaves, criminal governing regimes, and other informal power structures. He acknowledges that such obstacles are not always predictable.

During our interview, Rodríguez Castañeda also recognized that risks constantly threaten representatives and national correspondents of *Proceso*, who almost always receive assignments to cover local politics as well as organized crime and public security, not to mention protest movements and serious human rights violations. The fact of the matter is that these reporters are almost always living on the edge, given that they cover what goes on out on the streets, muckraking in hostile territories where the rules of plurality and democracy that apply in the nation's capital hardly exist. "Correspondents from national media are also subjected now and again to these sorts of risks or threats," he remarked. "Such was the prototypical case of Regina Martínez, our correspondent in Xalapa, who was the victim of a crime that has not been sufficiently looked into."[67]

The field risk in journalism is distributed unequally. This is particularly unjust, as is well pointed out by the researchers Celeste González de

Bustamante and Jeannine Relly, for those journalists who live and work on the field's professional, economic, social, and geographic peripheries.[68] There is far less risk for the owners and top brass of the media outlets in major cities across the country, especially Mexico City; such is the case with international correspondents and the most well-known investigative journalists, commentators, and editors. But journalists' exposure to risk is not distributed capriciously; instead, it follows specific causes and patterns, such as demographic particularities, the professional characteristics of each journalist, or the place where they live and work. The sociopolitical and professional arrangement that structures unequal risk distribution in journalism is unjust, materializing heterogeneously among different press sectors.

There is no even playing field to practice journalism in, and this has had a determining influence not only on the level of risk newsmakers are exposed to but also on how it is calibrated. The injustice of unequal risk takes it out on those who, because of their gender or ethnic origin, trigger a hatred that multiplies when they are reporting or, rather, exposing enclaves of influential figures. It also significantly affects those journalists whose professional or economic conditions place them at the margins of the profession, such as fixers, freelancers, and journalists who work full throttle with neither labor contracts nor health care; photojournalists and videographers who document social protests, repression, and repressive environments; crime-beat journalists; part-time local press; and community, indigenous, and emerging reporters. It is especially harsh on those who live and practice journalism from isolated locations where they do not enjoy the anonymity offered by the big city but, on the contrary, may be easily identified by their aggressors, with whom they coexist.

In the following section, I will explore several dimensions that are fundamental in the exposure of journalists to the risk of violence: (1) demographic characteristics (sex, gender, ethnic origin), (2) access to symbolic and material resources (such as years of journalistic experience, prestige, professional profiles, the type of media they work for, and reliable connections in the field of journalism, among others), and (3) the place where they live and work.

THE WAVE OF VIOLENCE AGAINST THE PRESS

INEQUALITIES: SEX, GENDER, AND ETHNICITY

"Not long ago, an official plowed into me just like that; I was trying to stop him so that he would give us a statement, and he cynically just kept going and practically ran us over with bodily force," said a journalist with over twenty years of experience covering the crime beat and citizen protests. "That's the sort of thing we have to deal with."[69]

On a day-to-day basis, many public and political officials still do not believe women are capable of discussing public affairs, much less maintaining a critical focus and line of questioning. In Mexico, women journalists, especially independent or critical journalists, have historically been blocked from newsrooms and relegated to the "more feminine" journalism sections, such as society news or culture.[70] Even now, as the journalist from Veracruz in the quote above told me, they continue to be looked down on and ignored in areas of journalism, such as politics and public security, that are heavily dominated by men, In a predominantly macho political culture like Mexico's, it matters little that some of the most outstanding work on political corruption and organized crime over the past few decades has been accomplished by brave women journalists.[71] According to one Mexican civil organization specializing in gender-related violence, most journalists who are attacked nationwide cover political issues.[72]

The great wave of violence against the press has affected men and women journalists unequally. The vast majority, 75 percent, of journalists murdered nationwide from 2006 to 2018 were men.[73] However, after women journalists are killed, their reputations are more likely to be smeared.[74]

As is the case in other countries with deeply rooted macho cultures—for example, in Russia, where the investigative journalist Anna Politkovskaya was murdered—in Mexico, the murder of women journalists is commonly associated, according to the authorities, with crimes of passion.[75] Allegedly, they are not killed while investigating stories but rather in the throes of passionate, romantic affairs. According to rumors spread by ministry authorities in Veracruz two months after her death, local investigative journalist Regina Martínez was murdered in a lover's quarrel.[76] This was an attempt by local authorities to derail the investigation by rarifying

81

judicial diligence while sullying her reputation at the same time. Soon afterward, painstaking journalistic investigations demonstrated with reasonable certainty that the motive behind her killing was her brave and outstanding work as a journalist, which had become a source of discomfort to the local powers.[77]

However, revictimization is not the only form of violence faced by women journalists. Unlike violence against male journalists, violence against their female counterparts and against journalists who belong to sexual or gender minorities is cemented in the structures of patriarchal domination. It feeds on intolerance, hatred, and sexual oppression. Consider how investigative journalist Lydia Cacho described her illegal arrest following the publication of the book *Los demonios del Edén*, her extraordinary investigation into a network of pederasty and sexual exploitation led by powerful businessmen and politicians: "Suddenly, it hit me that I would spend a journey of over fifteen hundred kilometers accompanied by two police officers and three other men in the back seat. I never felt so alone, so vulnerable, so aware of the fact that I am a woman."[78]

From 2012 to 2018, there were 422 cases of violence against female journalists in Mexico, according to an NGO study.[79] Such violence consists mainly of sexual threats and digital defamation, psychological aggression, physical harassment, various degrees of sexual assault, sexual torture, and rape.[80] The numbers are even more chilling than they may seem at first, given that one-fourth of these aggressions take place in the workplace at the hands of their abusive male colleagues.[81] Unlike them, women are never safe, not even when they are at the office.

In direct forms of violence perpetrated against the press, such as the kind wielded against women journalists, structures of domination and violence prevalent in general society are reproduced.[82] Hence, demographic characteristics, also called identity traits by some investigators, are a catalyst for violence against journalists.[83] In this sense, women, not unlike others who are socially vulnerable, are more susceptible to assault for practicing their profession.

Like women journalists, those who belong to sexual and gender minorities are exposed to greater violence for exercising their profession. As a transgender person, I know from personal experience the many limitations we experience in a conservative Catholic country with a deeply embedded macho culture, not to mention one of the highest rates of homophobic and transphobic crime in Latin America. In addition to the barriers to labor access to the field of journalism that transgender people often face, another significant limitation is the stigmatization and demonization that our community is subject to in the media. With few exceptions, major outlets tend to silence and erase our voices. Rarely are we allowed to generate and convey our own narrative. Worse yet, whenever we publicly raise our voices on social media, we are greeted with substantial hatred and intolerance in return. In March 2021, the journalist Láurel Miranda announced that a national newspaper dropped her column from the webpage where she denounced "transphobic feminism". The reason it gave for its decision was to "avoid confrontation with trans-hating groups."[84]

Exercising journalism as a cisgender or transgender woman increases the risks habitually associated with this profession. Something similar occurs with journalists who belong to, represent, or possess traits from indigenous communities. As in the other cases mentioned here, the risks reflect the high levels of discrimination that these communities have historically experienced. According to a national poll by the Instituto Nacional de Estadística y Geografía (INEGI) published in 2017, a quarter of the indigenous population declared they had been discriminated against within the past five years.[85] Skin color may also play an essential role in attacks against journalists. Ioan Grillo, a British investigative journalist who has resided in Mexico for the past twenty years, told me: "If you are a non-Mexican white foreigner, the risk is reduced."[86]

Also exposed are those journalists who report cases defending indigenous land and autonomy. In 2014, the Mayan journalist Pedro Canché was arbitrarily jailed for giving voice to and documenting the protests of Mayan indigenous people against the increased cost of water utilities in the state of Quintana Roo.[87] In 2013, a journalist who has documented the rise in community police in Guerrero, where three-fourths of the population is indigenous, was fired from the newspaper due to pressure from the mayor. In a communiqué, social, indigenous, and Afro-Mexican organizations

WHAT'S GOING ON HERE?

from La Montaña de Guerrero repudiated his dismissal.[88] To them, he was an informative ally, but to those in power, he was a thorn in their side.

UNEQUAL ACCESS TO RESOURCES

We are modest entrepreneurs with four or five people working with us. And then we must strengthen that small business the government finds so uncomfortable because people trust us to raise our voices for those who have no clout.[89]

—ANTONIO RAMOS, TIERRA CALIENTE, MICHOACÁN JOURNALIST

Antonio Ramos of Michoacán, who passed away as I was writing this book, performed impossible journalism: he investigated and wrote editorials while exploring the dark waters of local narco-politics. "In Tierra Caliente, in the Apatzingán Valley and the El Infiernillo Basin, working as a journalist means living on pins and needles," he told me in an interview.[90] In that region, Ramos was considered a kind of deacon of journalism whose place it was to witness how the rot of corruption and criminality had taken root in a historically inequitable zone linked to the traffic of illegal narcotics and merchandise.[91]

Despite the visibility provided by contributing from Tierra Caliente to periodicals like *El Cambio* of Michoacán or *La Jornada*, Ramos was a journalist who ran a great risk. As former mayor of his town, the veteran journalist knew that his op-ed work for media like his newspaper, *El Regional*, was a source of discomfort to the authorities and local pressure groups. As he put it so well in the above testimonial, the independence of his weekly newspaper resided in his conviction to practice journalism, which he considered important to the community and disgruntled citizens, and in resisting the temptation to accept government resources. He paid the price for his relative journalistic autonomy with a high quota of anxiety, uncertainty, and danger. "My health is shot," he told me, "precisely because of how I write."[92]

Ramos told me how, in 2006, he survived an abduction at the hands of organized crime cells. He also narrated the threats of federal and municipal authorities caused by his disconcerting publications. Even so, he considered himself fortunate to continue to practice his profession from no man's land. During our talk, he mentioned that other colleagues who reported from Tierra Caliente were not so fortunate. He is especially hurt by one absence: the forced disappearance in 2006 of his colleague José Antonio García Apac, who denounced the local criminal climate through the weekly newspaper *Eco de Tepalcatepec*.[93]

The story of Antonio Ramos helps me illustrate how different levels of capital that a journalist possesses can influence, on the one hand, the kinds of risks they face and, on the other, how they confront these risks. As in other social fields of action, in journalism, forms of capital are distributed unequally among actors, in this case, among journalists. Depending on their professional profiles and careers, journalists possess different levels of cultural, economic/organizational, and social capital. Consequently, the tools required to mitigate the risks they face while working as journalists are also distributed heterogeneously.

Taking the above into consideration, those who are found at the margins of journalism— for example, those who have received less training and accrued fewer years of professional experience covering sensitive issues—are more exposed to violence and possess fewer tools to mitigate the risks. Also, those who, like Antonio Ramos, narrate the devastating local reality in the print or digital pages of precarious media outlets operate without organizational support. Powerful locals may easily silence them. Also at greater risk are those who are alone, with a weak or nearly inexistent network of journalistic contacts and reliable civic allies.

Given his status as the owner of a small local media outlet, *El Regional*, Ramos could not rely on the protection and ongoing organizational support regularly enjoyed by the outlet's representatives or national and international correspondents. "Here, the privileges are for national correspondents. They have all this recognition. It's tough for them to come under attack. I don't know of any cases where they have suffered aggressions, and there are some very combative colleagues among them," another journalist from Morelia, Michoacán, commented.[94]

Critical journalists like Ramos, who report from closed communities, are not the only ones at significant risk. So, too, are emerging digital journalists and YouTubers who, via their social networks and internet pages, carry out informative reporting on community issues and crime, as well as in response to citizens' demands. According to scholar Marco Lara Klahr, this kind of commentator runs a high risk, given that they frequently do not follow the same information verification standards traditional journalists do. Political rivals and criminals easily manipulate them. Their high visibility within their communities also increases their risk.[95] The murder rate among emerging digital journalists and citizens killed or assaulted while carrying out their duties has swelled over the past decade.

Young journalists who set off on dangerous reporting assignments without weighing the consequences, often without adequate training for high-risk situations, are also exposed to a much higher risk of violence.[96] Other journalists, like Ramos himself, reduce their risk by acquiring a special talent for reporting from the "jaws of the wolf" and knowing how to "handle the situation," as he put it. In his case, one point of inflection, which other journalists I spoke to also mentioned, was the high level of awareness of personal protection tactics he acquired after suffering different forms of aggression and attacks for doing his job. That awareness denotes a higher level of social capital. All lived experiences—including aggressions and attacks—may be used to enhance risk mitigation in journalism.

Like journalists with low levels of cultural capital, others at greater risk do not possess substantial social and symbolic resources. It has been documented that some journalists who were murdered or assaulted for exercising their profession were found alone on the job, without a network of protection or camaraderie to support them.[97] In contrast, some journalists, like Antonio Ramos himself, could mitigate the risks of reporting amid dangerous scenarios through collective mechanisms of professionalization and support. In Ramos's case, this was made possible by encounters with and networks among local journalists in all regions of Michoacán. These mechanisms usually surpass typical pack reporting and have even, as in Ramos's case, generated greater awareness and professionalization among journalists, as well as collective forms of support and resilience to confront adverse situations collectively.[98]

THE WAVE OF VIOLENCE AGAINST THE PRESS

As I will review in chapter 5, the resistance networks among journalists and civic allies have multiplied over the past decade, principally among certain strategic sectors of the press. However, the truth of the matter is that when confronting acts of violence, marked differences between class and region often prevail, as do professional jealousy and mistrust.

GEOGRAPHIC INEQUALITIES

In the La Montaña region, [major aggressions stem from] municipal governments and radical organizations—teachers, Normal School students. And in Tierra Caliente, their main threat is organized crime because they also border Michoacán. So, those two cartels are at war. In the middle, we have a combination of all of the above. The same applies in Acapulco. But there, it's still mostly the government, organized crime, and radicalized groups.[99]

—GUERRERO INVESTIGATIVE JOURNALIST

The place where journalists live and work is one of the main determining factors in violence against the press. From a birds'-eye view with a regional slant, an investigative journalist describes the main threats against the press in Guerrero in the above testimonial. Although this is one of the most high-risk states for the press, the level and source of that danger varies depending on where reporters are based.

The scholars Daniel Hallin and Paolo Mancini have suggested that underlying sociopolitical and economic structures determine media and journalism structures.[100] If this is the case, the simplistic yet accurate geographic division described above is correct. Mexico's journalism is not homogenous and is constituted, broadly speaking, by media outlets in central Mexico that are politically influential and financially powerful, economically strong media outlets in the North, and highly precarious and vulnerable media in the South. This geographical composition mirrors the income inequality distribution in the country, where the North is commonly more developed because of its proximity to global chains linked to the U.S. At the same time, the South has been historically marginalized.

The reporter directly refers to figures representing a statewide danger to the critical press in her testimonial. These range from organized crime cells and corrupt authorities to radical social organizations, depending on criminal activity and local power structures.

At the core of her testimonial lies the idea that violence against the press has a strong component of territoriality. For the political geographer Robert Sack, territoriality is "a spatial strategy to affect, influence, or control resources and people by controlling area."[101] Following this definition, the logic of violence against the press is territorial, executed from a determined location, even when its repercussions transcend digital geography and barriers. Someone always pulls the trigger from somewhere. In other words, even when violence against the press defines the limits of something as abstract as public space, the truth is that the mechanisms through which the press is silenced are deeply material, so much so that they can be traced through coordinates. As the historian John Nerone says, "If the history of violence against the press in the United States demonstrates anything, it is that people have always understood the materiality of the press. Violence is always an assertion of materiality."[102]

In the case of Mexico, violence against the press is historically reproduced in states with high political and economic value. This means regions that are broad in territory and strategic in terms of population control. Territories like Tamaulipas, Veracruz, Oaxaca, and Jalisco also display high commercial and economic activity, with multiple trade routes, ports, or border crossings. Indeed, although journalists have been murdered in twenty-three states, between 2006 and 2018, 65 percent of those homicides were concentrated in Tamaulipas, Veracruz, Chihuahua, Oaxaca, and Guerrero. Do these states have something in common that makes them especially dangerous for journalists? In a quantitative study that attempted to answer this question, I found that, from 2010 to 2015, the murders of forty-one journalists occurred mainly in those states with greater indices of violence and criminal internal conflict, serious human rights violations on the part of the state, democratic underdevelopment, and social inequity.[103]

THE WAVE OF VIOLENCE AGAINST THE PRESS

Despite the historical persistence of these patterns, violence against the press can also migrate geographically. As comparative studies of violence against the media have suggested, aggressions against journalists tend to follow larger patterns of social and criminal violence.[104] In 2015, the year I interviewed the reporter who provided the opening testimonial for this section, such patterns were in flux, as were crimes perpetrated against the press. From 2006 to 2015, because of local criminal reconfigurations, homicidal violence became greater and migrated from the North to the South. The same thing happened with violence against the press, according to data from civil organizations. "Whereas five years ago, the wave of aggressions against the press was concentrated in the northern states, now the dynamic has changed, and they are centered mainly in Veracruz and Oaxaca," wrote the journalist Javier Garza.[105]

In 2009, geographically, the greatest number of aggressions against journalists was concentrated in Oaxaca, Veracruz, and Chihuahua. There were also many attacks in Durango, Sinaloa, Guerrero, Michoacán, and Quintana Roo. Seen on a map, these states form a hook that starts in Sinaloa, extends through the Bajío region down to the Isthmus of Tehuantepec, and ends in Veracruz. Quintana Roo remains an isolated territory on the Yucatán Peninsula.[106]

By 2016, states like Veracruz, Chihuahua, Guerrero, Oaxaca, Quintana Roo, Sinaloa, and Durango had sustained elevated numbers of aggressions, while Chiapas, Puebla, Tamaulipas, Nuevo León, Michoacán, Coahuila, Baja California, and Mexico City gradually experienced this trend. The most severe violence was concentrated, above all, in states located on the isthmus, on the Gulf of Mexico, and in the northeastern part of the country along the border with the United States.

Another relevant geographic characteristic is the size of cities. Journalists are safer in large urban centers than they are in small communities. "There are always more run-ins on a local, municipal level, and those gradually fade. I think it has to do mostly with the proximity of sources to journalists because they know each other, they see each other every day," comments Artículo 19 Mexico's Rodrigo González.[107] A top official at the

Mecanismo de Protección para Personas Defensoras de Derechos Humanos y Periodistas told me something similar: "Often, these are very local problems. The threat is very local. But that depends on the journalist, the subject, the power of the aggressor . . . every case is different."

From 2006 to 2016, 120 journalist homicides were concentrated in just 89 cities and 25 states. On average, Mexican cities where journalists are killed have a population of 250,000. However, the relation between the distribution of localities and the number of residents is more or less similar: these murders have taken place in towns with fewer than 50,000 inhabitants (20), cities with fewer than 100,000 inhabitants (22), cities with fewer than a half a million inhabitants (32), and cities with fewer than one million inhabitants (11).

However, journalists are also murdered in major cities with populations of over one million, like Mexico City or Monterrey. One emblematic case was the Mexico City murder in the summer of 2015 of Rubén Espinosa, a photojournalist for the influential magazine *Proceso*.[108] For many journalists, his murder meant the overthrow of "the final bastion of safety for journalists nationwide."[109]

This chapter demonstrates that this country's great wave of violence did not come from out of the blue, nor did it follow random patterns. This wave of attacks is deeply rooted in the political, social, economic, and criminal traits of Mexico. Violence against the press is not sound and fury, signifying nothing; instead, it follows logical specificities and regularities, exposing everyone to risk, especially the already most vulnerable.

Not all journalists are equally imperiled. When practicing journalism, the playing field is uneven: some factors accentuate risk or make it harder to mitigate. Geography likely determines the degree to which journalists are exposed to risk. Another factor, however, is the beat a journalist covers at the time of the attack, a story to be explored in the next chapter.

3

VIOLENT CENSORS

You don't know whether just to be on the lookout for organized crime delinquents, specifically drug traffickers, or whether you also need to be on the lookout for public officials, for those who govern. . . . We are in a constant state of tension because we know we have to publish something unpleasant, but we don't know how the gangsters or certain politicians will react. And, well, that can cost you your life.[1]

—JOURNALIST AND COFOUNDER OF *REVISTA RÍODOCE* IN SINALOA

Reporters operate under the watchful eye of violent censors. Members of teachers' organizations, as well as caciques or strongmen, authoritarian politicians, and gangs of drug traffickers, work in collusion with municipal police officers, among others, to silence the press. Although it is not the only tool at their disposal, these groups employ different means, including violence, to intimidate critical journalists and control the flow of information.

With more than thirty-five years of journalistic experience, the journalist quoted above has faced down these powerful enforcers of silence. In 2009, the magazine he cofounded, which specializes in topics related to security and drug trafficking, was attacked with a grenade launcher. In 2017, two years after our interview, another cofounder of that same magazine, Javier Valdez, was murdered after publishing an article that did not sit well with the children of a powerful drug trafficker. In Culiacán, the hometown of the journalist quoted above—historically, the birthplace of drug trafficking in Mexico—violence and censorship come not only from organized crime cells but also from intolerant, corrupt politicians. Valdez used to say that what he feared the most was public officials and politicians, not organized crime.

WHAT'S GOING ON HERE?

Within their territory of influence, violent censors build themselves up as de facto arbiters of public information, deciding what remains a secret and from whom. Politicians, criminals, and self-defense units are well aware of how effective it is to control the flow of information and demand silence. In some cases, control over information is even profitable: the future of an ambitious, corrupt politician could be undermined if a scandal goes public. A drug trafficker, if his location is revealed, could either be murdered by rivals or extradited and spend the rest of his days behind bars. These actors often seek to co-opt or buy off journalists. In a country like Mexico, with high rates of unsolved premeditated homicides, they often choose violence to maintain and expand their control. Knowing themselves to be above the law, they wield this violence indiscriminately. In extreme cases, they harass, abduct, or murder journalists. In others, threats and intimidation are sufficient to achieve their goal of silence through fear.

Based on interviews with journalists, as well as archival and scholarly sources, in this chapter, I explore the motives and contextual factors surrounding violence and threats against journalists made by politicians and public officials, organized crime syndicates, public security forces, caciques, violent civic organizations, and labor unions.

THE PUBLIC SPHERE, CENSORSHIP, AND SELF-CENSORSHIP

In most cases, violence against the press expresses some kind of judgment about the proprieties of public discourse. Anti-press violence is and has been political in the deepest sense: it has been about the definition of polity.[2]

—JOHN NERONE, *VIOLENCE AGAINST THE PRESS*

Anti-press violence does not constitute a novel phenomenon, given that the news has always been a source of conflict. Violence may be found in the history of journalism every step of the way. In the conclusions of his historic study regarding violence against the press in the United States, historian John Nerone argues that violence against the press is habitually a vehicle for public expression. It is an undesirable form of communication that frequently accompanies crises, such as armed conflicts or political transitions, significant debates, and other social, economic, and cultural transformations that invariably lie behind these attacks. According to Nerone, violence also indicates the level of tolerance, acceptance, and attention desirable for certain actors or subject matter to possess. Their particularities may be of public interest and, at times, may fall into the ambiguous realm of privacy, such as in disputes over reputation. Therefore, violence against the press as a form of public expression indicates social momentum and the properties and limits of public discourse.

Central to the notion of violence against the press is the role played by practices of censorship and self-censorship. These two concepts have rarely been explored from a comparatist perspective. As historian Robert Darnton argues, censorship involves a regime of laws, moral norms, mercantile forces, and ideological imperatives deeply rooted in sociopolitical and cultural particularities.[3] This is also true for the practices of censorship in journalism. However, self-censorship in journalism involves self-imposed silence regarding pieces of information or journalistic interpretations.

The margins of nonviolent censorship in Mexican journalism have expanded over the past three decades since the beginning of the democratization process. The legal precepts around freedom of expression and freedom of the press have remained consistent since the Constitution of 1917. However, as Sallie Hughes and Chapel Lawson have found, since the first decade of the twenty-first century, there has been an outburst of plurality in thematic and journalistic focus concerning what may or may not be investigated and published.[4] This is in response to advances in political plurality and representation and a few legal changes, like the Federal Law of Transparency and Public Information Access, cultural openness brought on by new technologies, globalizing market forces and their impact on the formation of public opinion, and professional transformations in journalism.

On the other hand, self-censorship, often a complacent practice that seeks to avoid confrontation with superiors in newsrooms or with powerful figures beyond their walls, is one of Mexican journalistic culture's most prevalent, widespread, and deeply rooted facets. As the columnist Miguel Ángel Granados Chapa pointed out, "environmental censorship," as he called it, was an unwritten norm in a period of electoral authoritarianism that set limits regarding what could and could not be investigated and published.[5] However, over the past three decades, the boundaries determining the limits of self-censorship have also faded. In this context, self-censorship continues to influence journalistic practice.

Within this context, more favorable cultural, economic, and political conditions to exercise critical journalism have arisen. However, many risks remain, even more than during the authoritarian era. As the historian Benjamin Smith summarizes: "Soft authoritarian Mexico was a much safer place for journalists than contemporary democratic Mexico."[6]

VIOLENCE, PERPETRATORS, AND MOTIVES

In most cases, violence against the press expresses some kind of judgment about the proprieties of public discourse. Anti-press violence is and has been political in the deepest sense: it has been about the definition of polity.[7]

—JOHN NERONE, *VIOLENCE AGAINST THE PRESS*

"In drug trafficking, you don't know who you are up against: your brother, your son, your cousin, your neighbor, who?" quips Francisco Castellanos, a veteran national correspondent in Michoacán.[8] Accordingly, self-censorship has become his primary tool for survival. One may investigate and publish a broader range of subject matter, yet there is still great uncertainty and risk, especially concerning specific topics from certain regions. Given the absence of precise parameters, journalism is often governed by self-censorship and, many times, forced to operate in the shadows, fearful of reporting on an increasingly violent society.

Newsmakers whose reporting crosses nebulous lines of self-censorship confront discontent, anger, and even reprisal. Violence is not necessarily the first option. Politicians, for example, regularly prefer to buy off or intimidate journalists through the legal system. They opt for violent means when this fails to produce the desired results.[9]

Still, identifying the perpetrators of violence is not always an easy task. This is especially true when the perpetrators of violence are not criminals but, rather, local government officials and municipal and state police officers who, paradoxically, are in charge of protecting journalists. In many cases, however, it is possible to identify those that harm journalists.

"For the reporter, it is almost always clear where an attack is coming from," commented the former deputy director of *El Diario de Juárez* during a period in which two of his journalists, a reporter and a photographer, were murdered.[10] Three of four journalists seeking federal protection know who their attackers are, according to a public servant I interviewed who works at the Mecanismo at the Secretaría de Gobernación.[11] Artículo 19 Mexico's annual reports confirm these numbers.

Moreover, perpetrators might have different motives to censor the press violently.[12] Some politicians and public officials retaliate against journalists out of intolerance and to avoid having their image damaged or because they fear losing influence.[13] Criminal cells, meanwhile, fear being exposed and losing their illicit enterprise, which motivates their violence and press intimidation.[14] Public security forces, such as the military and the police, are generally employed by someone else to strongarm or cover up journalists.[15] Finally, other civil actors, such as self-defense groups, unions, and local caciques, attempt to control what is said about them, especially in territories under their domain.[16]

Additionally, journalists and news organizations are increasingly coming under attack online by people who are not happy with what is being published, above all on the topics of migration, drug trafficking, intelligence services, arms control, and high-profile politicians. This "mob censorship" is a phenomenon that Silvio Waisbord describes as a "bottom-up, citizen vigilantism aimed at disciplining journalism."[17] There has been a significant increase in digital attacks against journalists, promoted mainly by politicians, public officials, and businesspeople. Efforts to surveil and influence journalists have included the tapping of telephone lines and digital espionage, as well as online intimidation, harassment, and smear campaigns that, in the case of women, tend to have sexual ramifications.[18]

Starting in December 2018, President Andrés Manuel López Obrador was a hard-liner who systematically attacked critical journalists, especially those who did not share his outlook. This is accomplished mainly through discrediting humiliation and verbal attacks during his daily morning press conference, which have had widespread repercussions on public opinion. This phenomenon not only undermines the informative process but also sends mixed signals regarding governmental support and guarantees of freedom of the press in Mexico. What's more, these continual discrediting attacks legitimize other actors in all three levels of government who attack newsmakers in an attempt to silence them.

However, not all aggressions against journalists are motivated by a desire to silence them. Sometimes, journalists are caught in the crossfire during violent confrontations between cartels or between cartels and the state's armed forces. Furthermore, journalists are also murdered because they have become criminal accomplices. So-called narco-journalists, who often are forced to collaborate by providing information services to criminals and their corrupt government allies, swell the ranks of the disappeared, murdered, and coerced.

The history of corruption in Mexican journalism is infamous. During World War II, as researcher José Luis Ortiz Garza has documented, the powers that be flooded newsrooms and radio stations with cash, turning broad swaths of national newsmakers into mercenaries.[19] Likewise, corruption in journalism gained traction on all levels during the period of electoral authoritarianism under the PRI. From 1929 to 2000, there was an unspoken arrangement, mainly among those covering the political beat: journalists, in exchange for financial compensation, practiced a more propagandistic and accommodating journalism. While some differences exist, this arrangement continues to prevail locally in many parts of the country.

With the emergence of powerful crime syndicates in the 1980s and 1990s, criminal cells infiltrated journalism, searching for allies in the media who would advance their interests. Narco-journalists became a strategic part of the communications battle between cartels or among cartels, the state, and self-defense groups formed by citizens for community protection in response to a lack of security and the rise in organized crime.[20] Narco-journalists perform various functions, ranging from publicizing information of interest criminal organizations to acting as press agents or media consultants for the cartels. Inevitably, many narco-journalists have fallen prey to reconfigurations in the local criminal arena or when they are deemed to have disrupted the cartels' illegal activities.

The work of narco-journalists in the criminal underworld has always been a touchy subject, mainly because the politically powerful have used this category discursively to delegitimize attacks on journalists. They were murdered "because they strayed from the beaten path," or so those in power say.

POLITICIANS AND PUBLIC SERVANTS: EMPOWERED INTOLERANCE

I believe it is more dangerous to disturb government interests at times than it is to downplay groups dedicated to trafficking narcotics.[21]

—ANTONIO RAMOS, MICHOACÁN INVESTIGATIVE AND OP-ED JOURNALIST

In Mexico, politicians and public officials are notoriously thin-skinned; they do not like to be scrutinized by journalists or any other citizens, for that matter. They do not tolerate criticism, according to one editorial deputy director who, for two decades, was a reporter and editor at an influential local newspaper in Culiacán, Sinaloa. Moreover, he says, these officials often lack commitment to democratic values. They are wholeheartedly opposed to the exposure of any of their actions or inactions; instead, they prefer to silence criticism by any means necessary, through verbal attacks, intimidation, bribery, legal action, and assault or murder. The political class is particularly intolerant of those journalists and media outlets that dare to dig deeper into corruption and the embezzlement of public resources, nepotism, government protection networks at the service of criminal cells and illegal traffickers, financial tax evasion and money-laundering schemes, criminal violence, serious human rights violations such as forced disappearances or mass graves, and other crimes against civilian populations, as well as violence against the press.

The deputy director explains that this is why, contrary to what it might seem at first glance from Mexico City or from the United States, what reporters fear most is not organized crime but political power. This is true, he says, even in places like Culiacán, where he lives and works, a city notorious for its association with the shipment of narcotics. He quoted statistics from Artículo 19 Mexico, which documented that half of the attacks on the press are made by a public servant or politician. "Whenever we are exposing or revealing affairs that the government does not want made public, that's when we are most afraid," he says.[22] "When we write and publish those stories, it scares us because politicians have a lot to lose. Unlike drug traffickers, who are already outlaws, politicians possess a lot of power, and they can lose it."[23]

Víctor Arrazola, an attorney and activist who has worked with dozens of local journalists after they have been attacked, describes this intolerance:

> Any political or economic power group in municipal, state, or federal government will always regard the critical press, the professional press, as an enemy of their interests. Once the press starts to question the actions of those in power, that's when the press becomes an enemy. And when coercion does not provide the desired results, when the groups in power can no longer buy off the press, that's when they start to exert pressure in a different manner because their objective is to silence journalists permanently.[24]

As Arrazola has stated, the Mexican political class remains deeply rooted in its intolerance and need for opacity. Every day, there are abundant examples of discourses and tactics intended to delegitimize newsmakers' critical stances intermingled with legitimate criticism. All too common are cases in which politicians, public servants, and bureaucrats dismiss, insult, or verbally attack critical journalists simply for asking uncomfortable questions. This open rejection of criticism is one of the most deeply rooted traits of Mexican political culture at all levels of government. There is a lengthy history of politicians and public servants silencing the press. In his historical study, Benjamin Smith found that legal attacks were one of the most common forms of violence under electoral authoritarianism. In Mexico, this trend has continued. From 2015 to 2018, Artículo 19 also documented forty-eight specific cases of harassment of journalists by politicians.[25] These practices remain common today.

The Italian researcher Piero Stanig found that topics of corruption received significantly less attention in states with more repressive laws of slander and libel.[26] Legal attacks as a means to silence critique is a method exemplified by the case of columnist and academic Sergio Aguayo. As a result of the publication of a critical op-ed in 2016, Aguayo was sued for moral damages by Humberto Moreira, a PRI member who was governor of Coahuila at the time. The journalist was found guilty and told to pay the former governor nearly half a million dollars. In 2019, a judge absolved Aguayo of all charges, but Moreira disputed the verdict, and Aguayo was again sentenced to pay. The case was then taken to the Suprema Corte de Justicia de la Nación. It was not until 2021 that the case was concluded in the journalist's favor after a costly legal battle of nearly six years. Influential political figures' weaponizing of the justice system didn't just harm Aguayo. It also affected his colleagues, especially in the country's interior, who will now think twice before publishing a story against a powerful politician. The same holds any time a journalist is attacked by seemingly legal means.

The political class also employs espionage to control and intimidate journalists. By 2015, civil organizations advocating for freedom of the press had already sounded the alarm about the use of spy software against journalists and activists by government agencies and state governments in Mexico at a cost of nearly US$5 million.[27] Scandals have emerged like Gobierno Espía, or "Government Spies," a political strategy adopted during the administration of President Enrique Peña Nieto from 2015 to 2016, which utilized the spy malware Pegasus to target human rights defenders and journalists.[28]

Many more tactics are currently being implemented to obstruct and hinder the press. Among those I interviewed, public officials, often close to power, denied critical journalists access to press conferences and interviews. When journalists publish criticism of politicians or reveal information exposing them in any way, the state government often responds by circulating complaints and threats against the journalists through its communications channels. "Calls are made, mainly by the government spokesperson. He phones certain journalists and makes comments. He yells at them and asks them to take down articles. I would say that's the main source of power," said an investigative reporter from Oaxaca.[29] Officials frequently demand that journalists be demoted or fired. Unfortunately, these requests may be honored because of sweetheart contracts between the state government and friendly media outlets and threats to withdraw all government advertising and impose a commercial boycott. "Officials are really bothered by a lot of things being published, and since they have the opportunity to bend the owners of the media to their will," commented an investigative journalist from Monterrey, Nuevo León, "there is a strong possibility that they may fire you if they don't like something or exert pressure on the periodical to fire you."[30]

Intolerance often increases during moments of political uncertainty, like elections. "There are times when the pressure is ramped up even more. For example, right now, since we are in elections, you can feel it," says a freelance journalist from Mazatlán, Sinaloa. "Colleagues are careful what they write, what they investigate, how they conduct their investigations, how they publish their articles."[31] While photographing a confrontation with rival political groups on election day, shock troops from a political party assaulted a journalist from Guerrero and his colleagues.[32] During the 2016 federal elections, a collective of civil organizations documented twenty-seven attacks per day during elections, including threats, theft of equipment, demands to erase documentary material, and cyberattacks.[33]

Other, more aggressive forms of violence have also been employed to silence the press. This occurs when politicians and state and municipal public officials perceive affronts to their reputation or feel their integrity, or that of their families, has been questioned, or when accused of abusing their power.[34] In her study of repression of the press in Latin America from 2011 to 2013, researcher Grisel Salazar examines local governors who, when their interests or power are threatened, particularly in states with high indices of criminality where the governor dominates the local congress and court system, often employ violence against the press.[35]

A reporter who specializes in police-related issues in the eastern part of the Estado de México, a densely populated territory with severe social marginalization. It was a historical bastion of the PRI until 2023, when the political party Morena won in the electoral race for state governor. A few years ago, he investigated how a mayor in the region used his power and influence to acquire certain properties illicitly. In response, "they sicced the entire [municipal] administration on me," he told me.[36] The mayor threatened to put him in jail, had his small media outlet shut down, and intimidated his family. This is no isolated incident but a widespread tactic used among public officials to silence journalists.

According to many I interviewed, the riskiest subjects to report on are corruption and political-criminal complicity. Over the past three decades, the national and sometimes local press has exposed major corruption scandals at all levels of government.[37] However, in many cases, even when revelations are well founded, they are buried in response to political pressure. "Reporting political corruption implies a certain amount of risk," said an investigative reporter from Guadalajara, Jalisco, "but many of the stories on political corruption never see the light of day due to censorship from the media outlets themselves."[38]

Reporting on narco-politics can be a death sentence, especially in regions where there is as much political repression as unbridled criminal violence.[39] The line between criminal cells and governors can be very thin. "If you tangle with someone from the government, if you dig up some sort of corruption," a radio broadcaster in Morelia, Michoacán, told me. "It will almost always be in collusion with organized crime."[40] Covering these

WHAT'S GOING ON HERE?

narco-political environments can be extremely hazardous to journalists. They have even been murdered while carrying out in-depth investigations, as was the case with Humberto Millán in Culiacán in 2011 or Regina Martínez in Veracruz in 2012.

ORGANIZED CRIME SYNDICATES: EATING LEAD

In Tamaulipas, you can't publish anything. There is no way to publish unless they want you to. This morning in Reynosa, there was a conflict, and everything we know about it circulated on social media. No press in Reynosa unless they have the cartels' say-so.[41]

—LOCAL MULTIMEDIA REPORTER FROM MICHOACÁN

Historically, journalists from Tamaulipas, a state bordering Texas and the Gulf of Mexico, have paid a high price in terms of bloodshed for living and working in a territory where the drug trade dominates. But the situation has worsened over the past two decades: from 2000 to 2015, thirteen journalists were murdered, six more disappeared, and eleven attacks were registered against media outlet facilities.

During this period of extreme violence, entire swaths of the state of Tamaulipas were transformed into a great black hole from which no information emerged. The vortex occurred in border cities like Reynosa and Matamoros and then spread across nearly the entire state, including the capital, Ciudad Victoria. During the bloodiest moments of this great black hole, as an investigative journalist commented above, no information was entered or left unless it had first been approved by the drug cartels (Los Zetas and the Cartel del Golfo). To enact this violent censorship, the gangs infiltrated newsrooms, just as they had with political parties and the justice and security apparatus. They did so by committing bribery, extortion, intimidation, and murder. In some cases, during extreme periods of criminal violence in places like Nuevo Laredo, Tamaulipas, the climate was so bad that even reporting an automobile accident was risky because it might involve members of a criminal cell: "You show up to take photographs," a police beat reporter told me, "and more often than not, someone pulls a gun, threatens you and [tells you] not to stick your nose in."[42]

Consider how, in March 2011, in the town of Allende in Coahuila, three hundred civilians were massacred. Yet this crime against humanity within Tamaulipas was not covered in the press. According to one investigative journalist, even years after the events, in the local media, "you still can't tell that story."

Tamaulipas is only the most cruel and extreme case of a phenomenon that plagues Mexico: Drug cartels and organized crime cells have gained ironclad control over information. Reporters are inhibited from doing their jobs; whole regions become information deserts. "There are times when the government asks you to release a story [quite often an official account], but the other party [formed by criminal gangs] tells you not to," said a journalist from Tamaulipas. "Obviously, we don't release it because no one can guarantee our safety."[43]

Of all violent censors of the press, organized crime gangs are the perpetrators of the most virulent type of violence. The majority of journalist homicides were allegedly committed by members of criminal cells, according to the Committee to Protect Journalists (CPJ). The researcher Edgar Guerra found that there were signs of torture and suffering on the bodies of many murdered journalists.[44] Indeed, from 2010 to 2015, the vast majority of journalist disappearances, attacks against media outlets, and documented cases of torture and forced abduction were attributed to organized crime.

Organized crime usually demands control over the news when a territory heats up after a violent confrontation or crime, and newsmakers are in the process of judging what stories and angles to run. According to several studies, including my interviews, crime syndicates interfere with the flow of journalistic information. This control ensures silence regarding the gangs' activities, including any discussion of where they operate and under whose protection they may be.

While these details are often an open secret among the populace, they cannot be revealed in the press. These include the coverage of the production and transfer of illegal substances and merchandise as well as other illicit forms of business derived from these, such as extortion, breaking and entering, human trafficking, sexual exploitation, blackmail, and abduction. In some cases, they also interfere with reporting on legal forms of business, such as customs commerce along border zones and in seaports, licenses for casinos and bars in Tampico and Ciudad Juárez, and real estate development in Guadalajara, Jalisco, among others. As I was told by an experienced international investigative journalist who used to cover some of the hotspots across the country, "The big-time gangsters don't care much if you are writing about their excesses or their violence. What they care about is whether you are affecting their local protection rackets or their money or if you are getting in the way of their business."[45]

The kind of violence that seeks to silence journalists possesses an "exclusionary" nature because, according to historian John Nerone, it attempts to exclude information from the public arena. However, exclusionary violence becomes chaotic when a criminal group wishes to conceal what someone else wishes to expose in the press. Journalists and media outlets often find themselves in the middle of narrative battles between criminal organizations or between these organizations and the state. This has been the case, particularly in areas with intense rivalry among gangs, who have a greater incentive to control public information.[46] I found that the murder of journalists from 2010 to 2015 was seven times more likely to occur in territories with open criminal conflicts.[47]

In situations with open criminal confrontation, coverage by journalists becomes extremely hazardous.[48] According to one analysis, twenty-three of the forty-one journalists murdered nationwide from 2010 to 2015 covered crime and public safety. "When journalists cover an execution, they're at risk because you don't know whether those interested in it being brought to light are among the bystanders or whether the criminals want to find out who has been assigned to cover those stories," comments a multimedia reporter in Ciudad Juárez.[49] From 2010 to 2012, this border city had one of the highest homicide rates in the world. I heard the same from safety and *policiaco* (police) reporters in Culiacán (Sinaloa), Guadalajara (Jalisco), Morelia (Michoacán), and Xalapa (Veracruz). In response, journalists and media outlets in some cities have reinforced passive reporting techniques and, before going out to cover a story, revisit only official bulletins. We "prefer to cover from a distance, without reporting many bloody incidents from the street, so as not to expose our colleagues," says an editorial director in Ciudad Victoria. This city experienced an unparalleled bloodbath from 2010 to 2011.[50] Criminal gangs also pressure newsrooms. A former general director of one of the leading daily newspapers of La Laguna, an urban area in Coahuila that became a central battleground for rival criminal groups from 2009 to 2013, told me that an illegal cell shot up their building in August 2009 because they felt the paper's coverage had made them look weak.[51]

Criminal organizations have used violence against the press to send a message of strength or fear to establish a particular news agenda. As opposed to exclusionary violence, Nerone calls it "inclusionary" since it seeks to include information in the public sphere. Inclusionary violence exploded in Tamaulipas, Coahuila, and Nuevo León from 2010 to 2012.[52] Amid territorial disputes between organized crime syndicates, members of these groups used rifles, fragmentation grenades, and car bombs to attack newspapers such as *El Norte* of Monterrey, *El Mañana* of Nuevo Laredo, *Expreso* of Ciudad Victoria, and *El Siglo de Torreón* in Coahuila. On some occasions, such as the one described above, these attacks were payback for running or not running a news item. Other times, they were merely a show of force to remind journalists who was in charge. When I asked the general director of *El Siglo de Torreón* where a second attack on his facilities in 2011 could have come from, he said, "We started reviewing recent coverage, trying to see what triggered their reaction, but we came up empty. It may have just been to send the message 'Here we are.'"[53]

Finally, organized crime has infiltrated newsrooms, corrupting them as they might any political organization. In mid-2009, when Los Zetas and Cartel de Sinaloa were fighting for control over profitable drug routes and other illicit activities in Tampico, a journalist in northeastern Mexico noticed that strangers were appearing in local newsrooms, including at her newspaper, which belongs to one of Mexico's largest media conglomerates. At first, she thought the newcomers were government ears, local reporters working for the local or state governments to enforce a given editorial position or to spy, sometimes exchanging information for privileged access. "Then we learned they did not belong to the government. They were, in fact, ears but for the drug traffickers. We had to be even more careful because they started taking our pictures, and you just didn't feel safe anymore."[54]

According to various testimonies, this phenomenon has been an open secret among journalists since 2005, especially in newsrooms in cities with organized crime syndicates, such as Ciudad Juárez (Chihuahua), Nueva Italia (Michoacán) and Ciudad Victoria (Tamaulipas). Julio Hernández López, a columnist and widely known media presence, summarized these censorship practices: "A writing partner next to your cubicle comes to you and says: 'Hey, I met with a friend, and he was mad because you ran that story. So, I'm just letting you know because he is really upset.'"[55]

How are journalists coerced into working for criminal gangs? According to the testimonies I have collected, most journalists who become go-betweens were forced to collaborate in exchange for money or protection. "There's no other option," said one local reporter at a Tamaulipas newspaper. "Either you're in, or you're out. And if you're out, you're an enemy."[56]

This criminal arrangement is as dangerous as it is unstable and can change as the balance of power shifts between drug cartels and local administrations. Narco ears represent an extreme form of interference in journalistic routines and codes and promote various forms of subordination of journalistic principles and independent editorial agendas to appease outside interests. This doesn't just limit journalistic autonomy; it spreads a wave of silence.

PUBLIC SECURITY FORCES: ABUSES ABOVE THE LAW

When we experienced a lot of trouble, it was with the police. When the violence was truly harsh, it was cops who were intimidating colleagues or even putting them in jail for going around reporting.[57]

—CIUDAD JUÁREZ INVESTIGATIVE JOURNALIST

In 2009, all hell broke loose in Juárez, a historically strategic city for the traffic of illegal substances and merchandise into the lucrative market up north. The rivalry between the Sinaloa and Juárez cartels, coupled with the intervention of public security forces, filled the city with bloodshed. Homicides soared sevenfold from 2007 to 2009. The city was roiled by gunmen, military officers, and municipal, state, and federal police forces.

At the same time, military and police abuse against journalists grew. According to the *El Diario de Juárez*, the most influential newspaper in the city, in nine months, twelve journalists were handcuffed, arrested, beaten, and threatened, all for documenting the actions of the municipal police.

In response, a journalist from *El Diario* and other local reporters organized collectives to defend journalists, publishing in various local media outlets a communiqué denouncing "the climate of insecurity . . . under which we do our jobs" due to the "aggressive behavior of municipal police agents."[58] The communiqué held the municipal police chief responsible for the attacks, a former military officer named Julián Leyzaola. The local press labeled him "the toughest cop in Mexico." According to some testimonies of the time, the allegedly methods employed by this officer, who, years later, was accused of homicide and torture to "pacify" Juárez, often clashed with the work of journalists at crime scenes.[59] Police forces blocked the way, confiscated photographic equipment, and intimidated and jailed reporters and photographers.

Police abuse against the press in Ciudad Juárez from 2009 to 2011 illustrates the habitual violence faced by reporters, photographers, and cameramen who cover police beats, crime scenes, and public security actions. "It seems like the cops are already under orders to rough up our colleagues," summarized a young journalist from Veracruz who was arrested after covering a protest at the seaport.[60] Artículo 19 Mexico estimates that in 2018, public security forces perpetrated 20 percent of attacks on the press, either the police (municipal, state, and ministerial), the army, or the navy. Abuse by law-and-order forces generally occurs at crime scenes or violent incidents, such as shootouts, arrests, decommissioning, and at evictions, street fights, public protection, and riots.

With a long and successful history in Mexican popular culture, the crime beat continues to be morbidly juicy and economically profitable for many newspapers.[61] The demand for sensationalist news has only grown, and journalists expose themselves to greater risks when they cover these stories. However, historically, they earn meager salaries, possess no minimum safety guarantees, and are looked down upon at their places of work. "Crime-beat journalists are mostly disregarded. They are largely forgotten as people without much training or who earn very little, especially in rural Mexico. And while they do sell a lot of newspapers, they are mistreated in terms of wages, economic support, and social support because they work elbow to elbow with the police and criminals, the dirtiest kind there is."[62]

While conducting interviews for this book, time and time again, crime scenes were mentioned as one of the riskiest locations for crime reporters because anything could happen.

A typical situation arises when police block journalists, especially photographers attempting to capture the scene, and "this results in intimidation practices that we may assume to be normal."[63] These kinds of clashes usually generate violence against the press. "Your first barrier is police officers. They will not let you work. More often than not, they won't allow you to take photographs. They bully you, they intimidate you personally, they threaten you, they throw you out, they try to confiscate your equipment."[64] Journalists know all too well that locking horns with a police officer or filing a complaint could subject them to violence.

Moreover, since 2008, armed forces violations against journalists have increased considerably.[65] Abuse and repression of Mexican citizens have upended journalistic performance. A quantitative study I led found that the risk of a journalist being murdered increases 1.7 times in local jurisdictions where the public security forces misbehave, for example, in those states where they are responsible for high numbers of human rights violations against the general public.[66] One investigative freelance journalist, who also collaborates with international human rights and security agencies, stated that they were subjected to multiple forms of intimidation by military forces after documenting a civilian massacre.[67]

VIOLENT CENSORS

CACIQUES AND VIOLENT GANGS: THE FRIEND/ENEMY POLICY

> *People, public figures, politicians, a lot of organizations that hold control over areas, over communities... those are the ones that assault and threaten. Since there are so many and they are everywhere, you are actually at risk all of the time.*[68]

—INVESTIGATIVE JOURNALIST FROM A OAXACA NATIONAL NEWSPAPER

Oaxaca has historically been a land dominated by caciques, autocratic political bosses who appoint local officials and control the distribution of public resources.[69] The above testimonial illustrates how these regional political bosses mark the boundaries within which journalistic work may be performed in their territory: they determine when a municipal area may be entered, who may be interviewed, and regarding what topics. Beyond Oaxaca, political bosses and social organizations with informal political control run rampant in states like Chiapas, Guerrero, Michoacán, and Oaxaca. Entire regions of these states register high degrees of social inequality, rampant crime, and abandonment of public services by the federal government.

Municipalities within these states run on an "informal order" that rules social and political existence. This order is defined by clientelist relationships that constitute a political intermediary between formal authorities and citizens, which in turn controls the access and distribution of goods, including public information, and services, and does so through networks of protection, cronyism, loyalty, and camaraderie.[70]

This informal order comprises not only political bosses such as caciques but also collectives and social organizations with access to political authority and resources in determined territories. These additional intermediaries of the informal order include civil rights movements, radical political organizations, and the self-defense movement. And in fact, these can be just as dangerous. For example, an independent journalist from Estado de

109

México clashed with the political pressure group Antorcha Campesina, a political organization linked to the PRI, which filed a criminal complaint against him. The group tried to have the journalist jailed over information he had published regarding one of its leaders. As he explained, "What they really want is loyalty."[71]

Dissident teachers' groups are especially violent with the press, according to an investigative journalist in Michoacán with over thirty years of experience in social and security conflicts. This is especially the case, he explained, when they believe that media coverage of the conflict will not favor them. In these cases, "they wind up finding ways and means to exert pressure. Sometimes they call out slogans against reporters, accusing them of selling out, or they will even resort to threats or direct attacks. We already have had several reporters and photographers beaten up by teachers."[72]

Beyond this, there are also the so-called self-defense organizations, groups of civilians who, in light of the collusion and ineffectiveness of state forces, have organized to defend their communities from organized crime cells. Mexico, like Guatemala and Colombia, has a long history of self-defense groups. But they reemerged with renewed intensity in 2013 in municipal areas of Michoacán, such as La Ruana and Tepalcatepec, that were practically co-opted by organized crime. Some of these groups developed communications strategies that attempted to counteract the narrative of the drug cartels and the government.

This represented a major challenge to local journalism. As a national correspondent in Morelia, Michoacán, commented: "Just like groups of criminals or even police or military corps, [self-defense groups] display a certain animosity toward reporters, toward communicators, because they somehow believe that many could be in the service of another band, be it the government, drug traffickers, or other self-defense groups. So there is also a certain distrust of the media, and all those elements can cause a lot of conflict in the coverage of these events."[73]

When it comes to covering autodefensas, journalists are trapped between these groups and drug trafficking cells. This is a risky position. A few years ago, the investigative journalist quoted above covered self-defense groups along the municipal border of Aquila, 430 kilometers southeast of Morelia.

After reporting and making a photographic survey of the zone, she was detained with other journalists and photographers by people from criminal gangs who asked them to go "talk to people from [self-defense group] Familia Michoacana because we need to get their angle of things, too."[74] When they refused, the journalists were surrounded and death threats were made. After being held for a few hours, they were finally set free.

Throughout this chapter, I have documented the means and motivations behind a series of censors, both internal and external to the state, who have used violence as a form of public expression. This has enabled them to take over a substantial portion of the public sphere, especially that which is created and disseminated through journalism. Frequently, these censors wield violence as a form of control to silence and inhibit journalism that could interfere with their activities, legal or illegal. In other cases—above all when violence is perpetrated by organized crime gangs and self-defense groups—they practice censorship to promote coverage of information and topics that serve their interests.

Journalists and media outlets have had to learn how to mitigate the risks involved in doing their jobs under these conditions and under the constant surveillance of violent censors. In the following chapter, I explore some of the tools and resources, in the form of cultural, economic/organizational, and social capital, used by journalists to mitigate these risks while practicing their profession while faced with such extreme hazards.

PART II

HOW DO JOURNALISTS PERSEVERE?

4
STRATEGIES FOR AUTONOMOUS SAFETY

ISLANDS FOR A CRITICAL PRESS

Ultimately, on the issue of insecurity and violence, if it was well understood how it was generated, why it was generated, and who generated it, well, that could help change things and solve it.[1]

—MONTERREY, NUEVO LEÓN, INVESTIGATIVE JOURNALIST

An investigative journalist from a national magazine who covers politics, security, and economics in northeastern Mexico, in Nuevo León, Tamaulipas, and Coahuila states told me that during episodes of increasing criminal violence, especially from 2009 to 2011, "a lot [of journalists] abandoned the profession, still more sank into anonymity and stopped covering many of the events related to organized crime and violence."[2]

Yet he, like other investigative journalists, beat reporters, and cronistas, has found ways of slipping through the cracks of censorship. Such strategies on personal, organizational, and social levels to innovate and endure as journalists are the focus of this chapter.

For years, he had engaged in high-risk journalism in Nuevo León, Coahuila, Tamaulipas, and Veracruz for a prestigious national magazine. But, in late 2012, everything changed. In Allende, a small town fifty kilometers from the border between Piedras Negras, Coahuila, and Eagle Pass, Texas, this investigative journalist from Monterrey documented a gruesome massacre of civilians. Today, it is known that Los Zetas and municipal police committed these murders as a vendetta against local operators.

He published a long report in December 2012 on this topic. His report was one of the first to publicly expose what for twenty-one months had been an open secret among locals: a rural legend of murders, extortion, and abductions that the authorities had attempted to silence.

Before covering such a high-risk story, he rethought his security guidelines. Unlike reportage in major cities, going to Allende as a recognizable journalist, with a population of only twenty thousand, would be like stepping in front of a fortified firing squad. Spies working for organized crime, known as *halcones* (hawks), watched the entry and exit routes from main avenues and places of business and followed outsiders who visited the town.

Given that journalism was prohibited, this journalist approached the town pretending to be a tourist. He even enlisted a colleague to play the role of his romantic partner. They were probably the first journalists to go to Allende after the terrible massacre. The two of them attempted to talk, not always successfully, with ordinary citizens like the parish priest or shoe shiners on the streets: "The journalism we were able to practice there was very limited because . . . at the time, it was impossible to assess the dimension of what had happened. Because back then, nobody knew anything; above all, the most complicated part was that people living in terror did not wish to speak. They went completely silent."[3]

Writing this long report allowed him to get to know part of the inner workings of the Allende massacre. Even so, he knew it was just one terrible episode in a long, complex story. He kept digging and published cautiously, sometimes anonymously. Knowing that he was "blocked from

STRATEGIES FOR AUTONOMOUS SAFETY

being able to discuss in-depth the topic of relevant events, such as certain massacres that had taken place," he learned to use a strategic self-censorship to bide his time and wait, tying the stories together and broadening his sources before going to press.[4] He knew that he was entering a minefield, something other threats he had received as a journalist made abundantly clear.

But this investigative journalist persevered. For several years, he documented, mainly for a prestigious national magazine and a news agency, the criminality that had pervaded that region of Mexico and the behind-the-scenes drug trade and other criminal activities. He interviewed dozens of sources, including former members of Los Zetas, military officers, and official sources such as security spokespersons, district attorneys, and governors. He also used testimonials from criminal capos in a series of trials he covered from 2013 to 2016 in the United States. He employed other journalistic sources, such as diplomatic cables from the U.S. government published on Wikileaks and the Archivo Histórico de la Secretaría de la Defensa Nacional (Historical Archive of the Secretariat of National Defense), where he consulted the files of military officers who had deserted to join Los Zetas.

This journalist benefited from the protections afforded by the country's most influential political magazine. But even these were insufficient. To remedy this, he joined with other colleagues in the press and founded the Red de Periodistas de Noreste in 2015, which enjoyed the support of the U.S. Agency for International Development.[5] He said, "We created a network of journalists to protect ourselves. . . . Back then, all the support and means to defend ourselves had to come from us. So, we formed a network to stay on the alert more than anything. For example, when I leave the city. If I am going to a high-risk zone, I need to check in with my colleagues every two hours, every four hours, to let them know where I am, how I am moving around, what I am there for, etc."[6]

This mix of hard work in the archives, undercover reporting, dogged patience, collective organizing with other journalists, and a willingness to conceal his intent, ultimately led him to publish several pieces of investigative reporting on this matter. This was also possible because, at that moment, he had been granted a window of opportunity: some of the main capos involved in his investigation were either dead or in prison, some in the United States.

The story of this investigative journalist reveals the main arguments of this chapter: engaged resilient newsmakers, driven by the importance they ascribe to their work, have learned to use the resources within their reach to implement creative strategies to continue documenting and reporting from inhospitable locations. These safety strategies, which may be applied personally, organizationally, and collectively, allow them to bring to light issues that affect their communities, such as criminal violence and its consequences, corruption and abuse of power, grave human rights violations, and environmental topics.

Some are more capable of implementing such strategies than others. Journalists like the journalist mentioned above possess a great deal of prestige (symbolic capital). Moreover, they possess significant professional experience covering sensitive topics (cultural capital) and some support from their media outlets (organizational capital). Finally, such journalists have also developed a network of reliable contacts that may even transcend the field of journalism to include other civic allies, such as activists (social capital). Not all journalists, of course, possess such high levels of these different forms of capital. However, resilient newsmakers can use and convert some forms to compensate for limitations in others. The investigative journalist from the beginning of the chapter, for example, employed his social capital (a reliable network of contacts) to compensate for his limited organizational capital (his media outlet, while prestigious, is based thousands of kilometers away from the coverage zone).

Also, he had high levels of cultural capital. This allowed him to attend various trials of drug traffickers in the United States, which, of course, added to his professional skills. His extended networks of support and trust made it possible for him to visit sites in the company of colleagues and generate collective self-protection mechanisms, such as the Red de Periodistas del Noreste. Finally, the various forms of capital gave him prestige (symbolic capital) that he could make the most of by bringing his manuscript to a publishing house.

STRATEGIES FOR AUTONOMOUS SAFETY

This kind of analysis of forms of capital, as is correctly pointed out by sociologist Robin Vandevoordt in his study on Syria, offers a more complete and complex analysis of how journalists can transform their material and symbolic resources into specific journalistic strategies.[7] Even when linked to national media outlets, journalists like the one I've just described are able, albeit with difficulty, to achieve cautious journalistic autonomy even in the most extreme cases of risk and violence. Of course, not all journalists possess the capital that he does. However, my interviews and similar studies in Mexico indicate that cases like his have become increasingly common among journalists who confront considerable adversity in their work. They are resilient newsmakers.

What this means is that journalists' life experiences, fears, and trauma have ultimately empowered new tools of the trade and even reinforced protection and bulletproofing against future aggressions. The criminal underworld has threatened one radio journalist specializing in politics and security in Culiacán, Sinaloa. He explained that after the trauma and fear, there was "understanding and accepting it, getting past it, and continuing my work."[8] Resilient newsmakers can capitalize on trauma and fear, converting it into self-preservation.[9]

These journalists have learned to operate strategically over the years, using their voice and especially their silence. Their journalism may be described as cautious because they avoid rushing to press when the government or criminal organizations prohibit the subject matter since that would increase their risk level. Verifying information can protect them but does not make them infallible. Patience, not immediacy, has become their ally, although this often goes against the demands of their editors or the market. Getting a scoop on information or visiting a crime scene is so risky that sometimes, they stop pursuing exclusives altogether. Even so, being a witness or speaking to witnesses is critical, especially to overcome the cover-ups and propaganda employed by elites. This is why cultivating a wide variety of sources has become something more than good journalistic practice, given that the puzzles of narco-politics and their myriad social costs can be reconstructed only by speaking to the victims and, at times, even to their victimizers. This is necessary not just in Mexico. Journalists in other parts of the world have implemented similar precaution tactics to create islands of freedom for the press within seas of repression, such as insecure democracies, autocratic regimes, and zones of military occupation or armed conflict.

While many studies agree that critical journalists continue to operate in such environments by combining tactics, only some explain how they do so. What kind of cultural, organizational, or social resources do these journalists use to adopt these more cautious tactics? In what way do journalists' personal, organizational, and social capabilities facilitate the adoption of one kind instead of another? Can such tactics complement one another?

I will attempt to answer these questions using my conversations with many journalists and other documentary and investigative sources. As in other parts of the book, I will focus on the forms of capital that journalists have at their disposition. I call the tactics that these critical journalists follow strategies for autonomous safety. Mellor's concept of "strategies for autonomy" has inspired that term. He uses it to refer to the discursive tactics that journalists employ to enhance professional autonomy in autocratic contexts.[10] In contrast to his term, which applies in authoritarian contexts, the concept advanced in the present work incorporates the concept of safety, which, according to the *Oxford Dictionary*, refers to "the condition of being protected from or unlikely to cause danger, risk, or injury." Additionally, in this book, I follow Slavtcheva-Petkova and colleagues, who define journalists' safety "as the actions and conditions that increase the risk of physical, psychological, digital, and financial harm to journalists as human beings and as institutional actors."[11]

Strategies for autonomous safety are tactics that critical journalists implement to maintain journalistic autonomy in high-risk, unstable environments or repressive atmospheres. Field theory explains that actors can react to their surroundings and use quantities of their resources (capital) to move about within their professional sphere. Their agency is valuable to their development as journalists, their survival in extreme situations and on a par with their ability to cover and publish challenging stories and endure social conflicts, violence, or other burdens.

STRATEGIES FOR AUTONOMOUS SAFETY

As a term, *strategies for autonomous safety* echoes other concepts that also refer to the practice of journalism in adverse scenarios. In their study of the occupation of Iraq in 2003, the scholar Piers Robinson and his colleagues found that, even in times of war, heightened patriotism, or government control, certain media outlets (and British journalists who were deeply committed to their journalistic ideals) created "pockets of resistance."[12] These took the form of media spaces that surpassed discursive consensus and government control, offering a more holistic, balanced, and critical vision of the conflict. Also, in their study about journalism during former Brazilian president Jair Bolsonaro's government, Joao Ozawa and colleagues referred to "catalyzing effects" as a form of resilience among journalists motivated by anti-press populist rhetoric and state censorship.[13] As in the case of the strategies for autonomous safety, catalyzing effects are manifested through more persistent coverage in the face of a hostile environment.

Strategies for autonomous safety act as boundary work tactics, given that they are used to strengthen the professional borders of their work while isolating journalistic logic from external interference.[14] These strategies, as illustrated below, include many tactics on different scales: individual (reporting and investigating precautions), organizational (strategic editorial policies), and collective (such as generating joint coverage and publication initiatives).

The strategies that I will explain include the following:

The Personal Level
1. Logistical foresight
2. Extreme vetting and strategic self-censorship
3. Adoption of discursive literary practices

The Organizational Level
1. Organizational training
2. Anonymous publication
3. Strategic news frames

HOW DO JOURNALISTS PERSEVERE?

The Social Level
1. Critical news startup
2. Collective monitoring
3. Collective reporting and publishing
4. Collective news agenda
5. News sharing

Adopting these strategies implies an empirical learning process of everyday work in high-risk situations and socialization with colleagues. In the case of Mexico, adopting these routines and their dissemination signifies a profound realignment among critical journalists. It means adopting an ad hoc journalistic toolbox for extreme conditions. In recent years, the broader acceptance of such practices has also benefited from initiatives of self-protection and prevention driven by or under the auspices of foreign government agencies such as the U.S. Agency for International Development, civil associations such as Artículo 19 Mexico and Freedom House, journalism networks such as Periodistas de a Pie, and universities.[15]

Below, I will analyze adopting and implementing strategies for resilient journalistic autonomy through the lens of cultural, organizational, and social capital. Rather than a detailed catalog of strategies, I will emphasize what led these journalists to adopt them with varying degrees of effectiveness.

CULTURAL CAPITAL: PROFESSIONAL EXPERIENCE, PRECAUTIONS, AND THE "SURVIVAL INSTINCT"

"Experience in and of itself," explains one correspondent for an influential national newspaper in western Mexico, "gradually marks certain parameters that allow you to carry out a certain kind of coverage."[16] Put another way, these journalists had to learn along the way, mainly because this daily newspaper provided no "specialized, integral" training to perform the kind of high-impact coverage that may trigger reprimands from influential local

STRATEGIES FOR AUTONOMOUS SAFETY

figures. As the correspondent, well-seasoned in covering local corruption scandals, criminal confrontations, military operatives, and social conflicts involving radical organizations such as the teachers' union, explained to me: "They suddenly ask us to carry out all the coverage on our own, not to share information, sometimes not even to seek out the company of another colleague if we are traveling to a zone of coverage that involves risk."

Working on their own, journalists at this newspaper received threats from organized crime and had been temporarily detained. These kinds of traumatic experiences, which were not reported to the authorities because of a lack of trust, generated a "fairly complex environment of panic."[17]

Like many resilient newsmakers, the adversities and aggressions they confronted made them more aware of possible dangers, leading them to protect themselves: "After those incidents took place, I ramped up my precautions," the correspondent told me, "and what I do now is to take my own steps."[18] They capitalized on their professional experience while covering sensitive topics, not to mention first-hand encounters with violence and repression, to generate new tactics. Later on, I will focus on three of the most common among journalists I spoke with: (1) logistical foresight, (2) extreme vetting and strategic self-censorship, and (3) adoption of discursive literary practices.[19] These have allowed them to continue publishing news, even from one of the most unpredictable and inhospitable locations for investigative journalism.

Resilient newsmakers adopt these new practices following a rudimentary process of reflection and trial and error based on their experiences. But when they begin, and when they lack adequate training, journalists can often be exposed to great risk.

A young digital reporter who worked for a legacy newspaper in Nuevo Laredo told me, "We didn't know what we were getting into.... We were going in there scared about what might happen."[20] This reporter, who had less than three years of professional experience at the time of the story, was referring to the groundbreaking initiative he took, together with other colleagues from the digital division, to "compile stories of migrants, above all those who were traveling by train."[21] The journalists were trespassing on abandoned roads and dangerous neighborhoods in cities like Nuevo Laredo, Reynosa, and Matamoros, through which "La Bestia" (The Beast), a cargo train used by migrants to cross Mexico, passes. These locations were in a no-man's-land, controlled or watched over by street gangs, organized crime cells, municipal police, and corrupt migration agents. The reporters of the legacy newspaper in Nuevo Laredo went in with no previous training, risking their lives over a news item that required special newsroom planning at the highest levels.

Journalistic inexperience, a lack of skill and support from their managers, and a strong desire for recognition are major risk factors among younger journalists. It is not enough for journalists to work for a media outlet like the legacy newspaper in Nuevo Laredo with a reputation for handling sensitive stories, especially since this newspaper didn't provide the support they needed. As in other unpredictable and dangerous contexts, the calibration of risk often falls to the journalist, given that even with a degree of preparation and collaboration, decisions in the field are usually made by the individual journalist: how far to venture into a zone of silence, when it comes time to go back to the copy desk, what sources to contact, and which ones to privilege in the story.[22] But as the young reporter's anecdote about this Tamaulipas newspaper illustrates, the draw of a major story can be irresistible to someone looking to make a name for themselves. Fortunately, this reporter wasn't killed or injured because of his reporting. Still, according to a national poll of journalists, it would seem to be a professional trend: "Youth also appears to put journalists at greater risk."[23]

"It's more like a nose for survival than a well-formed security protocol. . . . We haven't received any training as such," according to a Culiacán, Sinaloa, columnist and experienced investigative reporter (aged fifty-five) who was a cofounder of the outstanding magazine *Ríodoce*.[24] That nose consists of a self-awareness regarding "how you can somehow dodge that bullet, how not to put your life on the line for a story. Knowing what you can touch and not crossing those limits."[25] Similarly, when I asked a journalist who covers politics and security with over twenty-five years of experience working for *El Diario de Juárez* just how risky it was to cover homicides and other violent news in Ciudad Juárez, they told me, "Not very, because the

STRATEGIES FOR AUTONOMOUS SAFETY

people already focused on that know how to take care of themselves. They know, for example, when you touch on certain dangerous subject matter, well, you don't just jot down sources or stuff like that related to drug trafficking."[26]

The vast majority of resilient newsmakers employ such self-awareness. It does not make them invincible, but it helps them navigate the minefields they must cross. Beyond the "survival instinct" mentioned by the Sinaloa journalist are strategies like logistical foresight, extreme vetting, strategic self-censorship, and adoption of discursive literary practices.

Logistical foresight covers a range of tactics to mitigate risks while reporting. These include changing commuter routes, activating geolocators, carefully reading the work environment, encrypting information, and emptying laptop computers or planning coverage in hot spots or locations with an overwhelming criminal presence.

In Sinaloa, as in other regions where the local government may not always be an ally, groups of journalists have learned to proceed with caution, implementing "highly practical measures," especially when reporting on narco-politics, corruption, and public debt. Having worked for twenty years as a copy editor, deputy director, special representative for *Noroeste*, and a contributor to *El Universal, Sin embargo,* and *Ríodoce,* one experienced journalist has received threats and other attacks. One example of the foresight he employs is "not keeping to the same old routine, one that is too fixed or established. . . . In our commute to work or home, some of us already are in the habit of taking different routes."[27] This is a tool for survival not only when he's reporting but also when one of his colleagues has been involved in an incident. This use of flexible routes has been adopted by 15 percent of journalists.[28] In some extreme cases, such as the journalists in Veracruz who witnessed the murders of many colleagues during Governor Javier Duarte's administration (2010–2016)—newsmakers like *La Jornada Veracruz*'s Norma Trujillo even took to sleeping in different locations, suspecting that they were under surveillance.

Logistical foresight also means reading one's environment, cautiously sniffing out changes in the local scene while, at the same time, identifying potential catalysts of risk. A reporter on security for the influential newspaper *El Informador* in Jalisco told me that at crime scenes, he learned to protect himself by following a few fundamental guidelines, such as "not crossing the security tape, [being] very cautious, and above all, watching out for the authorities themselves."[29] He also learned to "see what mood people are in—that means everyone, from the neighbors to the people affected, as well as the police or the authorities—to learn who you can get information from by feeling your way through the terrain."[30]

Beyond crime scenes, such foresight is also essential to covering tumultuous events such as social mobilizations, disturbances, and police operations where, every year, dozens of journalists are wounded or beaten due to police abuse or confrontations. This means keeping one eye open, moving cautiously, getting ahead of fatalities, and preparing escape plans. A journalist who covers social issues in Guerrero told me that they decided to abandon the scene of a violent incident between teachers and the authorities just before the conflict intensified, causing the death of one of their close sources. They said, "I don't know what would have happened if I had stayed there where they killed him."[31]

Francisco Castellanos was a Michoacán correspondent for the nationwide magazine *Proceso* for thirty years. In a conversation, he remarked that whenever he gives courses in protection to journalists, he always emphasizes that "no manuals are any good" when you are covering drug-trafficking-related stories. He has been threatened, kidnapped, and forced into exile. Castellanos told me that when carrying out in-depth coverage, he "always makes sure no one is following" and stays "in a hotel one or two days" before going home. He has even lived apart from his family, lodging someplace where no one can peg him as a journalist.

Like other journalists I talked with, Castellanos takes precautions when traveling to any area he will cover, assessing how long he will be there, identifying possible contacts, and maintaining very low visibility. "Look, what I do is act as though I were clueless," he told me. "For example, when I was in Apatzingán and all the reporters were there, I wore my ball cap, my shorts, my T-shirt—nothing that would identify me as a reporter. I have a little camera. I take my photos and disappear. I never identify myself."[32]

STRATEGIES FOR AUTONOMOUS SAFETY

However, identifying yourself as a journalist to select local authorities can sometimes lessen the risks involved, particularly when visiting regions where influential informal figures dominate. "When I have to travel to a community, I try to contact the municipal authorities so that they know I'm on my way or that I will be crossing the zone so that it doesn't come as a surprise and there is no risk of aggression," a national correspondent for an influential national newspaper in Oaxaca who commonly moves around zones controlled by radical civil groups told me.[33] A renowned investigative journalist from the United States said his physical appearance made him stand out in towns and ranches when reporting. So, he usually goes "to the chief of police or municipal president to announce my arrival, not to be 100 percent honest with them about what I'm after, but for them to know that I am there reporting on an event or something important, with the awareness that the bad guys have their eavesdroppers and snitches on the inside there as well."[34] Moreover, whenever he works in the Tamaulipas border zone, he is only on-site for a few hours and then spends the night on the other side of the border. At times of intense violence, he avoids visiting the area altogether.

In addition to logistical foresight, many journalists have adopted extreme vetting, a set of tactics used by journalists to ascertain the reliability of their sources and determine the information they plan to publish and how they will publish it. They gather as many angles of a story as possible to verify authenticity. And they take extreme precautions whenever a meeting is scheduled with a sensitive source.

Environments of political and criminal repression require the careful handling and evaluation of a wide variety of sources. Investigative and chroniclers (long-form journalists who use literary journalism), who commonly have a lot more time than reporters to craft their stories, know that only a panoramic view can capture complex issues such as forced displacements, massacres, the elaborate schemes of money laundering and corruption. For British journalist Ioan Grillo, covering the Mexican underworld presents a distinct challenge. Grillo uses dozens of sources for his extensive stories and books, including farmers who work on poppy plantations, politicians, police officers, military agents, representatives of foreign governments, and informants from the criminal underworld.[35] "When you are talking about the criminal underworld in Mexico," he said, "you are talking about a world of enormous size, you are talking about hundreds of thousands of people involved in this, maybe even millions, we don't know, and we have to touch on a lot of data we know nothing about."[36]

An investigative journalist of Zapotec origin in Oaxaca is conscientious about vetting the sources she works with. She contributes to a national newspaper and digital initiatives offering her greater freedom, such as *Página 3* and the platform Connectas. Her stories, commonly about human rights, gender, and environmental megaprojects, have made powerful local politicians and major corporations alike uncomfortable. Once, after she published a sensitive article, she was given a gag order by the emissary of an influential local figure: "You'd better dial it down because something might happen to you."

She makes room for citizen complaints in her stories but is generally cautious when someone contacts her, not wishing to put them at risk. So, when necessary, she maintains their anonymity: "Sometimes I have to ask the person for permission," she told me, "and if I am going to put them at risk, then I don't publish it." In some cases, she said, fear has overwhelmed her, but she always bounces back. She said these episodes have "helped her become more meticulous" when writing her stories: "If I failed to include a source here yesterday, the next time, I won't drop the ball. I have to cover all the voices so that no one says, 'Why didn't you include me?'"[37]

Aside from being considered good journalistic practice, it has become a protective measure that resilient newsmakers adopt to mitigate certain risks. A cofounder of the investigative magazine *Espejo* and *Ríodoce*, publications known for their combative stories on the criminal underworld, corruption, and narco-politics, commented that he always keeps a very low profile, trying to keep the stories he is investigating "very confidential and very secret."[38] Another reporter, who worked for *El Diario de Juárez* and now collaborates with initiatives such as the Hub de Periodismo de Investigación de la Frontera Norte, told me, "The main [strategy] is to be certain of what you're publishing, of the evidence, to be sure of what you're doing, and with

STRATEGIES FOR AUTONOMOUS SAFETY

that, you have no problem."[39] This could eventually become a problem if a criminal or a politician does not like the story.

Resilient newsmakers have used logistical tools, careful routines, and literary practices. Using words and literary scenes, sensitivity, and their perspective to humanize all they have experienced, these journalists have adopted new discursive mechanisms to document and honestly convey the raw complexity of the Mexico they live in. What has helped them increase their autonomy is the adoption of a more literary style. This differs from the day-to-day *diarismo* (journalism), which does not offer the reported reality's context, voices, and faces. Adopting this style also provides more time for checking sources and enables a more meticulously crafted coverage.

For example, the crónica is a hybrid journalistic format some resilient newsmakers employ. Cronistas belong to a long tradition in Latin America that uses literary elements such as the use of the first person, the recreation of facts through detailed scenes and descriptions, and multiple sources of investigation. Cronistas, as Martín Caparrós puts it, employ a particular perspective to write about reality, an "extreme" and honest gaze, providing a way "to tell the stories that they taught us did not qualify as news." For many years in Mexico, where media outlets noncritically reproduce the official government version of events, the victims of the war on drug trafficking and other marginalized populations were not considered to be news.

Cronistas amplify the voices of others—the victims or people along the margins—who are commonly omitted from the news agenda.[40] For example, Diego Enrique Osorno focuses on townspeople devastated by a "war machine"; Marcela Turati, the mothers, wives, and daughters of missing persons; Daniela Rea and Pablo Ferri, the foot soldiers or perpetrators of military abuse;[41] Javier Valdez, the orphans of drug trafficking and silenced journalists; Sergio González Rodríguez, the murdered women of Ciudad Juárez; and Emiliano Ruiz Parra, those who dwell in the urban periphery or oil workers killed by negligence.

Many contemporary cronistas in Mexico came to this genre out of a disenchantment with daily news and investigative journalism. "I arrived at the crónica as a resource to better establish what I was seeing and documenting. It's the most suitable genre," said Diego Enrique Osorno, a husky and adventuresome cronista who always wears cowboy boots and is the director of several documentaries and short films about politics, culture, and the media. After giving a crónica workshop to my journalism students, Osorno, who contributes to *Gatopardo, Milenio,* the *New York Times,* and *Vice,* told me he changed tactics while covering a social uprising in Oaxaca in 2006. "My breaking point was Oaxaca, where the reality is so screwed up I couldn't express it with a news article, so I started to write chronicles," he said. This feeling was made more acute by the boom in criminal brutality, something he realized the daily news could not describe since the violence in northeastern Mexico had become so prominent. "In 2006, I wanted to go to Africa, like Kapuscinski, in search of conflict. And then all of a sudden, here I am covering a war in my own country."[42]

Authors of crónicas, like many other resilient newsmakers, were pushed into narration by the extreme circumstances they were compelled to experience, using literary techniques to describe the social consequences of violence and repression. Osorno himself wound up deciding to write a crónica on Los Zetas after the criminal gang's kidnapping of a beloved fellow journalist.[43]

Authors of crónicas are uncommon in Mexican journalism. Their work, which often requires immersing themselves in weeks and months of investigation and writing, does not always enjoy backing from prestigious media outlets. This has pushed them to navigate alternate seas, turning their prestige into literary capital that allows them to publish their work as authors.

ORGANIZATIONAL CAPITAL: A LEARNING CURVE, EDITORIAL COMMITMENTS, AND PROTOCOLS

The night of Saturday, August 20, 2011, seemed like a tranquil evening to Javier Garza, editor-in-chief of *El Siglo de Torreón* from 2006 to 2013, but it would turn out otherwise. While he was getting ready to attend a concert,

STRATEGIES FOR AUTONOMOUS SAFETY

Garza's cell phone began buzzing with messages just after 8 p.m. A shooting had taken place in the most important soccer stadium of the city. How should the paper respond? Reporting on the shooting would require assigning various reporters, from the sports section to the crime beat. It was crucial to gather information and verify, given that social networks were abuzz with rumors. Moreover, since Garza and his staff didn't know who was involved in the shooting, they couldn't know who might not want them to report it. Such concerns were amplified by aggressive media monitoring of criminal cells, which fosters anxiety in the newsroom: "What do we do if one of the leaders of Los Zetas threatens us, knowing that his logic consists of hushing up all of the violence they've unleashed? They never contacted us, and due to the story's magnitude, we would have ignored them anyway, but we didn't know at what cost."[44]

The shooting took place in La Comarca Lagunera, a prominent metropolitan area with a population of over three million between Coahuila and Durango states, situated along a strategic route for the passage of drugs into the United States. For years, Javier Garza and his team had covered violent confrontations there between criminal gangs and government forces. Then, in 2007, precisely one year after Garza became editorial director, the violence grew worse. By the time of the stadium shooting in 2011, *El Siglo de Torreón* journalists had learned to continue covering criminal incidents by applying a series of editorial mechanisms and reporting precautions. "The treatment of information ought to be defined case by case," Garza told me, "because there is no single recipe. The facts are so diverse that each publication merits different decisions regarding their location and development within the newspaper."[45] The uncertainty and turmoil endured by *El Siglo de Torreón* staff illustrate the difficult decisions other media outlets face, especially those publishing information of public interest within high-risk environments.

With the outbreak of criminal violence, *El Siglo de Torreón* began a learning curve. In practice, this meant that the paper worked just as hard in ensuring the physical safety of its employees as it did in handling sensitive information. Garza and his team were committed to learning how to practice cautious journalism in a tense, ever-changing, high-risk environment.

They took safety measures at their facilities when carrying out high-risk coverage. They also carefully reviewed all information before publishing and made critical editorial decisions to avoid becoming spokespersons for criminals or corrupt politicians. In adopting these measures, they privileged some journalistic angles, such as violence's social consequences and statistical analysis, over others, such as the sensationalist coverage of violent events. They learned to navigate this environment while, at the same time, coping with fear in the flesh, dodging direct and veiled threats, and experiencing the kidnapping of some of their staff. The newspaper's facilities were attacked with hand grenades and machine gun fire on at least three occasions in 2009, 2011, and 2013. However, they persevered in doing their jobs because, said Garza, "the only viable alternative was self-censorship."[46]

The transformation experienced by *El Siglo de Torreón*, which in 2013 had a circulation of close to thirty thousand, relatively high by local standards, forms part of a pattern among an exceptional group of publications that possessed the organizational resources to adopt a set of strategies for autonomous safety. Generally, these media outlets had prestige—high symbolic national or local capital built through years of quality critical journalism. This group includes major media outlets with a broad network of national correspondents like *Proceso* magazine or the newspaper *Reforma*, and influential local media like *El Siglo de Torreón* in Coahuila, *El Diario de Juárez* in Chihuahua, *Noroeste* in Sinaloa, and the magazine *Zeta* in Tijuana. These media outlets benefited from an ad hoc organizational culture dedicated to civic journalism.

They also benefited from the owners' and upper management's support and commitment. In practically all cases, adopting a cautious approach requires decisive support from owners committed to their outlets' societal role. This is particularly relevant given that most media outlets lack minimal security standards or risk mitigation protocols. In a country plagued with the pernicious proximity of media moguls and governing politicians, who often engage in violent censorship, these protocols are critical to ensure the safety of newsmakers.

A closer relationship with politicians would ensure greater safety for a media organization. However, a closer relationship actually increases the possibility of violent retaliation from a political or criminal enemy. That is why editorial independence is crucial in illegal conflicts. It also allows for portraying events in a more detached and independent manner.

The owners of *El Siglo de Torreón*, a wealthy local family that also owns other businesses, had the financial means to invest in the security and protection of the newspaper while at the same time embarking on an organizational transformation oriented toward the digital market. Garza told me: "There are plenty of owners who don't take it in that direction [provide more security]. I don't know why. I don't know whether it's because they're stingy, I don't know if it's because they lend little importance to the newspaper or if the newspaper is nothing more than an instrument for other political or business interests they might have . . . but in this case, fortunately, I was able to do my job."[47] Although his organization's support for staff ought to be commonplace in Mexico, Garza lamented that this is not the norm: "In the case of *El Siglo*, the family that owns the newspaper comes from a tradition of a lot of engagement. Other media owners in other parts of the country don't want to follow suit. I don't know if it's mere stinginess or being miserly when they fail to appreciate the value of the newspaper and just see it as a political instrument."[48]

Inside newsrooms, the backing of institutional entrepreneurs was decisive in the adoption of these strategies of precaution. For sociologist Paul DiMaggio, institutional entrepreneurs are visionary figures who initiate and support changes in the organizational culture they are immersed in, implementing and institutionalizing new values and ways of doing things.[49] Javier Garza exemplifies the kind of entrepreneurial organizational transformers who, together with their colleagues and top executives, facilitated the adoption of precautionary mechanisms of reporting and publication.

With an unmistakably northern accent, Garza is a weathered professional who was a journalist and editor in Mexico City, as well as a correspondent in Washington, DC, for publications like *Reforma* and the radio team of the influential independent journalist José Gutiérrez Vivó. Before joining *El Siglo de Torreón* in 2006, Garza completed journalism studies at a prestigious journalism program in the United States. In addition to his notable career as an executive, Garza possessed well-developed organizational skills and worked closely with his team of executives and editors to define safety measures, coverage parameters, and editorial angles. Institutional entrepreneurs act not only as catalysts for change in newsrooms but also as go-betweens with owners and employees: "If I saw that it was necessary, I would think it over and make a proposal: 'We need to do this,' and [the owners] would consider it," Garza told me.[50]

Garza benefited from a workplace environment that supported fluid exchanges with beat journalists, editors, and other top executives. Institutional entrepreneurs like Javier Garza can also utilize support and cooperation networks outside newsrooms, such as businesspeople, politicians, or members of civil society, to take the pulse of the region and make better-informed decisions.[51]

Adopting many of these measures was a process of joint organizational learning, which depended on the prevailing organizational culture of risk assessment among newsroom staff. Garza commented that *El Siglo de Torreón* routinely identified what stories might be objectionable to criminal organizations or the government. It was a process of organizational self-reflection. "First," he told me, "you have to analyze what your risk factors are, who your aggressors are, what their methods of aggression are, what may set them off. And starting from there, you move ahead working on your protocol."[52]

However, Garza was uncertain how effective this institutional experience would be when applied to other contexts. He seemed skeptical when we discussed transferring this experience to similar risk zones elsewhere in Mexico. During the period under study, the media outlets' margins for maneuvering were sharply reduced, particularly for cities in Tamaulipas state suffering the ravages of criminal violence like Ciudad Victoria or Nuevo Laredo. That is why Garza was convinced that lessons from his publication couldn't be easily replicated. Instead, he felt that the learning process is, above all, a road that each organization must travel on its own terms, depending on whether it is a large or small outlet, while at the same time taking into account the criminal, political, and economic circumstances it operates under.

STRATEGIES FOR AUTONOMOUS SAFETY

Across the board, adopting strategies for autonomous safety on an organizational level is often more reactive than proactive. That is, as in similar cases like Colombia, such changes commonly happen only after an atmosphere of fear, intimidation, and violence intensifies. Adoption on an organizational level takes place after media organizations and their reporters have suffered attacks because of their reporting. For example, some national correspondents from the weekly *Proceso* told me that following the murder of the journalist Regina Martínez in 2012, they reinforced their security measures by reducing their travel to towns and cities co-opted by organized crime. At *Ríodoce*, a Sinaloa investigative magazine, they strengthened their security guidelines among reporters only after the murder of cofounder Javier Valdez in 2017.[53]

Many media outlets opted for mechanisms favoring an organizational culture that took greater newsroom precautions, such as adopting some specific organizational training to cover sources and events related to security issues. This usually includes field training, especially for journalists who cover security issues, where inexperienced journalists learn the tools of the trade by observing their more experienced peers.

Although important concepts are often learned in college or journalism school, the apprenticeship in journalism commonly takes place through trial and error. In other words, professional skills are learned from transmitting knowledge and experiences across generations of journalists covering similar issues. Intergenerational apprenticeship is traditional in journalism and, in recent years, particularly crucial to covering crime and corruption.

A director of a Sinaloa internet, radio, and television broadcaster (aged 41) told me that in the city of Culiacán, the historic birthplace of drug trafficking, public safety reporters have benefited from their more "experienced peers."[54] A journalist who covers public safety (aged 37) for the Jalisco newspaper *El Informador* commented that a decade ago when they got their start, they benefited from a similar mechanism: "They didn't send me, . . . just like that, out there, to cover public safety. I went with an experienced colleague practically everywhere to see how you covered public safety and security."[55]

However, similar experiences were barely mentioned by others I interviewed, even those who covered other political issues like corruption or serious human rights violations. Moreover, as the journalist and investigator Víctor Hugo Reyna pointed out, given constant labor uncertainty, continual rotation of staff, and economic precariousness, the transmission of intergenerational experiences within media outlets is drastically limited.[56]

Most media outlets in Mexico fail to provide risk training for reporters working on sensitive stories. This is particularly shocking in cities and zones that have endured repression and criminal and political violence. In some newsrooms, as a top official of *Reforma* told me, the need to provide training on an ongoing basis has started to seep in.[57] However, at the time of this book's writing, not much headway has been made in this area at the major national daily newspapers. After all these years, why is it that major media outlets still can't provide risk-prevention training?

The straightforward answer is that, in most cases, they don't care about the safety of their staff. In other words, they are not committed to their employees or, more importantly, to their social responsibility. In other cases, among small media outlets, this omission may be due to other difficulties, such as a lack of material and financial resources.

"Management monitoring" is one of the most widely used precautionary mechanisms. This seeks to establish fluid communications among colleagues in the field and their superiors—editors or directors—on the editorial staff to evaluate the coverage risks and how best to respond if there is potential danger. This practice commonly occurs when journalists are out on the streets covering crime, police corruption, and other sensitive topics or between national correspondents and representatives at work on special assignments.

According to a former deputy director, management monitoring has become a recurring practice at *El Diario de Juárez*. From 2009 to 2013, the paper operated in an environment of elevated criminal violence and police and military abuse. So the journalists began monitoring, meaning they were "in constant communication." They would say, "I am at point A, yes, and now I am going to move to point B," and "constantly check in to ensure nothing was going to happen to them."[58] According to the former deputy director, such fluid communication helps journalists decide on additional measures, evaluate risks, and make decisions. They recommend that their reporters report any situation that might represent a threat or risk: "When you interview someone, if you feel there is a certain hostility that might generate aggression or some other issue, you need to report it immediately and make the call whether or not to continue."[59]

This mechanism is also broadly used by correspondents and special representatives of nationwide media outlets like *Reforma*, *Proceso*, and *Vice*. An experienced *Proceso* correspondent in Michoacán told me that when there is coverage in high-risk areas like Tierra Caliente, they interact with the copy desk practically every hour. In fact, should they not check in, the desk contacts the correspondent's partner in the field, a photographer.[60] Something similar happens at *Reforma*. A correspondent in a state with informal organizations such as caciques, social organizations, and teachers' unions told me that their copy desk insists that reporters remain in constant communication. This allows them to evaluate the risk level in real time and provide additional assistance if something goes wrong during fieldwork.

However, amid the stress of high-risk coverage, there is tension between the pressure to turn in materials such as news items and photographs and journalists' red flags and boundaries. Another correspondent from the *Reforma* newspaper told me that, when communicating their illegal arrest to the copy desk, they "felt no backup" because staff in Mexico City were more concerned about getting a scoop.

Precautionary strategies on an organizational level are fundamental in gathering information and bringing it to light. One of the most common practices is anonymous publication, especially when the news concerns the criminal underworld.

Although, in some cases, anonymity is requested by the journalists themselves, it has increasingly become more of a routine practice. For instance, a contributor to *La Jornada* in Veracruz does not sign the news items she submits regarding abductions because they involve abusive military agents who have already identified her.[61] A nationwide poll found that four out of every ten journalists opted for anonymity on at least one occasion.[62]

Anonymous publication reduces certain risks. However, this tactic has clear limitations in local environments, where it is very easy to identify journalists who cover certain sources.

Another common mechanism is the establishment of strategic news frames by media outlets to cover sensitive stories. Put another way, news organizations publish certain elements and omit others as a protective mechanism, applying strategic self-censorship at an organizational level. In the Anglo-Saxon tradition of journalism, this compromises reporting. Still, as in Mexico, strategic news frames are always in place to safely publish news in a repressive environment.

This umbrella strategy helps diminish risk through editorial tactics that evaluate topics and select suitable language and journalistic angles. "Everything that is published relating to violence, organized crime, or even corruption is examined under a microscope," explained executives at the Sinaloa daily *Noroeste*.[63] "Look, if it has to do with drug trafficking and whatnot," said executives at Chihuahua's *El Diario de Juárez*, "the proposal always has to be taken to the director or managing editor. There is even a roundtable discussion to determine what kind of implications the topic may have and whether it is too risky."[64]

Such editorial framing is sometimes visible in seemingly minor word choices or linguistic precision. For example, stories on criminal violence in local dailies like *El Siglo de Torreón*, *El Diario de Juárez*, *Vanguardia of Saltillo*, or *Noroeste* were written with extreme precision, free of adjectives and omitting any details that could place the newspapers at risk. These papers are extremely careful with criminal information, removing any traces of interpretation and vetting stories in detail. An editor at *Noroeste* told me, "We try to run very impersonal publications in that sense, for that purpose, as if these were sensible, well-documented issues."[65] This includes omitting certain particularities, such as the names of criminals and other data that would help identify them.

This strategy, however, is not supported by other publications such as *Proceso*, *Ríodoce*, or *Zeta*. The longstanding Tijuana weekly *Zeta* has run front-page stories for years featuring photographs, names, and further details regarding members of organized crime. Adela Navarro, the newspaper's director and an outstanding, brave investigative reporter, believes publishing these stories is a fundamental contribution to society and that denouncing criminal acts performs a public service.[66] This editorial policy has come with a bloody quota. Since the magazine was established, it has received numerous threats and direct attacks, and two of its more highly regarded managers have been killed.

Another way to understand such editorial framing is how publications depict the violence they cover. Offering lurid details of a murder might be accurate, but it might also amplify the goals of the perpetrators. For example, Javier Garza told me how a dismembered body carries a greater symbolic weight in the criminal underworld than a simple murder, given that the spectacle of an attack on a rival is always read through the prism of dominance. "Very early on," he explained, *El Siglo de Torreón* realized "that the cruelty with which criminals committed certain crimes was part of the message."[67] To avoid becoming echo chambers of criminal disputes, the paper decided "to try and run everything on equal footing, try not to make pronouncements from the top or from the headlines about the cruelty with which a crime had been committed but describing it instead in the body of the article, taking great care in which photographs were published."[68]

As he recognizes, there were obvious exceptions to these rules, especially when a criminal act, one with significant news impact, could alter the life of a community. In these cases, such as the 2011 shootout at the soccer stadium, the information was fully published in print and on social networks.

Reporting on criminal violence that upsets daily life requires alternative news angles that favor more holistic coverage, focusing on the broader impact on society. In 2010, two camera operators and a reporter for influential national television broadcasters Televisa and Milenio were kidnapped in Durango.[69] In response, Javier Garza and his team at *El Siglo de Torreón* recalibrated their coverage of violent crimes to avoid blowback. That is, they didn't directly cover the kidnappings to avoid violent reprisals from the perpetrators, but they did offer a broader picture of criminality to continue to shape the public's understanding of what had taken place: "We found a way to make up for it with stories about crime statistics, the spike in armed robberies, the social and economic impact of violence, testimonials of people living under its shadow, and linkages between poverty, unemployment, and crime."[70]

Similarly, when covering waves of violence in Sinaloa, an experienced editor at *Noroeste* told me that they also sought to offer a more social perspective, focusing on the victims of violence. "A Money Factory Called the Sierra Madre Occidental," an outstanding report published in 2013 in conjunction with the daily *El Universal* and the platform Connectas, gave broad coverage to the dozens of people whom the violence had displaced. They did the same in their coverage of criminal organizations' use of torture and abduction. "Our coverage was focused on what the obligation of the government is concerning the victims of crime and violence. And we shed light on whether these ... have been attended to or not," he recalled. "So, our thing is not related to self-censorship but about achieving solutions to problems."[71]

SOCIAL CAPITAL: TRUST, COLLECTIVE TACTICS, AND DIGITAL INITIATIVES

Over the past decade, rowing against the current, groups of resilient newsmakers have created journalistic collaboration and networking spaces that act as bulwarks of journalistic autonomy. Fostered by journalists, these spaces may take the shape of a critical news startup, such as native digital journalistic initiatives focused on human rights violations and corruption that practice in-depth, investigative, and literary journalism. Moreover, these initiatives have a far more horizontal organization than traditional media, which allows participants to define the editorial policies instead of a management team. Similar initiatives have popped up across the country, including those states characterized by repression and political and criminal control. One of these places is Veracruz. In this region, hard hit by violence and abuse of power, groups of journalists have created

STRATEGIES FOR AUTONOMOUS SAFETY

emerging critical digital initiatives over the past ten years, such as *Voz Alterna, AVC Noticias, Plumas Libres*, and *La Marea*.

Norma Trujillo has been at the epicenter of this cooperative awakening. Recognized by her colleagues for her generosity and spirit of solidarity, she has been a cornerstone in the founding of *Voz Alterna* and *La Marea*. Trujillo told me in a pleasant but firm voice that *Voz Alterna* emerged, overcoming fear and sharing sorrow, as a collective of protest by and for journalists in Veracruz. At first, they were brought together by fear and rage, linked by a shared set of experiences relating to political persecution and criminal violence. These included the profound pain caused by abductions and missing persons cases. Afterward, they went from protest to journalistic action. Although the cycle of violence against the press was at its peak—in 2015, photojournalist Rubén Espinoza, a member of that collective, was murdered—the group slowly transformed into a digital journalistic initiative. In 2017, after overcoming other obstacles, including organizational and administrative challenges and paucity of resources, they obtained additional financial backing from the Open Society Foundations through the Red de Periodistas de a Pie.[72]

Following various disputes among its members, *Voz Alterna* folded in 2020. Nonetheless, it led to the creation of *La Marea*, a digital publication that follows this same critical line of thinking.

Norma Trujillo—a tenacious reporter who has covered stories such as the rape and murder in 2007 of an indigenous woman at the hands of the military—told me that *Voz Alterna* and *La Marea* share a journalistic commitment to public service. In these digital spaces, she and her colleagues investigate and publish stories that conventional media outlets will not touch: "Something we had begun to contemplate in traditional media was cutting out paragraphs. They would remove them to modify an impact. And what this was about here was not vetoing, but finally being free." Through these digital initiatives, critical journalists in Veracruz amplify the voices and elevate the visibility of historically marginalized populations, such as Indigenous peoples) and those relegated from the official discourse, like victims of criminal violence. The inaugural report of *Voz Alterna*,

"Geography of the Missing in Veracruz," attests to this.[73] "Journalism in Veracruz has a long way to go to get to the most remote places, where the real problems are," Trujillo told me.[74] She was referring to the social consequences of political and criminal violence, and the social, environmental, and community effects of mining and hydroelectric megaprojects in the region.

In studying how news startups formed in Toulouse, France, and Seattle, Matthew Powers and Sandra Vera Zambrano found that high levels of prestige and experience (symbolic capital) are often needed to create these critical digital journalistic initiatives. However, this is not always the case.[75] In other words, critical news startups, like *Voz Alterna* ("Alternative Voice") and *La Marea*, rely on their founders having the kind of prestige and symbolic capital Norma Trujillo possesses. Similar paths followed other news startups in the country like *Página 3*, founded by a national correspondent; *Espejo*, created by a Sinaloa columnist-reporter; or *La Verdad de Juárez*, founded by a group of female journalists from *El Diario de Juárez*.

By turning the tables on government and market-based priorities, critical news startups have focused on carrying out journalism, from news items to in-depth coverage, on topics of social impact and with a human rights perspective. In a study regarding eleven critical news startups that emerged across the nation from 2011 to 2019, researchers Sarelly Martínez and Diego Ramos found that these publications practice a kind of journalism that challenges the mainstream agenda, which tends to be stigmatizing and acritical.[76] Their analysis of these news items found that these startups highlight human rights—especially among historically marginalized populations such as women, migrants, and Indigenous peoples—and journalistic work on public security, justice, and environmental mega-projects.

The creation of critical news startups like *Voz Alterna* and *La Marea* forms part of a broad repertoire of collaborative journalistic actions that have emerged in Mexico in recent years. Like other countries in the region, news startups took off nationwide while the epidemic of violence against the press was raging.[77] Hence, this wave of critical digital journalistic initiatives is deeply marked by an environment of violence, repression, and abuse on a local level and continuous restrictions on the

STRATEGIES FOR AUTONOMOUS SAFETY

publication of sensitive material in traditional media. These forms of collective action qualify as perhaps the strongest example of strategies for autonomous safety.

They are so powerful because such collaborations are collective tactics implemented by journalists to turn the tables on the repressive and violent environment they are experiencing and the organizational limitations they are subject to. These social tactics go beyond institutionalized collaborations, such as forming critical news startups. They also include more informal practices, such as sharing journalistic exclusives with other colleagues who enjoy greater autonomy and prestige so that sensitive stories get published and generating sensitive pack reporting in zones of silence and other areas under the control of the powers that be. These collaborative tactics value public information over personal prestige, and the journalists who use them view their vocation as a network rather than professional individualism. Given that security is not equally distributed among journalists and regions and that, consequently, security and autonomy are privileged, the critical journalists who implement these collaborative tactics are willing to lose an exclusive for their own protection.

The wave of violence against the press in Mexico has deeply marked these collective practices. Even so, collective journalist autonomy is part of a global trend.

Collaborative journalism endeavors to conceptualize, gather, analyze, and disseminate information collectively between journalists and/or media outlets beyond their regional or national borders.[78] While collaborative journalism is nothing new, in recent years, this trend has taken off worldwide, in advanced and developing countries, because of significant transformations in journalism.[79] The main catalysts of collaborative journalism are (1) the crisis in the business model of traditional journalism and the growing precariousness of workers in the press sector; (2) tensions between the control over news production in professional journalism and the increasing adoption of a participatory culture in a digital environment;[80] (3) a trend toward civic coalitions in labor between journalists and nonjournalists to document, investigate, and increase the prominence of major social issues;[81] and (4) the need to act as part of a coalition, using networking to gather and analyze material regarding transnational topics such as networks of money laundering or migration, among others.[82] For some observers, this kind of collective journalistic effort, or networked journalism, redefines the press worldwide.[83]

Collaborative journalism faces professional, economic, and security challenges in Mexico and other Latin American countries. Collaborative journalism upends journalists' natural predisposition to compete, pushing them to produce work of high quality and impact. Here, another major obstacle is mistrust among the journalists themselves, especially among those who operate in places where external agents have infiltrated the profession, whether from the political sphere or the criminal underworld.

Despite these barriers, initiatives like the Veracruz digital initiatives *Voz Alterna and La Marea* suggest that collaborative journalistic action is viable and that journalists can work together, even amid suffocating and repressive contexts. Like the strategies for autonomous safety adopted on individual and organizational levels, these collective tactics have made it possible to continue to practice a brand of high-quality, cautious, and critical journalism. Collaborative tactics break some of the editorial limitations established in more traditional newsrooms, imposed by owners and directors who are loyal to the powerful. The practices of collective journalism can also often compensate for the shortcomings of resources, in terms of reporting and publishing, experienced by professionals who do not enjoy the support of their editorial staff.

Moreover, collaborative journalism has developed alongside and with the support of civic, political, economic, and other nonjournalistic organizations. Collaborative strategies with these tactical allies can range from government contacts to entering a high-risk zone to co-financing mid- and long-term editorial projects.

Beyond the formation of critical news startups, among the main strategies for autonomous safety on a collective level are (1) collective monitoring, (2) collective reporting and publishing, (3) collective news agenda, and (4) news sharing.

One of the strategies most often used by resilient newsmakers is collective monitoring. This alert system involves two or more trusted colleagues

STRATEGIES FOR AUTONOMOUS SAFETY

maintaining close-knit communication while carrying out high-risk coverage. In contrast to monitoring by the copy desk, which is limited to journalists who work for legacy media outlets, collective monitoring is a widespread practice among independent journalists, freelancers, and cronistas who participate in risk coverage. Like other collaborative strategies, one extremely relevant factor for collective monitoring is the trust journalists sustain among themselves: "We all try to watch each other's backs," said an investigative journalist in Guadalajara, Jalisco.[84] Some journalists say that when they carry out high-risk coverage, they have family members monitor their location.[85]

Collective monitoring is commonly applied by journalists covering the streets and reporting on sensitive areas. Journalists on the police beat have developed highly detailed monitoring schemes, especially in cities with violent criminal activity. A reporter and academic scholar in Guadalajara, Jalisco, who typically covers issues related to public safety and human rights said, "I share these protocols with a group of colleagues I trust, specifically so that we may monitor ourselves by telling each other where we are going, under what circumstances, what time we arrive, and what time we leave."[86] The investigative journalist, whose story opens this chapter, told me: "When I leave the city, I have to keep touching base with my colleagues if I enter a high-risk zone, every two hours, every four hours, telling them where I am, how I'm moving around, what I'm there for."[87]

Groups of resilient newsmakers have also implemented sensitive pack reporting initiatives to continue reporting from high-risk zones. The idea behind this practice is that journalists' security increases when they carry out high-risk coverage together. "The first and most important [security mechanism] is the buddy system: in many areas of Mexico, the conditions do not allow journalists to work alone," Ioan Grillo commented emphatically. "Four eyes are better than two," he told me.[88]

Group coverage of news stories is an old practice among the so-called crime-sheet reporters who may visit several locations in a single day or night to document bloody incidents. However, in some cities buffeted by criminal violence, such as Ciudad Victoria (Tamaulipas), Ciudad Juárez (Chihuahua), and Ecatepec (Estado de México), this practice has become a rule of thumb among police beat reporters. Once they learn of a story, they let each other know so they can arrive as a group. One television journalist who covers public security stories in Estado de México with over twenty years of journalistic experience spoke to me about this and mentioned the "war code" they use to cover crime scenes in specific neighborhoods or locations that are known to be high-risk: "I don't show up alone anymore, only with local, state, and national media," he said.[89]

This collaborative strategy is also widely used among national correspondents and investigative journalists, who report on areas and roads far from the big city and are subject to the law of might makes right. "Generally, I try to come to an agreement with my colleagues, with the ones I go in with, and we try to all watch each other's backs," a special assignment reporter for the *Milenio* newspaper in Guadalajara, Jalisco, told me.[90] In his investigations, he usually travels hazardous roads monitored by the military, state police, and crime cells. The small groups consist of only four to five journalists, including photographers; their composition is usually deliberate.

During periods of intense violence in some places, such as Coahuila and Tamaulipas, sensitive pack reporting also helped police reporters agree on what kind of information to print and what to leave out, a practice I call creating a collective news agenda. At times, when the authorities fell short and criminals sought to control the news, this kind of agreement allowed journalists to get the facts straight.

A journalist of a newspaper in Ciudad Victoria told me that from 2010 to 2012, after confronting intimidation and suffering direct attacks from organized crime syndicates, reporters on public safety, editors, and directors came together and agreed on what kind of information their publications would print to avoid any further reprisals: "When we were under pressure from organized crime to publish things against the authorities or against some other group, or something in favor of them or someone they were protecting, we would arrive at an agreement between editors and reporters of all the newspapers in the city to run a similar story so that no one would print any more or less."[91] Something similar occurred during the same period in Coahuila. As Javier Garza, editorial director of *El Siglo de Torreón*, told me, "Something would happen, and there was communication above all between *Milenio* and our end to say how we were going to handle such and such a story so that tomorrow, when we go to press, it won't trigger some kind of reprisal."

Some journalists who enjoy prestige and symbolic capital also benefit from receiving information, materials, and data from other, usually local, colleagues who cannot publish this material in their outlets. This strategy, which I call news sharing, is one of the most common ways to ensure that information of local and even national relevance sees the light of day, particularly when journalists are prevented from running the story. A national poll found that two out of every ten journalists have used this practice to get out news and information that would otherwise have been caught in the nets of self-censorship.[92]

Noé Zavaleta is an investigative journalist from Veracruz who speaks without filters and is eager to share information, stories, and analysis. He worked for various local media outlets before joining *Proceso* as a correspondent in 2013, following the murder of Regina Martínez, his predecessor. Unlike the editorial freedom that the nation's leading political magazine enjoys, Zavaleta tells me that for many years, he suffered censorship now and then: "Listen, this is pretty strong stuff," "Hey, don't go there," "Run that in some other periodical but not here." Now, as a result of working for this prestigious magazine, dozens of local colleagues have contacted him on countless occasions to share information and data of public interest with him, information they cannot publish in their own media outlets: "There are colleagues in the southern part of the state, to the north, in the mountainous zone, who may have some piece of information they were not allowed to run, but that they consider important for public opinion. So they seek me out and facilitate that, and I verify it or contrast it with other information I might have from the area. Then I use it."[93]

This kind of collaboration works thanks to the prestige of these journalists and their publications and because networks of trust have been built between them. Such information-sharing practices can also take the shape of regular, often anonymous collaborations between local journalists and national media outlets. One reporter from Tamaulipas told me that she regularly collaborates with media from Mexico City since her local paper won't run certain material [especially stories linked to organized crime]."[94]

Throughout this chapter, I have explored several strategies at the personal, organizational, and social levels that resilient newsmakers employ to report some of the most dangerous and necessary stories in their communities. But in Mexico, if you want to be a journalist, you must do more than keep reporting; you must actively fight for your rights. In the next chapter, I will explore how resilient newsmakers have become advocates for freedom of the press.

5
STRATEGIES FOR RESISTANCE

EXISTENCE IS RESISTANCE

No crime has shocked Mexican journalism as much as the murder of Javier Valdez Cárdenas. He was renowned, admired, and beloved by his peers, followed assiduously by his readers, and recognized with awards from his hometown, Culiacán, and beyond. Through his crónicas, Valdez Cárdenas amplified the voices of those marginalized by the machinery of political and criminal violence: minors who had become hired guns, children orphaned by criminal violence, mothers and daughters of the missing, and journalists who fell under attack.

On May 15, 2017, in Culiacán, Sinaloa, just a few blocks from the newsroom of *Ríodoce*, the courageous weekly he cofounded in 2003, two armed men ended the life of the beloved cronista, AFP contributor, and correspondent for *La Jornada*. A few minutes later, the news broke on major national and international media. "If they can kill Javier Valdez, our beloved Javier, the best known, the winner of the most prizes, the most protected in the profession," wrote his friend Froylán Enciso, a historian of Sinaloa, "then what about the rest of us? It's like we are all wearing a bull's eye."[1]

Joined by public figures and hundreds of readers, Valdez Cárdenas's friends and colleagues posted their consternation, pain, indignation, and rage on social media. Friends and journalist colleagues joined the protest in the face of such violence and flooded the streets. Just a few weeks earlier, they had protested the murder of investigative journalist Miroslava Breach in Chihuahua (see introduction). Now, to the cry of "They are killing us!" hundreds of journalists and a handful of citizens came out to demand justice for his murder in a dozen cities across Mexico, at the emblematic Angel of Independence in Mexico City, and outside the Sinaloa government palace. A dozen media outlets went on a twenty-four-hour strike to protest the cronista's shocking murder.[2] "It was important to do something different than what we normally do," Daniel Moreno, *Animal Político*'s director and founder, told the BBC.[3]

The crime also achieved something unprecedented: political figures took notice. For the first time in five years of his presidential administration, after thirty-odd journalists had been killed, President Peña Nieto condemned this crime. He even called an urgent meeting with his cabinet and all of the state governors to combat violence against the press. The event was held at the official residence of Los Pinos and was as solemn as it was inconsequential. Following years of heavy silence, this political stunt lacked legitimacy in the eyes of the trade and society.

Many feared that Valdez risked becoming just another number. But his fellow journalists were not about to let that happen. A small group, including Karla Medina, Diego Enrique Osorno, Antonio Martínez Velázquez, and Guillermo Osorno, among others, channeled that pain into a collective effort. In time, this effort would grow into a national journalists' collective, an outlandish notion in a country without an independent national journalists' association, to increase protection. Thus, through the support of a dozen media outlets, civil society organizations, and networks of journalists, universities, and publishing houses, not to mention financing from the Ford Foundation, Agenda de Periodistas was founded, a national collective that sought to develop from rage to diagnostics, from protest to taking concrete steps. This initiative allowed hundreds of journalists to see and recognize one another, combining their strength, rage, and pain. Journalist and

STRATEGIES FOR RESISTANCE

co-organizer of Agenda de Periodistas Guillermo Osorno commented, "It was one of the few occasions where journalists were relatively successful in meeting on their own terms to reflect on what was happening in their profession regarding violence and murder."[4]

Agenda de Periodistas came together for multiple reasons, but the loss of someone with the stature, professional reputation, and many friends of Javier Valdez Cárdenas played a fundamental role. "It was the first time that the threats had reached a journalist who, due to his prestige and national and international recognition, was considered relatively well protected," cronista and editor Guillermo Osorno told me. The political and social timing was also ripe for such a movement—or, as Sidney Tarrow put it, political opportunity—particularly one drawing from collective networks of journalists and activists arising from a crucible of violence over the previous ten years.[5] Even those civil organizations defending freedom of the press had hit rock bottom after a decade of intense labor. They, too, were ready for something new. Lastly, the group capitalized on people fed up with the government turning a blind eye and incapable of channeling citizens' demands for justice and security.

From June 14 to 16, 2017, Agenda de Periodistas met in Mexico City as a heterogeneous group of 381 journalists and organizations from 20 out of 32 states nationwide. Many of the journalists were young, under thirty, and from remote areas, including those most battered by political and criminal violence. Among those in attendance were canonical writers, personal friends of Valdez Cárdenas, university professors, activists, and journalists with budding or lengthy careers. This collective emerged from the journalists themselves, not the owners of media outlets. Owners had already sought to co-opt this initiative through efforts launched by various media and sending reporters to the meeting to infiltrate the proceedings.

What these outside observers found inside the Palacio de Correos in the heart of Mexico City was unprecedented: dozens of journalists organized, in a deliberative and horizontal format, to collaborate on enhancing security and justice within the profession. In discussing the immediate dangers, the journalists assembled illuminated other shared battles, such as labor precariousness, abandonment by the state and society, and the indifference of news organizations' owners. The experience was cathartic, fueled by pain and rage. It had a reflexive and positive character, transforming impotence into diagnostics and burnout into proposals.

By the end of the sessions, the organizers had created a guide for action that addressed the press's existing vulnerability. One of the main demands that emerged, one central to the future of the collective, was to form a national trade organization that would bring together journalists and channel their demands for labor rights and security.

However, the initiative almost immediately faced an obstacle. In Mexico, labor unions are associated with corporatism and authoritarian practices, and the notion of a collective was met with skepticism. Remote participation by journalists was viewed as cumbersome. Local organizations founded years before to grapple with violence resisted control by a new group based in the capital. However, the decisive sticking point was the coalition's inability to move from diagnosing the problem to a plan of action, which made it impossible to move forward. For these reasons, Agenda de Periodistas failed to evolve into a more institutionalized nationwide organization.

Even so, this watershed moment showed that the unthinkable was possible. There was now an option to bring together journalists from all over the country for sporadic protests in reaction to attacks and for proactive collaboration on a common agenda. Most importantly, Agenda de Periodistas showed that given a hostile state, indifferent media, and weak civil society, solutions had to come from the journalists themselves. If they didn't do it, no one would.

Thus, Valdez Cárdenas's murder was not in vain. Even in death, the Sinaloa cronista planted a seed for change in journalism's collective culture. This profound transformation did not come cheap, nor did it happen overnight. However, it is tangible across the country, even in territories and regions where a robust press has never taken root.

Seven years have passed since Cárdenas's murder. During that time, a Mexican judge sentenced two of his killers to fifteen and thirty-two years in jail. In the U.S., a third man involved in the murder remains in custody.

* * *

STRATEGIES FOR RESISTANCE

According to the author Carlos Fuentes, in 1910, the violence of the Mexican Revolution made individuals all over the country recognize one another as fellow citizens. Something similar might be said one hundred years later: the political and criminal violence of the early twenty-first century has helped journalists from across the nation truly see one another.

This collective awakening reflects the dawn of new resilience and resistance in civil society. On the heels of a bloody decade, dozens of social movements, collectives, associations, and networks have emerged in various parts of the country to demand security and justice. However, this awakening is tenuous, given that, as Andreas Schedler correctly points out, in many sectors of society, violence is still considered someone else's problem, the problem only of those engaged in criminal activities, and not a phenomenon in which society engages. Nevertheless, no matter how tenuous, this social awakening has resonated with journalists, doctors, professors, and others in public service.[6]

As the level of violence has ramped up, so, too, has collaboration, resilience, and awareness, fueling further resistance. Mexican civil society has, perhaps, entered a virtuous cycle that accelerates positive change.

After all, the relations of power, as French philosopher Michel Foucault argued, always leave open the possibility of resistance.[7] No form of domination is total, nor is anyone ever entirely dominated. There is always room or desire for resistance. Where there is power, says Manuel Castells, there are always forms of counterpower.[8] In field theory, actors accrue resources throughout their life trajectories that catalyze their agency. Agency not only reproduces social life but also transforms it. Like journalists, actors commonly aid situational agencies to circumvent adversities. They are rarely passive receivers; on the contrary, they are agents who can transform their circumstances, taking advantage of adversity and generating opportunities even when it is an uphill struggle.[9]

Thus, counterpower is channeled by the means the resource's agents have at their disposal. This channeling is the bedrock on which much of this book's analysis is built. Journalists have become figures accustomed to building the abilities and tools to turn the tables on adverse circumstances and fulfill their social role. Although the capacity of journalists for resistance is nothing new, it has only begun to be discussed.

HOW DO JOURNALISTS PERSEVERE?

Many questions regarding this phenomenon are still being explored. What role do symbolic and material resources play in acts of resilience, resistance, and confrontation adopted by journalists? How and why do some journalists acquire and employ resources to resist and face adverse surroundings? What compels them to continue their journalistic labor, even when they might lose lives? What enables courageous editorial staff to stand firm against and challenge power? What leads groups of critical journalists to adhere to broad collectives that demand justice and an end to attacks against them? Why do journalists form social movements, and what do they seek to accomplish through them? Guided by the experiences of the journalists I conversed with, and by documentary sources and investigations, I will attempt to answer these questions. As in other parts of the book, I explore the cultural, organizational, and social capital journalists have at their disposal.

The tactics employed by these critical journalists may be called strategies of resistance. They implement tactical maneuvers to adapt to, resist, and even confront challenges. Their higher capital levels enable journalists to acquire the resources needed to deploy these strategies. Strategies of resistance also include actors' capacity to develop mental schemes, tactics, and practices that serve as coping mechanisms and thus protect individuals from the negative impact of stress, attacks, intimidation, or other traumatic events. Resistance is, therefore, a state of mind that channels coping strategies and counterbalances the limitations and adversities journalists face in daily practice. With only a handful of exceptions, many of these tactics emerged after self-reflective processes occurring at an individual, organizational, or collective level. In these cases, as David Snow comments, the foundational affront, or series of affronts, is associated with a set of feelings, such as fear, impotence, indignation, and rage.[10]

Most critical journalists who implement these tactics fervently believe their profession is relevant, whether they hold certain journalistic values or think their profession has social impact. While it is true that journalistic values are not always homogenous, newsmakers' lofty social and community aspirations are. Rosemary Novak and Sarah Davidson explain that journalists motivated by professional and social values develop an emotional

STRATEGIES FOR RESISTANCE

connection to their work that compensates for the "sacrifice" implied in risking their physical integrity.[11] For Sallie Hughes and a group of researchers, the satisfaction and passion journalists feel in doing their jobs, especially in witnessing their work's social impact, is reason enough not to give up; for them, journalism is a lifestyle.[12] An empirical study by Violeta Santiago reached similar conclusions: the majority of a group of Veracruz journalists indicated that, despite their profession's risks, they would continue to work as journalists because fighting injustice motivates them. They have the sense that their work contributes to a more critical, democratic society. It also brings them social recognition.[13]

In what follows, I describe in detail the strategies of resistance implemented by critical journalists.

The Personal Level
1. Developing meaningful resistance
2. Learning precautionary actions

The Organizational Level
1. Applying precautionary measures
2. Providing emergency assistance and support

The Social Level
1. Fostering collective professionalization
2. Becoming emergency responders
3. Promoting social protest
4. Lobbying

Strategies of autonomous resilience allow journalists to practice their craft in adverse environments, but the strategic framework I propose here goes beyond professional journalistic practice to outright resistance.[14] The Agenda de Periodistas journalists shared their pain and indignation over the loss of Javier Valdez and then counterattacked. They created a space for catharsis in which to work, where the struggle was not limited to their profession. It was also a struggle for their lives: existing meant resisting. It was a place where they expressed sorrows that were catalysts for action. To be flexible under adverse circumstances: For the journalists I spoke to, flexibility under adverse circumstances was the first step toward transforming them.

As we observed in the previous chapter, the greatest form of resilience in the journalistic profession is to continue to provide media coverage. This means not only overcoming danger or trauma but clinging to professional practice even when facing the kinds of danger described extensively by reporters throughout this book. For example, a study explains how Colombian journalists confronted self-censorship: they built journalists' networks or made alliances with independent editors to continue investigating and publishing facts of public interest. Even in cases where their safety was at stake, some preferred to hand information over to other colleagues for publication rather than remain silent.[15]

Critical journalists' strategies of resistance necessarily require taking political stances informed by personal rigor, objectivity, and ethics. In covering Mexico, journalists confront violence that turns them into both victims and activists.

In the following sections, I analyze the adoption and implementation of strategies of resistance through the lens of cultural, organizational, and social capital. Rather than catalog the strategies in detail, I emphasize the mechanisms that allow critical journalists to adopt these strategies effectively.

CULTURAL CAPITAL: UNDERSTANDING, LEARNING, AND PERSEVERING

"Despite all these circumstances, we must continue to fight back," remarks Emilio Lugo, who abandoned Guerrero after local criminal groups threatened his life.[16] We met at a café in Mexico City. He chooses a seat with a view of the street, his back protected by the wall.

He tells me in a long conversation about his epic journey since fleeing Acapulco five years ago. In his blog *Agoraguerrero*, he documented the social deterioration and violence of a famous tourist seaport and the

STRATEGIES FOR RESISTANCE

surrounding Guerrero region from 2010 to 2013. When society was demanding news of public interest not found in traditional media outlets, his blog filled the information gap with a yellow journalism style, mixing citizens' reports and news items, frequently embellished with graphic descriptions and explicit images of bloody events. Much of the information came from anonymous complaints and informants from criminal groups, local and federal authorities, and military sources. Among other sources of financing, contributions from relatives of the missing sustained the blog. They would dig through its contents in search of clues regarding the fate of their loved ones.

Covering this criminal environment came at a high cost to Emilio Lugo in terms of his well-being and security. This resilient newsmaker told me that during that period, he was subject to attacks and threats from authorities and criminal groups that included digital attacks on the blog in 2012 and other kinds of threats. He remembers that in moments of the highest pressure and greatest fear, the community encouraged him to keep at it: "They gave me the strength to continue to practice journalism."[17] But this precarious balance, already under great strain, was upset in 2013, when he faced death threats from a powerful criminal organization attempting to enter the territory.[18] The threats began after he refused to publish propaganda from the cartels in *Agoraguerrero*. From then on, he spent his personal and professional life on the run.

Lugo and his partner took refuge for a few weeks at a local police station. Later on, supported by organizations that defended freedom of the press, they moved from Guerrero to Mexico City, which was then considered a refuge for displaced journalists. By 2015, that oasis was marred by the murder of the photojournalist Rubén Espinoza (see chapter 2). He told me he became one of the first beneficiaries of the Mecanismo de Protección de Periodistas housed by the Secretaría de Gobernación. The Mecanismo, as stated in chapter 3, suggests to members at high risk that they stop practicing journalism to reduce their exposure. However, this is practically impossible for many journalists, for whom this trade is a way of life that provides of purpose. This proved to be the case for him, and he continued to publish on his website.

HOW DO JOURNALISTS PERSEVERE?

Soon after in 2014, working with the Associated Press, Emilio Lugo learned how government military forces executed two dozen civilians in what is known as the Tlatlaya case. His work helped tear down the official version of the facts because it made it clear that this, like many other cases, was a massacre committed by the state rather than the result of a criminal confrontation.

At the time of our interview, his situation remained precarious. "You have to continue to work even though everything is against," he commented as we ate. "It's something that needs to be done."[19] Just a few minutes later, his panic button, provided by the Mecanismo, started beeping, signaling that the battery was about to die.

It would be incorrect to assume that this process of overcoming complex and high-risk situations is linear, given that on more than one occasion, this journalist was incapable of continuing to do his job, primarily because he was fearful. However, in the long run, his story demonstrates that clinging to the value of his profession was critical to helping him move forward. The same has held true for journalists in other countries who have embraced the ethical principles of journalism as a form of resilience.[20]

This case may seem extraordinary at first. But it is part of a broader pattern I and other investigators have found among committed journalists who endured harsh periods of stress and trauma from covering natural disasters, terrorist attacks, wartime situations, political and criminal violence, or even planetary challenges like the consequences of climate change or COVID-19.[21]

As this case illustrates, one of the main characteristics that guide resistance behavior, allowing resilient newsmakers to move forward, is the high value journalists place on their profession, commitment to society, and journalistic values. A series of investigations over the past few years suggest that critical journalists are highly resistant and can confront and overcome the traumatic and high-risk situations they have experienced.[22] However, to transcend their fear and continue to work, they need resources in symbolic and cultural capital acquired through life experience. According to George Bonanno, the capacity for flexibility and adaptation among people typically follows specific stages. The first, "context sensitivity" refers to the subject's

STRATEGIES FOR RESISTANCE

analysis of the environment, the ability to read and understand the demands of the situation requiring the subject's action. The second stage, "repertoire," involves developing strategies to confront the situation. These may include engaging in other activities (whether beneficial, such as meditation, or harmful, such as abuse of alcohol). The third is "feedback monitoring," the process by which the subject constantly analyzes the feasibility of the strategies used in the second stage. This process results in meaningful personal resistance.[23]

A study by Laura Iesue and other investigators found that journalists in stressful or traumatic situations have good and bad ways of adapting to the changes they face.[24] Sallie Hughes and other academic scholars detail these positive methods: resilient newsmakers may turn to collective and individual practices based on emotional healing, like practicing a sport or exercising, writing poetry, meditating, or enjoying a hobby.[25] A journalist from Veracruz who experienced intimidation via social media commented that he began exercising to minimize stress in response.[26] However, Hughes' investigation states that other journalists have mentioned maladaptive strategies to deal with this type of stress, such as the abuse of substances like alcohol.[27] A local Oaxaca journalist who belonged to a civic organization devoted to helping journalists commented it was working with newspeople to address their alcoholism, especially those subjected to high levels of professional and personal pressure.[28]

But in addition to these strategies, elements central to making the journalistic vocation a meaningful process are a strong commitment to journalism's social value as an agent of change and a deep-rooted adhesion to professional values. Studies have found that Mexican journalists in high-risk contexts, like those who work in Tamaulipas, have continued to practice their trade because of the professional identity they derive from "satisfaction from work and commitments to public service norms."[29] Novak and Davidson make a similar argument. They found that journalists working in hazardous situations constructed protective factors within their professional performance: "The journalists described the importance of prioritizing the job over other commitments to achieve, for example, in making sacrifices in their personal lives and the necessity of going to hazardous situations and being exposed to danger."[30]

HOW DO JOURNALISTS PERSEVERE?

In my fieldwork, I commonly encountered cases like the displaced journalist's that opens this section: journalists embrace professional ideals to cope with the reality they confront. When I asked why he hadn't abandoned journalism even after an attempt on his life, a veteran editor and investigative reporter from the Sinaloa legacy newspaper *Noroeste* told me: "Well, yes, at the very least, you have to understand it, accept it, bear it, and continue working. Under those circumstances, you carry on. It forms part of the risks of our profession."[31] A Oaxaca correspondent for a national political magazine who often criticized local government wrongdoings was beaten and psychologically tortured for twelve hours in 2008. In an interview, he talked about how, after receiving support from his community, he became more aware of the relevance of his work and felt more motivated:

> After I was abducted and then freed, the next day was like a party at my house because people who I didn't even know stopped by. Organizations and religious people would tell me, "Well, we heard what happened, and we came to tell you that we are with you, and we support you." That's when I felt that my work had a purpose, that it had some leverage, some influence, and that people think it's important. That motivated me a lot, and it made me believe this is where I belong.[32]

This testimony summarizes how a strong commitment to performing a professional role and social recognition stemming from one's work can allow resilient newsmakers to continue practicing journalism. His story illustrates how those who witness, investigate, and publish stories on extreme situations or work under tremendous pressure may develop physical and emotional integrity issues and suffer psychological trauma from fear and life-threatening conditions. Nonetheless, they feel the worst thing that could happen to them would be to abandon journalism.

Additionally, after living and working in extreme situations or under great pressure, the resilient newsmakers interviewed for this book have not only carried out their vocation with "meaningful resistance" but derived meaning from close encounters with fear, danger, and trauma and learned to be more cautious. In Sinaloa, an editor-in-chief threatened three times—twice by local authorities and once by local traffickers—said he had learned a lot from these traumatic episodes: "They have no reason to detain you or anything of the sort. You simply have to learn to be more responsible and more cautious."[33] A national correspondent for a legacy newspaper based in Morelia, Michoacán, was abducted while covering local drug trafficking activity. He commented that while he continues to practice journalism, he is extremely careful: "Now, as a result of those incidents, I have maximized my precautions. What I do now is adopt my own measures."[34] An experienced Oaxaca investigative journalist for legacy newspaper *El Imparcial* said: "Sometimes, it can be a week or a few days when I start to think about it a lot. But sometimes I also say to myself, 'No, you have to carry on, you chose this profession, so you do it with passion.' And every time, I try."[35]

These testimonies suggest that journalists have learned from their negative experiences and continued to do their jobs even when they take special measures, such as preventive actions. Empirical findings suggest that journalists transformed these forms of cultural capital into specific strategies for newsgathering.

In light of this, the following sections demonstrate how journalists translate their encounters with violence—and those of their colleagues—into creative strategies for reporting within their news organizations while avoiding further negative consequences.

ORGANIZATIONAL CAPITAL: SUPPORT, SECURITY, AND PROTEST

The Veracruz correspondent for the weekly *Proceso*, Regina Martínez, was murdered on the afternoon of Saturday, April 28, 2012.[36] The next morning, "we were already at a meeting with the governor, led by the magazine's founder, Julio Scherer, and the director," recalled Jorge Carrasco, an investigative reporter.[37] They were part of the entourage from *Proceso* that promptly left Mexico City for Xalapa, Veracruz, the enclave of Governor Javier Duarte of the PRI. From 2010 to 2016, under Duarte's administration, seventeen journalists were killed and many more were targeted. The period also stood out for its elevated violence and brutality, in which thousands of people disappeared, and hundreds of bodies were later found buried in clandestine mass graves.

At the meeting, escorted by top state security officials, Governor Duarte, now serving a nine-year sentence for embezzling billions of dollars while in office, took the floor and said, "You may be sure that every avenue will be explored."[38] Scherer retorted: "What we have just heard barely scratches the surface. Regina Martínez's death is the product of a decomposing state and nation. We want to know what lies beneath that surface. In short, Mr. Governor, we don't believe you."[39] Rafael Rodríguez Castañeda explained that the magazine knew Martínez faced a "hostile environment" because she dug into local narco-politics. She had been threatened several times before her death. After the meeting, the journalists retreated to a back room to write a press release, in which they set down *Proceso*'s position on Martínez's killing and stated their lack of trust in the promise of justice from Duarte's government.[40]

Since then, the magazine has taken on an important public role, leading the investigation into the brutal murder and demanding justice. Its advocacy is uncommon since Mexican media all too frequently dismiss aggressions perpetrated against their staff or deliberately maintain an accommodating silence regarding atrocities. When I asked Rodríguez Castañeda about this historic episode, he said, "The fact that *Proceso* placed such strong emphasis on the case became very important."[41]

Proceso journalists supported the magazine's timely and robust response to this outrageous crime. Historically, the publication has gone against the grain, dodging intimidation and government censorship since its founding in 1976. "I'm not saying there isn't one, but I can't think of any other case of a journalist who was murdered where her news organization was so persistent about investigating the case," commented Jorge Carrasco, who took over as *Proceso*'s editorial director in 2020. While the magazine has continued to stand up to power, it has also introduced safe journalistic practices: "We continue to inform. We have not changed our editorial line, but we are much more cautious about safeguarding the lives of our staff."[42]

STRATEGIES FOR RESISTANCE

A longtime friend and trusted colleague, Carrasco confirmed Martínez's death. From 2009 until her murder, he worked closely with her, reporting on risky topics like narco-politics. So he became a prominent figure in the murder case investigation. Early on, assisted by a legal figure called a *coadyuvante* (adjuvant), he collaborated with the local state prosecutor. However, his collaboration raised important ethical and professional issues as he was forced to act as both a journalist and as an investigator, two complementary yet contradictory roles:

> On the one hand, it put us in a compromising situation because, having gained access to information through the preliminary investigation, we could not make that content public. On the other hand, what we could do and did do was to inform our readers about what was being investigated, how the authorities were investigating, and what they were no longer investigating. We were always very careful not to publish a single detail of the file so we wouldn't have to assume any responsibility for a leak that could sidetrack the investigation.[43]

As difficult and stressful as this situation was, these experiences allowed him to witness the repressive state apparatus from within. He experienced firsthand how the state undermined his efforts to access information about the crime. From the start, the public prosecutor tampered with crime scene evidence and ignored substantial proof that Martínez's death was related to her journalistic activity. Persons closely linked to the local governor backed a misinformation campaign claiming that she was murdered during a botched robbery or crime of passion.

One year after Martínez's murder, Carrasco and his family, with the magazine's support, had to abandon the country because of threats against his life. As is common in situations of forced displacement, journalists find themselves compelled to cut personal ties and journalistic activities to remain safe. "It had a tremendous impact," he said. "I disconnected from my journalistic work for about a month, with all the personal implications."[44] But he also had to face the fact that he could no longer investigate the murder of his colleague.

Twelve years have passed since the crime was committed, and the murderers remain unpunished. However, the demands for justice continue as if it were day one: in Veracruz, journalists continue to protest in the public square, unofficially known as Regina Square, outside the Palacio de Gobierno. As Scherer wrote, "Regina touches our hearts."[45] Eighteen national and international *Proceso* correspondents published an open letter warning that they would not abandon their demand for justice. Other colleagues and friends of the deceased led a public demonstration in Mexico City. They marched to the capital's official Casa de Veracruz, where they demanded justice. Media moguls, legacy newspapers, and national TV channels did not support the demonstration, attended by three hundred journalists. Media owners warned their staff not to participate in the demonstrations, proclaiming the need to preserve professional objectivity.

The magazine's brave, firm, and determined response sparked a wave of discontent and resistance in the journalism field. For many journalists, especially in Veracruz, the crime became a space for showing, sharing, and boosting courage, outrage, and solidarity.

The prominence of symbolic, organizational, and social capital helps explain why Martínez's murder triggered this wave. Martínez was a well-known, seasoned investigative reporter with over twenty years of experience who was highly respected among her peers in Veracruz and whose "ethical conduct was impeccable" (symbolic capital).[46] Martínez worked for *Proceso*, the most prominent political magazine in the country (organizational capital). Moreover, she had solid networking ties with colleagues in Mexico City and beyond (social capital). Additionally, the series of protests and the turmoil caused by her death, combined with the fact that the alleged perpetrators formed part of a well-documented corrupt and criminal local administration, created a climate of terror for journalists.

Martínez's death "caused a commotion in journalism nationwide," as columnist Julio Hernández López put it.[47] It also greatly impacted journalism in Veracruz, changing how journalists perceive and react to violence against them. For Noé Zavaleta, who became *Proceso*'s national correspondent in Veracruz, "there is a before and after in terms of Regina's death." For him,

STRATEGIES FOR RESISTANCE

"Regina shook journalistic unity in Veracruz to the core because we thought, 'If they got to Regina, they can get to anybody.'"[48] This crime had important legal and professional consequences because of mass demonstrations in several locations and the public pressure brought to bear by *Proceso*. Days after her death, overwhelming majorities in both houses of Congress approved a bill that protects journalists and human rights defenders. Her murder also bolstered the emergence of the so-called Cartel Project. This ambitious journalistic collaboration encompassed a group of sixty journalists from twenty-five international news media outlets, including *Proceso*, the *Guardian*, *Le Monde*, *El País*, *NPR*, and the *Washington Post*, who teamed up to continue investigating some of the stories that Martínez was working on when she was killed.[49]

Her murder exemplifies how confronting risk, fear, and violence in the wake of the brutal murder of a colleague may also trigger a set of behaviors that demonstrate resistance. Shared violence and fear can bring about some form of counterbalance whereby resilient newsmakers find a way to cope and resist despite highly adverse conditions.

Confronting violence is not solely an individual matter. Organizations may engage in confrontational actions mirroring those of journalists. So, what sets off this kind of resistance in a profession? In some cases, violence in Mexico and how power is wielded pose challenges to the exercise of freedom of expression. This may support forming civic-minded editorial staff who seek to practice critical, independent, and resistant journalism. Just as journalists have the capacity, individually and collectively, to exercise counterbalancing actions, organizations may also take that step if and when managers, directors, or owners back them.

The most important strategies frequently referred to by the journalists, editors, and directors with whom I conversed for this book are: (1) applying security measures; (2) providing emergency assistance and support; and (3) exposing aggressions.

Because they may be cumbersome, security measures are one of the self-protection tactics that have received the most attention from the international press. They are also highlighted in reports on freedom of the press and security. Security measures are a series of preventive and precautionary actions that range from installing security cameras in newsrooms and purchasing bulletproof vests to incentivizing digital and personal security protocols, such as changing routines, among reporters. Investigations like Márquez and Hughes's have found that reporters, above all, should transform their work routine, such as following orders not to cover certain stories and practicing journalism in groups.[50] It was necessary to change routines for continued reporting in an environment of extreme violence and as an organizational reaction to direct and veiled attacks against news media facilities. From 2006 to 2016, there were more than fifty such attacks in thirteen states of the federation, mainly in Tamaulipas, Sonora, and Veracruz.[51]

Some legacy periodicals, like *Noroeste*, *El Diario de Juárez*, and *El Siglo de Torreón*, made significant investments in security at their facilities, which often included installing security cameras in their newsrooms, hiring security personnel, and implementing specific logistical protocols. At *El Siglo de Torreón* in Coahuila, where protective measures were taken at the facilities after a series of attacks against them and their workers, "the directors did whatever was necessary to try and mitigate a situation of insecurity or violence against the newspaper or vulnerability. If you had to invest to reinforce the entrances, it was done. If you had to invest to purchase equipment, it was invested. In that sense, they spared no expense."[52] An experienced *Noroeste* editor told me that they installed security cameras because of a wave of attacks they experienced, including an attack on the newspaper building in 2015.[53] Other media organizations purchased bulletproof vests and other security equipment for their reporters, especially for those working the crime beat.

Some legacy news organizations and certain civic digital news startups have undergone a process of "organizational learning," which occurs when, after a direct attack against colleagues or media facilities, members of a professional organization learn from the experience and incorporate additional tactics of coping and resilience into their daily routines.

A researcher from Colectivo de Análisis de la Seguridad con Democracia A.C. (CASEDE) who studied the Sinaloa newspaper's experience said

STRATEGIES FOR RESISTANCE

Noroeste demonstrates how media can develop strategies and a protocol to face violence against the press: "El *Noroeste*, for example, is a newspaper that has also been subject to a lot of aggressions. Together with their reporters, they developed a self-protection protocol that applies only to them. They have their own networks of prevention, accompaniment, and cooperation among journalists to keep tabs on one another."[54] This newspaper learned to prepare and equip itself better. In 2010, its facilities in Mazatlán were the target of an armed attack. Still, the problem is such protective measures are taken only after the attack. A journalist from Sinaloa remembers: "When there was a drive-by at the newspaper *Noroeste*, they shot up the front of the building. Not until then were reporters given a course on journalist protection and then only the ones working the crime beat, even though the shooting happened at the *Noroeste* building."[55]

This consolidation of security protocols among Mexican media involved a pronounced learning curve through trial and error, attacks, and resistance. "It was like when you thought you already had the solution to a situation you were facing, the final challenge, the final difficulty, or the final problem, another would pop up," Javier Garza Ramos said about *El Siglo de Torreón*, adding that for them, the main lesson consisted of realizing that security measures went beyond physical protection and choosing journalistic angles during coverage. They also became aware of "watching our surroundings for people who might be on the lookout, surveilling, or tailing you."[56]

According to Garza, the situation they lived through triggered a reaction of mutual support among those who worked on the editorial staff. Although "the journalists from the company, the reporters and editors, could assume it was an inherent risk, they decided to work there for the newspaper. . . . It was admirable, the way they reacted, because it showed solidarity within." Nonetheless, he believes it is impossible to fully transfer everything the organization did to protect its personnel to other media, perhaps because no national protocol applies equally to all editorial staff. Garza argued that what *El Siglo* did worked only in Torreón because it analyzed local risk factors, such as the main aggressors, their methods of generating violence, and the situations triggering the attacks. He is still an optimist. The former editor believes that if a journalistic organization considers these points, "you can work on creating your own protocol."[57]

Media organizations also protect their personnel through individualized actions and attention to personal cases, especially when the risk involves not the outlet itself but reporters, mainly those who cover crime, justice, or violence. A Michoacán correspondent for a national newspaper abducted there stated that threats against his person started following the appearance of *narcomantas*, banners used by cartels to communicate among themselves.[58] His employers ordered him to suspend his activities, leave home, and flee with his family to a "safe haven." Without knowing what relocation really involved, it was clear he had to leave the state. Although he secured his own security and that of his family by leaving Michoacán "until the situation calmed down," the reporter remembers the emotional consequences: "It was a situation that kept us in a state of psychosis, of constant panic. It's very complicated because as I said, it involves the safety and integrity of your family." He added that at least he felt a greater sense of certainty and calm because the periodical was in constant communication and collaborated in the decision-making process.

Erick Muñiz, who was intimidated following the publication of an investigation into national networks of corruption with links to businesspeople in the state of Nuevo León, describes something similar. The news outlet suggested that he act cautiously, helped him get his daughter out of the country, and accompanied him when he filed a complaint with the Procuraduría General de la República (Office of the Attorney General of the Republic).[59] Before the attack, he had enrolled in journalism courses for high-risk situations, taught by Israeli instructors. "We took three [courses]. They were all focused on reporting in situations of stress, armed conflict, and also kidnapping. So I think we received adequate training." Such programs, he reflected, helped him act with a cool head amid a high-risk situation, which in turn allowed him to make better decisions with the support of his media outlet: "At least as far as I'm concerned, I feel it has helped me a lot."

According to a top *Reforma* executive, the assistance generally provided by the editorial staff allows not only a risk evaluation in real time but also provides aid in the event something happens to them while working in the

STRATEGIES FOR RESISTANCE

field: "The first reaction is to provide them with coverage, humane medical assistance solely for what touches on their own integrity. We do want them to feel our backing and the support of the institution they belong to."[60] A Oaxaca journalist says, "I remember I did talk about it at the newspaper. Let's just say it's a dynamic practiced at *Reforma*. Even if it seems minor, you have to report every incident immediately so that the newspaper becomes aware of it and can take the necessary precautions."[61]

However, this training is not always present for many reasons, among which journalistic inertia stands out. In the heat of high-risk coverage, there is pressure to deliver news and images. Journalists face deadlines and limitations. When is it time to stop is a question even the most experienced must answer. A correspondent for the same newspaper told me that despite clear warning signs, journalists continued to report in a zone controlled by self-defense groups. When they reported to the office that some of them had been abducted, they felt unsupported because management in Mexico City was mostly concerned about going to press with the story so they could scoop the competition.

In my research, I found that to produce strategies of resilience and resistance, news organizations must have editors and owners unafraid of public confrontation. A good example of this occurred at *Noroeste*, one of the few Sinaloa publications independent of the economic resources provided by state authorities, which has allowed it to be civically minded since its foundation in 1973.

On April 5, 2014, the daily published a full-page statement holding Sinaloa authorities responsible for what it called a "premeditated attack": General Director Adrian López Ortiz had been shot in the leg after a group of men forced him to get out of his car, beat him, and robbed him shortly after midnight on the streets of Culiacán. He sought treatment at a local hospital. In the statement, which ran in all major national media outlets, the daily denounced that since 2010, they had suffered as many as sixty-two attacks, which included threats, harassment, and armed assault. Many of these attacks were allegedly perpetrated by local authorities, in response to *Noroeste*'s critical coverage of collusion between local police officers and authorities, and drug traffickers were allegedly behind the attacks.

After multiple assaults on its facilities or personnel, the daily learned how to react to these situations: "The first aggression was not made public. We were not at that point yet; we were just starting to learn. Now if something happens to us, we make a scandal. But back then, we didn't know what to do," commented the newspaper's deputy director.[62] In 2014, soon after the attack on López Ortiz, *Noroeste* deployed a forceful public response, denouncing the aggression, and kept up coverage for many days to exert pressure on local authorities. As in previous cases, it ran a story in the newspaper first, then published a public statement. "From there, we begin a series of road shows, doing interviews, talking to the media." The day after the attack, early in the morning as the resilient newsmaker convalesced at a local hospital, the deputy director fielded a series of calls. "We got plenty of solidarity from local, national and international colleagues," he said.[63] Two days later, in an interview with a prominent national radio show, López Ortiz said, "I was showered with support and solidarity from both family and colleagues."

Noroeste has practiced quality independent journalism for years. The daily is part of a network of press freedom advocacy organizations in Mexico and Latin America. The deputy director says, "We have a very good personal and institutional network that includes nongovernmental organizations." After the Lopez Ortiz attack, Carlos Lauría, the Committee to Protect Journalists' senior program coordinator for the Americas, stated: "The authorities must guarantee the safety of the daily's staff and ensure they can continue to report on sensitive issues of public interest."

However, *Noroeste*'s deputy director says that once the news dies down, the news media and public opinion start to forget, resulting in the silence of impunity: "Then what happens? When the facts, the scandal, and the story were right there, everyone was interested. The problem is the follow-up because, like everything else, it falls into oblivion, except for those of us who are investigating all the time, publishing news and follow-ups. But that's just because we're in charge. The profession has already moved on to something else."[64]

It is not always possible for news organizations to go public regarding attacks. Some enterprises cannot contain the violence even when they're financially stable. One such case is the Tamaulipas daily *Expreso*. On the night of March 19, 2012, a car bomb exploded just outside the presses. Shortly thereafter, it was learned that the attack was premeditated. The flames consumed five automobiles parked nearby, and eight more were damaged. Fortunately, no one was harmed, but the impact on workers' morale was severe, especially because in Tamaulipas, there had been four previous attacks on Televisa facilities in Nuevo Laredo, Matamoros, and Ciudad Victoria. To make matters worse, Tamaulipas would soon become the state boasting the highest number of attacks using explosives on media outlets: as of 2016, there had been eleven attacks, one more than in Coahuila and two more than in Nuevo León.[65]

"It was very difficult," recalled a newsmaker, describing what happened in 2012. "In my case, I'm responsible for some of my people. The first thing I did was go to the editorial department to check if everyone was alright, collect myself, and remain calm.[66] Our colleagues were all scared." As a result of the attack, the directors decided that the Tuesday, March 20, edition would never see the light of day. A local reporter said, "It was a Monday. . . . There were no papers on Tuesday. Since it is an editorial group, . . . two or three pages about what had happened were published in Tampico and Matamoros but not in the papers of Ciudad Victoria."[67] Although the *Expreso* journalists wanted to protest symbolically, by running a blank first page, they were overcome by terror: "We came to the conclusion that we didn't have enough security and couldn't guarantee not only the safety of the directors and editors but of the people who work in circulation, the reporters, the people on the streets," the journalist said. They decided to remain silent, at least locally. Other periodicals and national digital media like *Excélsior*, *El Norte*, *La Jornada*, and *Animal Político* ran stories on the attack. They somehow succeeded in denouncing what had taken place in Tamaulipas. Said the journalist, "The local press did not publish anything out of fear."

Their fear was warranted. Less than four months after the car bomb explosion, a grenade was tossed and exploded against the facade of the *El Mañana* newspaper building in Nuevo Laredo, which fortunately sustained only material damage. The media responded publicly to the attack—with silence: the daily's editorial board and administration announced that it would abstain from publishing news related to criminal confrontations in Mexico.[68]

How should a newspaper respond to such targeted violence? In one investigation, Márquez found that journalists have sought to become more professional and embrace the value of objectivity as a journalistic canon.[69] Yet journalists uphold the premise that reporters should not become the news, something they consider unprofessional. So, when the news is about the violence done to them, that objectivity is more challenging to maintain. As the national director of a leading newspaper in Mexico City puts it:

> As for journalistic coverage, in general, we don't make a big deal out of it. We seek to confirm the facts for official purposes and maintain a record of any aggressions, and eventually, we go to the authorities to file a complaint on the incident. We do this without exaggerating the news. Meaning that we don't want to be subjected to arbitrariness or aggressions resulting from exercising our professional duty, but we also don't want to turn the journalist into a news story.[70]

Sometimes, despite this notion that journalists should stoically suffer aggression without responding publicly, violence provokes a response. As mentioned earlier, transparent positioning does not mean abandoning quality reporting, at least not for resilient newsmakers. *Proceso, Noroeste,* and *Ríodoce* could not keep silent in the face of these attacks and murders As journalists and organizations, they felt it was imperative to take public stances and warn criminal and state actors they would not stop reporting in their pursuit of freedom of expression and justice.

SOCIAL CAPITAL: SOLIDARITY, PROTEST, AND COLLECTIVE VOICES

Periodistas de a Pie, composed of journalists from some of the most prominent media in Mexico City, occupies a unique niche among the

STRATEGIES FOR RESISTANCE

organizations that have emerged nationwide over the past fifteen years. It gained a foothold by generating awareness of violence against the press among its members, promoting training throughout the country, and practicing journalism with a human face and social impact. This influential collective appeared in 2007, when a handful of journalists, most of them women, joined forces to "raise the quality of journalism." They were disenchanted with the way major media outlets in the nation's capital were practicing the profession.[71]

But explosive episodes of violence against the press pushed them to fully commit to the subject of freedom of the press and journalist training. Daniela Pastrana, one of the cofounders of the group and a journalist who got her start in the 1990s in critical journalism outlets like *Reforma*, said "We thought, if reality is shifting and you are watching your colleagues drop like flies, you need to get a move on. Things changed from 2006 to 2008."[72]

Later on, the murder in 2008 of Ciudad Juárez journalist Armando "Choco" Rodríguez would have a tremendous impact on the group. "They killed Choco, which I believe was the first time that we were really affected and understood what was going on," she comments. Another event with major repercussions for the collective took place in 2012: four journalists were kidnapped by the Cartel de Sinaloa in the vicinity of the penitentiary located in Gómez Palacio, Durango. Among them was Raymundo Pérez Arellano, a personal friend of Pastrana's, whose captors forced him to convey narco-messages.[73] This led Periodistas de a Pie to organize Mexico's first major journalists' protest, under the slogan *Los queremos vivos* (We want them back alive).

"I believe that's where everything detonated. It was when we launched the Los queremos vivos march," Pastrana concluded. The summons was a success because they presented a common front from the start, distancing themselves from the limelight, leaving out any logos from media outlets or freedom-of-the-press defense organizations. It also helped that even the media most reticent to take this sort of action, such as the newspapers *Reforma* and *El Universal*, allowed their journalists to choose whether to participate personally. Held in Mexico City, the march attracted nearly two thousand participants, from top journalists to beat reporters and some civil society allies. "Although those of us who are here represent different media that compete with one another and have our differences, we are here for a common goal, which is to say enough already. We want to continue reporting stories, but we are not going to be able to do so if they keep abducting and murdering journalists. We want to be able to cover stories and come back alive," stated the cronista Alejandro Almazán.[74] The march started from the emblematic Angel of Independence monument on Reforma Boulevard, then headed for the Procuraduría General de la República and Secretaría de Gobernación. Although intended as a silent march, some organizers read out the names of journalists who had fallen in recent years, their rage resulting in cathartic protest. As columnist Miguel Ángel Granados Chapa put it, this great march endowed journalists with a conscience: "It is important to know that the fate of our profession matters to everyone, that we are not indifferent."[75]

The protest was echoed in half of the country's thirty-two states, including cities subjected to constant criminal violence like Ciudad Juárez, Tijuana, and Xalapa. As the days passed, the Los queremos vivos website became a space where journalists could denounce violence and pay tribute to their colleagues. Beyond that, the collective was also critical in staging other protests and relevant actions, such as the creation of the group Prensa no disparen to demand justice for the murder of Veracruz journalist Gregorio Martínez de la Cruz in 2014, referred to in the introduction.

Aware that social mobilizations, no matter how historic, would be insufficient to bring about structural change, Periodistas de a Pie led other collective mid- and long-range actions. Many of these took place with the help of an alliance among dozens of regional collectives, organizations defending freedom of the press, and international organizations, such as Freedom House, the Open Society Foundations, and the Ford Foundation. From 2010 to 2012, Periodistas de a Pie advocated the creation of a nationwide government protection mechanism for journalists, an initiative borrowed from Colombia. Soon after the Los queremos vivos march, Periodistas de a Pie sponsored a national debate that, after several months of negotiations and discussions in the Senate, culminated in the approval of the law creating the Secretaría de Gobernación's Mecanismo de Protección para Personas Defensoras de Derechos Humanos y Periodistas, whose functions I refer to in chapter 2.

The establishment of an agenda for creating the Mecanismo benefited from the tremendous public impact of Los Queremos Vivos. Also contributing was the multilateral organisms' involvement and legislative branch members who, together with the Secretaría de Gobernación, sponsored roundtable debates on the issue. The law that gave rise to the Mecanismo and other legislation supporting victims of the so-called War on Drugs was approved in the final year of the administration of President Felipe Calderón, in office from 2006 to 2012, just as political and electoral pressure compelled him to provide respond to the humanitarian and security crisis that originated during his six-year tenure.

The protest and lobbying by Periodistas de a Pie exemplify the range and limits of journalism organizations that have appeared over the past two decades in Mexico. As Daniela Pastrana correctly recognized, the harsh reality faced by Mexican journalists was key to creating this journalist co-op, which has been fundamental to the renovation of Mexican journalism. This case also illustrates some of the tensions inherent to professional organizations of this kind—such as the canonical idea of journalists not becoming news stories. Time and time again, their hardship forced them to go out into the streets, form alliances, and attract attention to make society aware of the imminent risk.

Periodistas de a Pie is committed to quality journalism promoting human rights. This collective, like other journalists' groups that have emerged in recent years like Red de Periodistas de Juárez, does not intend to compete in the ecosystem of organizations that defend freedom of the press; rather, they seek to extend strategic alliances to grow and, as a profession, advance an agenda that benefits national journalism.

Periodistas de a Pie wields enormous influence nationwide, and though it stands out from the crowd, it is part of the trend in politically and economically independent networks, collectives, and organizations that have emerged far and wide in recent years. Several factors, such as precarious labor conditions, have spurred the creation of these initiatives; however, the most significant factor has been political and criminal violence. Such initiatives display varying degrees of institutionalization. Some, like Los queremos vivos, are collectives with concrete objectives and a short lifespan, protesting to garner public attention and establish a public agenda to address violence against the press. Others, such as Prensa, no disparen and Agenda de Periodistas, have objectives that require more time, such as investigation into the murder of a specific journalist or the stimulation of a nationwide dialogue to enhance journalists' protection and security in Mexico. Once those objectives are met, they tend to disperse. In other cases, such as Periodistas de a Pie, the members come together with mid- and long-term objectives. To achieve their goals, they generally undergo a period of institutionalization that allows them to constitute themselves as an organization, endowing them with a greater capacity for action and mobilization and granting them access to greater resources and influence.

In the following paragraphs, I focus on formally constituted organizations of resilient newsmakers. This type of initiative, which has a longer, more structured existence, has succeeded in implementing a series of collective strategies of resistance, professionalization, lobbying, and protest.

These organizations are journalists' resistance movements. They are professional journalists' organizations based on horizontality and mutual trust, coalitions introducing strategies that denounce, combat, and mitigate the climate of vulnerability experienced by the press.[76] In 2017, the civic organization Propuesta Cívica, promoting freedom of the press, baptized this kind of organization. Conceptually, they belong to what investigators María Soledad Segura and Silvio Waisbord call media movements, which are "civic initiatives aimed at transforming media policies to promote pluralism in public communication."[77] Like other social movements, these are structured, collective efforts that make demands of authorities and other actors to achieve democratization, pluralization, and openness in journalism and public communications.

In contrast to media movements, where citizens commonly participate, journalists' resistance movements consist of compact groups of active

STRATEGIES FOR RESISTANCE

professionals who share ideals. Unlike media movements, which make many demands, ranging from internet regulation to promoting equity in electoral coverage, journalists' resistance movements focus on eradicating the climate of vulnerability in the press. Specifically, they seek to mitigate the risks inherent to the practice of the profession, elevate the professionalization and quality of journalism and safety practices, and protest violence against the press. Members of these organizations meet regularly offline; however, in some cases, they also enter into coalitions with other civic allies or engage in collective online actions to obtain specific objectives, such as attracting public attention or mobilization. They are the antithesis of the clientelist organizations that emerged during the dictatorial years and, in some places, still endure. Because of this clientelist past and present, journalists' resistance movements seek to avoid any association with labor unions or corporatist ties.

Journalists' resistance movements are the social spaces where praxis, resistance, and peer support enter into dialogue. The actions generated by these collectives fulfill immediate objectives, such as professionalizing reporters or raising alerts, and strengthening journalistic autonomy by empowering and endowing members with enhanced relations of reciprocity. While these organizations have proliferated, substantial barriers persist within the trade that prevent unity. As stated in chapter 2, one of the main characteristics of Mexican journalism is its need for more cohesion and a low level of solidarity.

However, according to most journalists, organization within the profession is vital to guaranteeing better safety conditions and combating an environment of profound vulnerability. Nearly 80 percent of the journalists I interviewed for this book feel the same way. These findings are consistent with the results of a national poll.[78] "Forming a group is better," commented a Oaxacan journalist who cofounded Grupo Prensa Oaxaca. "It's solidarity. It's telling our colleagues that they are not alone."[79]

Indeed, for many journalists, independently organizing the trade is the only viable way to ensure the safe practice of their profession and force authorities to meet their demands. "I believe that [organization] is very important," a journalist who covers security in Estado de México told me, "because if we don't take care of one another, if we don't protect ourselves as colleagues, no one else will."[80]

However, generating journalists' resistance movements requires the alignment of multiple factors. According to my interviews, factors favoring their creation include (1) one or a series of foundational, egregious events that feed an indignant outburst; (2) the emergence of a solidarity network; (3) the creation of a formal organization; and (4) dense regional social capital that favor its development.

As in other social movements, a foundational, egregious event or an accumulation of such events is fundamental to an initial outburst. Every major act of violence is met with a response on the part of those who are affected. Professional solidarity emerges among a handful of journalists in the most traumatic and trying times, commonly after a lethal attack against one of their colleagues takes place. A journalist and cofounder of a Sinaloa magazine commented that when journalists are threatened or intimidated, it tends not to generate an initial outburst of this kind, perhaps because the attacks are not public knowledge or are too frequent.[81] Thus, one more does not cause further discontent. However, when a violent event occurs, it can detonate indignation and sow the seeds for a journalists' resistance movement, especially aggressions that have a significant impact because of the victim's stature or their local or national influence, such as the murders of Regina Martínez (2012) and Javier Valdez Cárdenas (2017); or because they cause indignation and give rise to collective discontent, such as the cases of Alfredo Jiménez Mota (2007) and Gregorio Jiménez de la Cruz (2014).

Thus, dozens of journalists in Mexico have transformed violence and mourning into a uniting force. Red Periodistas de Juárez was founded in 2011 following the murders in Ciudad Juárez of Armando Rodríguez and the photographer Luis Carlos Santiago (2010). In Coahuila, the murder of Eliseo Barrón (2009) led a group of colleagues to form the collective Voces Irritilas in 2015. A wave of murders, notably that of Regina Martínez (2012) and Rubén Espinoza (2015), compelled several independent Veracruz journalists to create the collective *Voz Alterna*. In the case of Agenda de Periodistas, solidarity in the national profession emerged following the murder of Javier Valdez Cárdenas (2017). In other cases, organizations like Grupo Prensa Oaxaca (2013), Encuentro Estatal de Periodistas in Michoacán, and the Red de Periodistas Noroeste (2015) were born after a series of attacks in a climate of constant hostility toward the press.

The seeds of the creation of these journalists' resistance movements were members' affinity of interests, their empathy, and a sense of urgency created by the ongoing climate of aggression. As a cofounder of the Red Periodistas de Juárez explained, "When we started out, we had very clear objectives. At first, we worked specifically on the issue of security. We found ourselves in a highly critical stage of violence."[82] This kind of network is commonly small and involves a small number of journalists because mistrust prevails in environments of repression and violence. They don't come together "by generating massive networks, as if they had already gone corporate and there are five hundred of them," says a Oaxaca national correspondent, "but by being selective, because within the journalistic profession, there are also people who have been compromised or who have business interests. So it's not about quantity if that means losing quality."[83] Although they come from different professional and personal backgrounds, network members commonly share the urgent need to join other colleagues and the high value they ascribe to their profession.

A sinuous, treacherous path lies between the emergence of a network of solidarity and establishing a journalists' resistance movement, one that it is not always possible to travel. The institutionalization of networks of solidarity is critical to the transformation in collective movements because it requires moving from individual instances of discontent toward a far more structured form of collectivity, one with fixed objectives. Such a lengthy process commonly comes at a high cost for members in terms of time and money invested.

Even so, this kind of organization has many benefits, including the capacity to gain access to greater economic resources and a broader public impact. The journalist Daniela Pastrana of Periodistas de a Pie told me that the collective used to form "alliances with organizations to hold workshops that would allow us to pay for expenses." In 2010, it created a civic association to "work with journalists from across the country on the subjects of security and self-care."[84] Forming a civic association was a long and torturous process, especially for a journalists' collective whose area of expertise was not human rights, However, as a civic association, it gained access to financial arrangements that allowed it to support at-risk journalists in rural Mexico. "[A civic association] allows you to go [to rural Mexico], come back, bring [journalists] in for workshops, pay them, and make sure they come," Pastrana adds. "Before, it was purely cooperation among ourselves, so you didn't have that possibility."[85] Other journalists' organizations in Mexico have replicated their process to a degree to access financing and resources. A cofounder of Red de Periodistas de Juárez told me: "There are very few resources you can gain access to when you are not well organized. That was something we learned with our colleagues from Periodistas de a Pie. We were not a civic association, and we had no resources. We started out with our own money. Then, they supported us so that we could connect with a foundation in the United States, which is the one that provided us with a grant in the end."[86]

Like other social mobilizations, journalists' resistance movements do not arise from a void; instead, they require a certain amount of regional social capital to subsist. According to Robert Putnam, social capital is the depth and density of social norms that create trust, reciprocity, and civic participation in a determined region.[87] Social capital is cemented largely in relations of trust and reciprocity that are determining factors in collective action.[88] However, within contexts of criminal civil war and violence, trust, reciprocity, and social capital tend to break down, making any form of collective action difficult.[89]

In the case of Mexico, exacerbated criminal violence and the marked state absence have made the creation of journalists' resistance movements particularly difficult in states like Michoacán and Tamaulipas, where the journalism trade has gone through a severe process of deprofessionalization, atomization, and mistrust because the criminal context that has prevailed. The most dramatic case is Tamaulipas, where during the harshest periods of violence, civic associations comprising journalists and other interested groups practically disappeared. A journalist in Tamaulipas commented:

STRATEGIES FOR RESISTANCE

"Our colleagues have not raised their voices, at any rate, not to the government, to demand greater safety guarantees. Not on any level—municipal, state, or federal. There's no unity on the subject."[90]

Like other social movements, journalists' resistance movements possess a repertoire of collective actions that they use to achieve specific goals, which include (1) collective professionalization, (2) emergency responders, (3) social protest and visibility, and (4) lobbying.[91] It is worth pointing out that this kind of strategy is commonly carried out through coalition with other civic allies, under the principle that they will achieve better results together. These civic allies include journalism organizations, organizations that defend freedom of the press, international foundations, multilateral organizations, political alliances, and other actors from civil society in Mexico and abroad.[92]

One of the first collective challenges was to elevate the degree of professionalization in coverage of risky or sensitive topics and training in physical and digital security. As Celeste González de Bustamante and Jeannine Relly point out, this collective professionalization process is a collaborative process of reflection that seeks to elevate cautious journalistic autonomy, especially within contexts of political and criminal violence.[93] According to the academic researcher Salvador de León Vázquez, these kinds of initiatives "seek to generate points of encounter and strengthening of collaborative work, while at the same time generating spaces to exchange experiences and generate new lessons."[94] Dario Fritz, a journalist and consultant, told me that, in the late 1990s and first decade of the twenty-first century, very few collective initiatives prioritized the training of journalists who operated in high-risk contexts.[95] Some of these initiatives, he told me, took place under the auspices of the Inter American Press Association to which he belongs. However, in the vortex of criminal violence, these collective actions would not take off until years later, backed by networks of critical journalists, often with the support of national and international NGOs based in Mexico.

Periodistas de a Pie emerged as a collective to enhance the training of a small group of critical journalists. Daniela Pastrana recalls that, at first, the training took place among a small group of journalists through workshops and talks with notable figures in Mexican and Latin American journalism.[96] Thus, little by little and with the support of local actors, including critical journalists, universities, and NGOs, courses and workshops on journalist protection were created, as were workshops on human rights, digital security, and ethics. From 2010 to 2012, the workshops, courses, and seminars were held in rural, marginalized, and relatively invisible locations far from the nation's capital, such as in Chiapas, Chihuahua, and Veracruz states. Since then, Periodistas de a Pie has been a cornerstone of these national collective initiatives.

Almost at the same time, groups of critical journalists from different parts of the country started generating their own training networks. In Ciudad Juárez, Chihuahua, the Red de Periodistas de Juárez was formed in 2011.[97] Founded following the murder of a colleague, the network has focused on the professionalization of coverage of sensitive issues. One cofounder told me this network has performed work in training and professionalization that other media outlets have abdicated.[98] "All the support and ways to defend ourselves had to come from us. So, we made the Red de Periodistas de Noreste," stated a journalist from Nuevo León, cofounder of this network, which encompasses critical journalists from Nuevo León, Coahuila, and Tamaulipas. Other similar initiatives have emerged across the country, such as the Consejo de Periodistas del Papaloapan in Veracruz and Voces Irritilas in Coahuila.[99] Many of them rely on the support and framework of other networks, like Periodistas de a Pie, as well as organizations that defend freedom of the press and international foundations and agencies.[100] The work of these organizations has affected critical local journalists: "There are national and international organisms that invite us to the courses, and what we learn there, we share with our colleagues," said a Oaxacan photojournalist, cofounder of Grupo Prensa Oaxaca, and local reporter. "Some NGOs started to develop here in Mexico financed by international cooperation organizations. A veteran journalist, the founder of Casa de los Derechos de los Periodistas commented, "We would have accomplished nothing without [their] presence, not even local organization."[101] These kinds of collective initiatives have been of great importance in a country where

STRATEGIES FOR RESISTANCE

training for the coverage of sensitive news is scarce, improvised, or simply nonexistent.[102]

In addition to promoting collective professionalization, journalists' organizations have also acted as emergency alert centers, responding to calls for help or alerts from journalist colleagues. As Howard J. Osofsky and his colleagues have documented, journalists who work in conflict situations, like war correspondents, may be found among the professionals who act as first responders in emergencies. Like other professionals, say, doctors, journalists find themselves on the front lines of confrontations, where they often need to aid other colleagues. As discussed in chapters 1 and 4, this kind of peer assistance is crucial in countries like Mexico, where media enterprises lack minimal security and assistance protocols for their contributors. Some researchers have found that peer assistance is also present among other workers from the media who operate along the margins of journalism, such as freelancers or fixers.[103] In this sense, journalists' resistance movements act as spaces of support and catharsis where journalists may find the kind of companionship they don't receive from their news organizations, let alone the state.

Given journalists' proximity and bonds of trust, journalists' resistance movements are often the first to know about attacks on the press. In many instances, they also provide follow-up and accompaniment for the victims. Periodistas de a Pie's Daniela Pastrana explains that because of intense networking in states with high levels of violence committed against the press, such as Veracruz, the collective has often provided consultation and support to colleagues who have suffered from aggression due to their work: "Trust has been generated [so that] sometimes we are even psychologists."[104] A journalist member of the Asociación de Periodistas de Ciudad Juárez has accompanied colleagues when they file complaints because the media outlets wash their hands of their contributors: "Businesses are the first ones to abandon them and leave associations of journalists like ours. Here in Ciudad Juárez, there are three, so they can take charge of protection and confront the government."[105] Journalists' organizations also alert members of other networks, even beyond subnational borders, when aggression occurs. A Red de Periodistas de Juárez journalist commented, "We have approached colleagues from other states because that also allows us to activate, for example, alert situations, in the sense that if something is happening in Veracruz, we find out what's going on and see how we can help from Juárez. We have strengthened those alliances a lot."[106] A Oaxacan journalist at the newspaper *El Imparcial* emphasized that, after it was targeted, they got a rapid response and backing from local journalists' organization Grupo Prensa Oaxaca and organizations that defend freedom of the press such as Casa de los Derechos de los Periodistas. The visibility provided by this collective reaction helped the authorities to act in an expedited manner in their case.[107]

Street protests, shows of social support, and public spaces, online and offline, are some of the most representative characteristics of social movements. In many ways, the appropriation of public space by journalists' resistance movements is an active, profound form of transgression. Not only do they occupy a space visible to all and shout slogans against established authorities but they also transgress the most traditional borders of the profession because they become the news. A national correspondent based in Guadalajara, Jalisco, highlighted this: "The reporter is rarely news. The reporter should not even have to become news."[108] In the case of Mexico, public protests by journalists are vital because they showcase the nonconformity many journalists must develop to demand a profound transformation of their structural vulnerability.

Over the past fifteen years, public protests have become one of the principal collective actions in which journalists and civic allies participate. I have mentioned several social protest cycles spearheaded by journalists throughout this book. Since the political and criminal violence escalated, costing dozens of journalists their lives, going out into the streets has become more common.[109] "At least over the past two years, there has been a greater development of awareness among journalists in emblematic cases that affect colleagues from other states," remarked a freelance journalist based in Nuevo León. "Protest marches have been organized with the participation of only a few colleagues, but at least there has been a reaction."[110]

Nonetheless, an investigative journalist based in Mexico City told me in an interview that these mobilizations often produce more light than heat:

STRATEGIES FOR RESISTANCE

"There's a group of journalists who are more independent, who have made a lot of noise on networks. Even so, it seems like very little for the country we are and the size of the profession. I find it to be a super lukewarm response."[111] All too frequently, such mobilizations may even lack journalists. "Most journalists do not actively participate in these shows of support or in these acts of protest," stated a newsmaker specializing in human rights.[112] A national correspondent based in Guerrero commented that the participation of colleagues in these marches is very uncommon because they encounter repercussions at work.[113]

Worst of all, these protests garner minimal sympathy from the population at large, revealing the profound lack of connection between journalism and the public. "Society in general does not support these kinds of marches," lamented a journalist for Agence France-Presse (AFP) in Mexico City.[114] Tragically, the public doesn't care because it doesn't identify with or believe in journalists, and that is why journalists' deaths get little public reaction.

Despite social street protests generated by deaths in the field, often all that remains afterward is a sense of emptiness, as if indignation had ceased once the streets were taken and oblivion prevailed. In response, some journalists' organizations, in alliance with other civic actors, have implemented different collective strategies, such as lobbying actions or wielding legislative and political clout. María Soledad Segura and Silvio Waisbord point out that such strategies have proven highly effective in media movements.[115] It is no coincidence that in the 1990s and 2000s, when the media and journalists became more relevant than ever in Latin America, a new legal framework arose to regulate public communications and journalism across the continent.[116] Supported by left-wing governments, many of these new legal arrangements seek to encourage, at least in spirit, more pluralistic and democratic public communication. Mexico is no exception.

Since the great wave of violence against the press began to rise, one of the main objectives of press activism has been establishing a more robust legal framework that favors protection for journalists.[117] As explained in chapter 2, broad coalitions of journalists, organizations that defend freedom of the press and international institutions have promoted that framework and now mete out justice and ensure security for journalists nationwide.

Beyond this, similar state-level coalitions have promoted the creation of institutional legal frameworks that address journalists' myriad vulnerabilities at a regional level. In association with other organizations, journalists from the collective *Voz Alterna* backed the creation of an early-response mechanism as an answer to aggressions against the press in Veracruz. Members of the collective Grupo Prensa Oaxaca succeeded in introducing a bill before the Oaxaca Congress for the protection of journalists in that state.[118] In Michoacán, a local group of journalists backed a similar legal initiative. Over the past few years, thanks to these collective initiatives, it is estimated that substantial numbers of these laws have been introduced before state legislatures.

However, as cronista Guillermo Osorno points out, after years and years of extreme violence against the press, these legal initiatives are perceived as Pyrrhic victories within the profession.[119] Ultimately, they have failed to bring about improved safety conditions.

CONCLUSION

PROSPECTS AND LIMITATIONS

Throughout this book, we have explored the many factors contributing to violence against the press. I have addressed major structural, social, economic, cultural, and symbolic factors that encourage attacks against journalists, as well as circumstantial factors, regular occurrences, and patterns they may encounter. It should be noted that such violence is rarely examined by specialists, beyond the field of journalism studies, or even journalists themselves. Despite this oversight, violence is more prevalent than ever in developing countries like Mexico and in developed democracies like the United States or Western European countries, which are no strangers to this global phenomenon.

Democracies offer better conditions than any authoritarian regime can for journalistic work. However, democracies when unsafe may be a mirage where a free and critical press is severely restrained. In this book, I have shown that electoral democracy is not necessarily a solution to violence against journalists, even when their work contributes to consolidating and maintaining democratic principles and practices. On the contrary, these

CONCLUSION

democracies, especially when emerged in critical situations involving internal criminal and social conflicts, often open a Pandora's box of violence against the critical press.

In contemporary Mexico, the democracy paradox forms part of three factors that have exacerbated violence against journalists. This is violence so extreme that every possible alarm has been sounded among international organizations, so much so that the country has even been labeled as "deadliest for the press." The year 2000 marked the end of seven decades under the control of the same party, the PRI. The people gained public liberties, and political alternance ensued. This brought about a revolution in press-state relations through the dawn of critical journalism. However, this mirage of greater freedom did not herald any guarantees for professional practice.

This change in political power augmented the power of Mexican rulers at municipal and state levels; they transformed subnational territories into personal fiefdoms. Although democratic in appearance, these local governments often behave in an authoritarian manner. And they have not taken kindly to any form of vigilance or criticism from the press. Something similar might be said of other actors on a federal level, such as high-ranking officials, public servants, and bureaucrats in charge of media relations. They also view with disdain and hostility the exposés and criticism that originate in an independent press. All this has become even more relevant because Mexico's main press censors are politicians, public servants, and bureaucrats. And we cannot help but mention the risks represented by the critical state of criminal violence in which the country has been mired since the beginning of the twenty-first century. The extremely high levels of violence committed against the press nationwide would be impossible to understand without this shadow conflict, which has set citizens against each other in an economic battle for control and profit, stoked by the complicity and connivance of the authorities.

Lastly, as a precarious profession, journalism also struggles with internal crises, lacking a social security system and health services, not to mention fixed schedules, future stability, professional unity, or support from the very society it attempts to serve. Moreover, journalism and the press industry find themself in constant flux and adaptation, resulting from tremendous

CONCLUSION

decreasing in institutional confidence, as well as drastic technological and digital advances and major transformations among audiences that no longer turn to traditional media for information.[1]

As described in chapter 2, all these internal and external factors laid the foundation for a perfect storm. The widespread murders and forced disappearances of journalists that began in the first decade of the twenty-first century would be merely a preview of the maelstrom of crime, persecution, and impunity that would soon be unleashed. In some cases, Mexican journalists truly operate in the worst of all possible worlds when they find themselves in the conditions explored in this book.

Yet, we should not gloss over the fact that violence against the press has a long history and is not limited to the twentieth century. During the Porfirio Díaz dictatorship that ruled Mexico practically uninterrupted from 1876 to 1910, journalists, writers, and thinkers were already being persecuted for confronting those in power. As John Nerone has thoroughly documented for the United States, violence against periodicals and writers on current affairs in Mexico was present even before journalism became the modern profession it is today. The fact that murders and aggressions against journalists in Mexico have been documented for over one hundred years allows us to contextualize violence against the press and understand it. This is probably the first step in society's attempt to mitigate the current wave of attacks against the press.

This book identifies most aggressions as originating from state actors, crime syndicates, or civil society organizations, although there are slight differences in their motivation: politicians seek to silence the press to avoid damaging their public image or affecting their interests; the police and military institutions look to cover up their violent acts; self-defense groups or caciques attack journalists to maintain territorial control; and organized crime employs direct violence to silence the press and send a symbolic message of terror to opposing groups or society at large.

Moreover, the interviews I carried out among journalists from different regions of Mexico also revealed that the distribution of risk is unequal. As described in detail in chapter 3, journalism reflects the same conditions of discrimination and inequality suffered by the nation as a whole. Hence,

CONCLUSION

being born indigenous, a woman, or identifying as a member of a sexually diverse group also implies having to face a brand of violence different than that affecting white men, cisgenders, and heterosexuals. For example, serious physical assault tends to be directed more at men, while gender becomes an issue for female journalists and other gender minorities are compelled to face the kinds of gender-related issues or even forms of sexual harassment or assault from which their male colleagues normally are spared. In this sense, experience also matters a great deal: being a young journalist with less professional experience and fewer professional contacts likely means running a greater risk than established journalists who have had long and outstanding careers. Nor should we forget the importance of organizational backing, because, as in the case of building individual careers, the support of a major prominent news organization goes a long way in fighting back against harassment or aggression. A freelance professional does not have that support.

Let's not forget that Mexico encompasses many Mexicos: where you live makes a great deal of difference. Journalists I interviewed told me it was not the same working in Ciudad Juárez during the second decade of the twenty-first century, when the homicide rate broke world records, as it was in Mexico City, the nation's largest metropolitan area and where political and economic power is concentrated. And it is not the same to cover the corridors of power at Palacio Nacional in the capital as it is to delve into the more vulnerable neighborhoods of marginalized communities.

Identifying these variables leads me to conclude that these local distinctions cannot be disconnected from what is happening nationwide. Violence against the press is only one of many forms of brutality and is, therefore, embedded in a cycle that spreads beyond journalism to engulf all of Mexico. It forms part of political stratagems, as an enemy held up to make a struggle more meaningful, a way of silencing the watchdogs of power, or a means to spread terror. Homicides and aggressions against journalists ought to be perceived as part of a climate of structural violence that, no matter how distant it may seem, is in the same constellation as the attacks against those who defend the environment or missing persons found in

CONCLUSION

clandestine mass graves. Journalism forms part of the whole of Mexican society, and that whole has been altered by impunity, death, and pain.

Throughout my investigation, I was aware of the connection between ongoing violence and high levels of impunity. According to Artículo 19 Mexico, 163 murders of journalists have taken place since 2000 in Mexico. Though, in many instances, the authorities have arrested the masterminds or perpetrators of aggression against journalists, the cycle of impunity remains little changed and has proven extremely difficult to break. This is not only a feature of crimes against the press; solving a crime in Mexico is the exception rather than the rule. Jackie Harrison writes that this "policy of impunity," which creates an environment in which crimes are ignored or investigations are ineffective, becomes an accomplice, reinforcing the notion that in Mexico, killing a journalist is no earth-shattering event and thus will go unpunished.[2] Knowing themselves to be immune, the aggressors—politicians, public servants, public security forces, caciques, or criminals—know they are immune and commit crimes against the press without a thought because they do not expect the state to sanction them.

The lesson, in the end, is a painful one: what does the government gain by failing to address acts of aggression and supporting the perception that it is dangerous to be a journalist in this country? In my interviews with journalists, I observed that this environment of generalized impunity results in self-censorship. As a result, silence spreads fear, hostility, and helplessness across the country.

But even under the most adverse conditions—of the kind that threatens to founder the practice of journalism and freedom of expression—the will of resilient newsmakers remains strong in the face of impunity and violence. I have attempted to capture this other side of the coin, one that is ordinarily overlooked, throughout the book. These are dark times for the press, but resilient newsmakers are finding ways to get through them together, without abandoning all hope.

As stated in chapter 5, journalists find ways to approach dangerous topics and protect themselves. Their method is trial and error; they assess what works and what doesn't. Their strategies come not from guidebooks or the

CONCLUSION

classroom but from lessons of the street, daily practice, and professional socialization. Self-protection developed empirically helps mitigate early risks, but it may be difficult to maintain over time, especially when the journalist has little or no experience working in contexts of violence.

As the testimonials in this book demonstrate, wherever resilient newsmakers possess individual, organizational, or social resources, they can successfully execute these strategies. However, their stories reveal that if one does not possess a minimum of these resources, any attempt to mitigate self-censorship and confront professional hazards may come at a very high cost. Hence, from the perspective of more experienced reporters who value a well-planned and thought-out protocol rather than operating by survival instinct alone, stories of heroism or risking one's life in reporting belie a lack of awareness and failure to implement self-protection strategies.

If the ship of journalism is sinking, survival depends on teamwork. Organization and, consequently, the commitment of owners, managers, and directors to the editorial staff have proven to be fundamental in confronting waves of violence. Wherever there are engaged news organizations or, to borrow Sallies Hughes's term, "civic-oriented newsrooms," the local ecosystem changes because news media outlets' preparing personnel for violence is often the first step toward avoiding risks. In my research, I have found that critical media back journalists who are equally critical and that this "organizational apprenticeship" functions as if the editorial staff were bees in a hive: knowledge and apprenticeship are shared, and through them, the possibilities for survival increase.

However, the future is not necessarily bright. Relying on organizational resources is an important factor for resilient newsmakers, but in Mexico, this is the exception to the rule. For the vast majority of the news media in the country, especially major conglomerates, journalists are considered to be nonessential. They are cheap cannon fodder, easily discarded through clientelist arrangements with the politically or economically powerful. While resilient organizations may generate support networks or form alliances to jointly publish some story that implies a measure of risk to reporters, such instances are rare in the nation's media ecosystem.

CONCLUSION

In my research, I became aware of the importance of the social dimension, journalists' capacity to come together and achieve collective journalistic autonomy. I must emphasize that the development of strategies for resilience is especially robust here.

Journalists' networks are the new bulwarks for freedom of expression. In territories overwhelmed by violence, critical news startups have emerged as a new model of communications media that confront repression, control, and violence. We have also witnessed the development of significant investigations made possible by networked journalism, enormous reporting networks that have given rise to projects of immense impact worldwide.[3] As others have stated, the future of journalism is collective because major social issues and humanity's great challenges require many eyes and voices to see and denounce them. In Mexico, some examples of significant investigations in recent years were La Casa Blanca of President Enrique Peña Nieto or La Estafa Maestra.

Journalists in Mexico have implemented some of these tactics. Academic journalistic practices attest to a rise in these strategies, especially since the start of the twenty-first century. In a broad study, Celeste González de Bustamante and Jeannine Relly found that Mexican journalists employ various tactics, implemented institutionally and individually, to turn the tables on political and criminal censorship.[4] Grisel Salazar found something similar in her recent book.[5] My interviews taught me that these cautionary tactics have been adopted in different parts of the country. All of this suggests that self-censorship is not the only way to cope with the stress of being a journalist amid high-risk situations in Mexico.

Thus, journalists must learn to overcome adverse conditions. And yet, questions remain. Why do reporters, editors, and photographers continue to practice journalism despite confronting its hazards?

The main answer lies in journalistic values and resilient newsmakers' commitment. Their dedication is a life jacket that allows them to hold on and persevere despite the risks involved. It is so powerful that, even when self-censoring, it motivates them to continue publishing. I focus mainly on this phenomenon in chapter 5. Awareness of their work's social impact is a guiding light that can encourage journalists to continue practicing their profession.

CONCLUSION

A ray of this light may be found in the journalistic figure's mythical construction. Major investigations that reveal monumental corruption have been idealized to the point that they have become an attainable aspiration for journalists. The reality is more complex and frustrating, given the external and internal threats they face, as discussed in chapter 1. However, I have concluded that they derive from their efforts a sense that it was all worthwhile, compelling resilient journalists to continue working in what Gabriel García Márquez once called "the most wonderful job in the world." Reaching this point requires self-reflection, a learning curve, and trial and error at an individual, organizational, and collective level. And yet, professional values and the passionate belief in the ideal of journalism as a force of social change for the better are fundamental to resilient and resistant behaviors.

It is necessary to emphasize that news organizations also play a critical role in apprenticeship and the development of strategies of resistance. Continuing to investigate topics of risk and proceeding with the periodic publication of news stories that other media have let slide require the full support of the profession. But for many editorial staff, denouncing aggressions and taking a stand against violence has come at a very high political cost, even if socially profitable. As the case of *El Siglo de Torreón* illustrates, solidarity among people who work in media and its audience can be forged despite fear. When they see that their newsrooms will take the necessary steps to protect them, whatever the financial or political cost, reporters develop a solid organizational empathy invaluable to resistance. Because resisting, unlike surviving, is not a solitary act.

In this sense, what I have learned from my interviews with journalists and theoretical reflection challenges the paradigm that a journalist is solely a journalist. The road to resistance in journalism is collective. According to Silvio Waisbord, the formation of journalists' movements aids the demand for justice.[6] Collective movements in Mexico like Agenda de Periodistas illustrate this idea. Waisbord also warns that this collective force must be actively sustained. Despite good intentions, organization, and collective outrage, I have shown that this goal is not always achieved. Some challenges persist as the lack of unity and trust in the trade.

CONCLUSION

Still, there is hope. The road is long, and it may seem there is little to be done other than to protest and denounce the violence. But journalists' collective demands to the state, media barons and moguls, society, and the international community have built momentum among core groups that seems unstoppable.

BEYOND MEXICO

In sociopolitical and cultural terms, the conditions that have prevailed in Mexico are highly particular and include internal conflicts of great intensity and complexity, the tremendous power and long tentacles of crime syndicates, high levels of impunity, geopolitical proximity to the enormous drug market in the United States, and a long history of arbitrary censorship of the critical press. However, in the following pages, I maintain that professional motivation, tactics, and strategies to keep working despite adversity and the resistance mechanisms adopted by resilient newsmakers in Mexico are similar to those in other latitudes. Resilience knows no boundaries, national or personal. On the contrary, it can flourish even in the most varied environments.

I do not seek to provide a detailed breakdown of the practices utilized by newsmakers to encourage journalistic autonomy and resistance. Instead, I offer a bird's-eye view of some of the tactics and strategies followed by the critical journalism trade in different regions, especially Latin America, as a resilient professional practice beyond all borders.

Individually, critical journalists have historically turned to strategies and tactics that enhance their levels of autonomy and deepen their spirit of resistance. The author Rodolfo Walsh, murdered by the bloody military junta of Argentina in 1976, utilized a great many tactics and mechanisms throughout his prominent literary and journalistic career to investigate and publish the most relevant stories of his time. In Operation Massacre, published in 1957, a watershed book paradoxically employing journalistic nonfiction and literary resources, Walsh examines and relates a series of military executions. Guided by a tip from a friend who told him a shooting victim had survived an attack, Walsh pursues clues, testimonials, and evidence to put together the pieces of this tragic puzzle. Like the chess player he was, he fell back on diverse techniques and skills while chasing down the story that would upend his life. In the prologue to his book, Walsh writes: "For nearly a year, I would think of nothing else. I would abandon my house and my job, go by the name Francisco Freyre, and obtain a false ID bearing that name. A friend would lend me his house in El Tigre, and for two months, I would live on a freezing cold ranch in Merlo and carry a revolver. And every step of the way, the actors in this drama would return obsessively, again and again."

The tactics mentioned by Walsh were used to cobble together a story using an innovative literary and fictional style that involved characterization, the inclusion of multiple points of view, and suspense, characteristics of a detective novel. This literary brand of nonfiction often allows writers to dodge the tentacles of censorship that shortsightedly tends to focus solely on raw journalism as its enemy. Walsh's proposal echoes the discursive and literary practices that resilient newsmakers use to delve into and narrate the stories they decide to tell.

Discursive practices are not exclusive to Mexican journalism. They have increased over the past two decades in Latin America through crónicas like those of Óscar Martínez in El Salvador, Ana Teresa Toro in Puerto Rico, Joseph Zárate in Peru, and Rocío Monts in Chile. Journalists implement discursive practices as tools to carve out greater space and autonomy. Citing journalists' memoirs from Egypt, Lebanon, and Syria, Noha Mellor suggests that in the late twentieth century, critical journalists posed as specialized commentators to maintain privileged access to political elites and publish critical views on the regimes in power.[7]

In other parts of the world, personal practices allowing journalistic autonomy have flourished, even in vertical political environments like China and Russia. In her studies of the relations between press and political power in closed regimes, Maria Repnikova argues that a new generation of Chinese journalists improvise creative tactics to resist pressure from the system, especially during periods of tension and crisis.[8] Repnikova suggests

CONCLUSION

that critical Chinese journalists take advantage of the system and maintain ongoing negotiations with state agents to gain access to official sources. Critical journalists have expanded their autonomy within the vertical system of Chinese control by sharing sensitive information with other colleagues or by seeking innovative angles for their stories.

In contrast, Repnikova suggests that critical journalists in Russia who confront Vladimir Putin's regime follow strategies that eschew collaboration with state agents. Repnikova emphasizes that collaboration is practically impossible in Russia, unlike for critical journalists in China, because state forces are far more unpredictable. Within this context, Russian critical journalists have implemented strategic self-censorship and self-preservation tactics while investigating as much as possible and publishing prohibited subject matter on the margins.[9]

Strategies of autonomy that enhance journalists' safety are beneficial in times of tension. In their study of survival tactics used by journalists in Africa during the coverage of Boko Haram terrorist attacks from 2009 to 2015, Umaru Pate and Hamza Idris recommend that the press follow cautious practices like the ones surveyed in this book. Such tactics include logistical actions, like altering routes or practicing undercover journalism. Moreover, these journalists implemented a broad network of reliable news sources and trustworthy contacts who could come in handy in high-risk situations.[10]

In finding ways to enhance their autonomy and ensure their safety, critical journalists resist and seek new forms of resilience in adverse situations. In what follows, I highlight international cases in which journalists have developed meaningful personal resistance strategies.

In one of the earliest studies on this topic, Gretchen Dworznik analyzed a group of photojournalists in the midwestern United States who commonly cover traumatic events such as homicides, car accidents, or fires. Dworznik found that specific personal narrative techniques helped journalists find meaning in their professional labor. They transformed traumatic experiences into meaningful learning events that helped them continue to do their jobs.[11]

In one of the more influential studies on coping and resilience among journalists, Rosemary Novak and her colleagues suggest that identifying

CONCLUSION

with journalistic values is one of the most sought-after and useful protection mechanisms where coverage is difficult and hazardous, especially in international conflicts.[12] Similarly, Elsebeth Frey found that newsmakers underwent "post-traumatic growth," a process where positive learning experiences occur despite an event's negative aspects. Frey found such growth among a group of nine journalists who had covered terrorist attacks and wars in Gaza, Iraq, Ukraine, Sudan, Libya, Kenya, and Norway and reported on the Tunisian Revolution.

In Colombia, Laura Lozano and Lucía Suescún found that journalists have developed psychological resources as a resistance mechanism in the face of constant exposure to violent acts.[13] This capacity for resilience is linked to the social role of journalism, where ethics and personal satisfaction are reflected in the narrative: to continue to tell stories allows newsmakers to overcome adversities.

One of this book's central premises is that although practiced individually, cautious journalism and resistance tactics also flourish collectively through journalism organizations or support networks among colleagues. Before reviewing instances of collective resistance, it would be worthwhile to survey the organizational strategies journalists employ to practice their profession in adverse settings.

The magazine *Novaya Gazeta* always springs to mind when one thinks of independent journalism in post-Soviet Russia. Until 2022, *Novaya Gazeta* was the most long-lived Russian independent media outlet; it was even awarded the Nobel Peace Prize in 2021. Over the years, *Novaya Gazeta* has capitalized on the prestige and influence of its top editors and directors to maintain a critical stance, neutralize attacks, and avoid editorial sabotage. However, in a repressive environment, no tactic is failsafe.[14] Like other combative publications, such as *Zeta* in Tijuana, *Novaya Gazeta* has paid a high price to preserve its liberty: seven contributors have been murdered since 2000. One of these victims was Anna Politkovskaya, who, at the time of her death, was devoted to in-depth coverage of the second war in Chechnya. More recently, shortly after the Russian invasion of Ukraine in 2022, Putin's regime suspended the *Novaya Gazeta* website and prohibited its physical and digital publication.

CONCLUSION

To keep the presses running sometimes requires taking unusual measures. In April 2023, the digital newspaper *El Faro*, one of the most critical in El Salvador, announced the transfer of its administrative and legal structure to Costa Rica because it lacked "operating conditions." *El Faro* has been internationally recognized for its work in critical journalism and has focused on denouncing nationwide corruption and gang violence. In business for more than twenty-five years, the digital periodical has faced an openly hostile environment from the start of the Nayib Bukele administration in 2019, including accusations of libel, government harassment, cyberattacks, espionage, and audits carried out by the secretary of finance.[15] Nevertheless, *El Faro* continues to practice critical journalism committed to some of the most important causes in El Salvador.

Elsewhere, the editorial strategies employed by the press range from implementing in-house security actions to strengthening ties to the community. In Venezuela, *Efecto Coyuyo* has dodged libel, harassment, repression, and persecution by government agents since its creation in 2015. Over the years, the digital portal has kept its journalists safe, especially during social unrest, political crises, and street protests. To strengthen its social stance, *Efecto Coyuyo* has put down roots in the community by covering social interest stories and hosting informal dialogues with its audiences, fine-tuning its news agenda by hearing them out.[16] One of its cofounders, Luz Mely Reyes, assures me that she will continue to practice journalism despite the hostile climate: "It's a lifelong decision. I don't see myself doing anything else."

In a recent study, Lucía Mesquita and Mathias-Felipe de Lima-Santos suggest that small- and mid-sized digital publications in Latin America (for example, in Brazil, Cuba, Colombia, Ecuador, Peru, Nicaragua, Puerto Rico, and Venezuela) have incorporated security strategies into their journalistic routines. For example, some of the media outlets they analyzed have implemented evacuation routes in covering stories that present physical risk and have reinforced support networks with other publications and contacts to alert them to any attacks. These publications have also implemented measures in the digital realm, hiring cyber specialists to address online threats and implement specific security protocols.[17]

CONCLUSION

However, publishing houses that protect their journalists are few and far between. In a study of international journalists and correspondents covering conflict situations, Frey found that the majority of those who had experienced trauma had received no assistance or support from their media outlets. And when they did, it was an insincere gesture lacking true institutional involvement.[18] In Brazil, Gisele Barão da Silva and her colleagues found that the lack of support from media outlets affects female journalists who face violence and trauma. These women have resorted to collective strategies of resilience and protection beyond their news organization.[19]

Throughout this book, I have pointed out that social capital is a key to increasing journalistic autonomy and resistance. Collective actions founded on trust and empathy have proven to be propitious spaces for resilient newsmakers searching for ways to resist adversity. These collective forms of resistance, which may take on diverse forms and deploy a wide range of tactics, may also transcend international borders.

Although this has recently changed, collaboration between media outlets has always been tense and complex. Unfortunately, this continues to be the case even though collaboration can successfully reduce attacks on journalists. During the Kosovo War, journalists and correspondents developed the Sarajevo pool. This mechanism favored a single cameraperson shooting scenes in high-risk situations to share with others. Unfortunately, this mechanism eventually failed because of competition between news organizations.[20]

However, in recent years, collaborative work has triumphed through the investigation, treatment, and publication of thousands of documents that tell long-range stories.

Over the past decade, in different parts of the world, collaborations have emerged between journalists and news media in different latitudes to report and publish stories of transnational importance. One of the most emblematic, the Afghan war logs, took place in 2010. A transnational cooperative effort by the *New York Times*, the *Guardian*, and *Der Spiegel*, it was a response to a Wikileaks revelation about the war in Afghanistan. The files allowed a glimpse into indiscriminate attacks on Afghan civilians by the U.S. Army.

CONCLUSION

Since then, cases of collaborative journalism have proliferated to chase down global stories. The publication in 2016 of the Panama Papers, which won a Pulitzer Prize, is another emblematic case. This investigation, led by the International Consortium of Investigative Journalists (ICIJ), was an exposé of the offshore business dealings of politicians, businesspeople, professional athletes, and celebrities. This investigation emerged from a megaleak of 11.5 million documents from the Panamanian law firm Mossack Fonseca to the German newspaper *Süddeutsche Zeitung*. Under ICIJ leadership, this project involved 370 journalist members of the organization in seventy-six countries.

Leaking stories to journalists is nothing new. What is new is a recent trend to work these leaks as a group, based on trust, following shared leads with certain digital coordination. Global stories, such as global drug trafficking, money-laundering networks, and illegal exploitation of natural resources, can be reported only in a collective fashion.

Beyond these global stories, collaborative journalism does not always include the participation of prominent media outlets or hundreds of journalists around the world. In 2019, a group of journalists from Peru, Chile, Colombia, and Mexico created Salud con Lupa, which sought "to expose the lobbying maneuvers of food and medicine corporations with the objective of favorably influencing their interests through the passage of public policy." In 2018, in Peru, a group of investigative journalists and independent media gained access to over sixty thousand recordings that showed people investigated for crimes such as murder for hire, extortion, and drug trafficking had ties to officials in the Callao justice system. The so-called Corruption Recordings case shook the Peruvian political system and unleashed investigations of those implicated.

Global experiences that collectively increase journalistic coverage may also include examples of collective actions that create bonds of resilience and strength among journalists, particularly in repressive environments and contexts that are adverse to a critical press.

According to the Colombian journalist Germán Rey, an organization within Colombian journalism supported by civil society and the state created

CONCLUSION

an environment of solidarity that has contained attacks by paramilitary groups and organized crime. The formation of early alert networks and a system of journalist protection backed by the state and other organizations are remarkable, as are roundtable discussions and institutions that defend freedom of expression and the presence of international organizations.[21] This capacity for resilience is linked to journalism's social role, where ethics and personal satisfaction are reflected in the narrative. The drive to tell stories and practice journalism helps overcome adversities. Martha Barrios and Toby Miller explain how Colombian journalists develop strategies to combat fear and self-censorship.[22] They create journalists' networks to disseminate information. For these reporters, it doesn't matter who publishes the news, only that the news gets out.

In Brazil, Sarah Anne Ganter and Fernando Oliveira Paulino found that a digital publications group developed "models of resilience" to mitigate and overcome attacks and adversity. Analyzing six emblematic case studies— *Agencia Pública, Brasil 247, Poder360, Nexo, Intercept Brasil,* and *Metrópoles*— the investigators identified strategies that included maintaining different business models, obtaining collective legal counsel and guidance to improve digital security, and models of collective psychological support. "Independent digital news organizations in Brazil can create cultural persistence by continuing to share their values, ideas, and norms, particularly in times of acute and multilayered crises," they commented.[23]

An empirical investigation by Marína Urbániková and Lenka Haniková describes how a group of Slovakian journalists managed the stress, trauma, and fear resulting from the murder of the journalist Ján Kuciak and his wife. They explained that to overcome their response, Slovakian journalists developed a dialogue with colleagues that led to news organizations publicizing Kuciak's legacy and allowed newsmakers to find meaning in tragedy.[24]

Comparative perspectives allow us to understand that Mexico's case is not exceptional. They show how journalists, as resilient subjects, will fight back against domination and find ways to make sure their practice endures. Resilience and resistance are not unique to Mexican journalists—some of them who are currently suffering the worst conditions for practicing journalism in the modern age. They are globally characteristic of the

CONCLUSION

profession. Professional values and social relations allow journalism to change people's lives, pursue justice and equality, and embrace freedom and nonviolence. From these emerge strategies for how to safely practice the craft.

The cases I examine here demonstrate that critical journalism tends to prevail when confronted by adversity and repression, driven by the vocation for public service that characterizes the profession. As the Nicaraguan journalist Joaquín Chamorro Cardenal, assassinated in 1978, put it: "As long as there is a typewriter, a piece of paper, a microphone, a public square, a balcony, or a space to speak from, even if it's a jail cell, we will continue to denounce immorality, especially when it traffics with the social wants of the poor. This is the main reason for our existence as humans, as journalists, and as citizens."

SAFETY AND SECURITY IN THE FIELD OF JOURNALISM: CURRENT STATUS, LIMITATIONS, IMPROVEMENTS, AND OUTLOOK

To unpack change and continuity in the status of risk and security, we must first talk about present-day journalism. Although some trends persist, there are also transformations.

A recent Worlds of Journalism Mexico poll, a nationwide exercise in which I participated with a dozen of other scholars, shows that in 2023 the press sector continues to employ more men (55 percent) than women (45 percent). The average age is forty-one, and 75.9 percent of journalists possess graduate education. Of this group, 85.3 percent studied communication or journalism.[25] The number of journalistic professionals who work in digital media and produce content for social networks surpasses the figure in past years, especially among women. Similarly, 44 percent of media outlets in Mexico are digital natives.[26]

According to this poll, of the total number of Mexican journalists, estimated at over twenty-five thousand, three-quarters hold a full-time job. In

CONCLUSION

rural areas, journalists commonly experience less economic stability than in Mexico City and practicing journalism is not enough to make a living, given that four in every ten journalists engage in a second full-time professional activity in addition to journalism. Moreover, on average, journalists earn from Mex$9,000 to Mex$14,000 (US$522 to US$812) per month, barely above the average nationwide salary, which rose to Mex$8,800 per month in the second quarter of 2023. Additionally, the gender gap means that no matter where women work or what position they hold, they always earn less than men.

As in other fields, the pandemic and its economic impact shook the job structure of the journalism industry. Nationwide, COVID-19 caused a GNP reduction of 8.7 percent in 2020. Despite a recent economic recovery, this plunge had a lasting impact on the media sector: there were massive layoffs, journalistic enterprises were shuttered, and permanent wage cutbacks were sustained even as the range of digital news and information expanded. Moreover, COVID-19 posed a tremendous risk to journalists, given that one in four do not have access to social security or the public health system.

According to the poll cited above, it is estimated that the pandemic changed labor conditions for four out of every ten journalists. Similarly, two out of every ten were compelled to cover environments with a high risk of contagion. And while many journalists worked from home to reduce their exposure to the virus, the risk was lesser among journalists from the country's interior of the country than among residents of the capital (60.9 percent and 75.9 percent, respectively).

Beyond the impact COVID-19 has had on industry and the unstable economic and labor conditions it brought to journalism, the country remains a veritable minefield for journalists and is openly hostile to the practice of this profession.

Safety conditions for Mexican journalists are abominable, a situation made worse by an ongoing nationwide public security and human rights crisis. According to figures from Artículo 19 Mexico, the number of journalists killed during the 2018–2024 period had reached forty-three by April 2024. There is no greater act of censorship than the murder of a

CONCLUSION

journalist. During the current six-year presidential administration, community journalists like Rafael Murúa Manríquez, director and founder of Radio Kashana in Baja California Sur, have been killed, as have national correspondents like Luis Martín Sánchez Iñiguez, who worked in Nayarit for the newspaper *La Jornada*, and local journalists like Yesenia Mollinedo Falconi, director of *El Veraz*, and her camera operator, Sheila Johana García Olivera. The latter two were murdered in Veracruz.

Homicide is only the tip of the iceberg. According to Artículo 19 Mexico, 696 attacks against the press were registered in 2022, making it the most violent year for journalists since 2007. The five states with the highest number of incidents of aggression against journalists were Mexico City, Yucatán, Quintana Roo, Tamaulipas, and Veracruz. In 2021, for the first time since 2007, Artículo 19 Mexico documented attacks on the press in each of Mexico's thirty-two states, illustrating the nationwide span of the issue.

The Worlds of Journalism Mexico poll reports that the most common forms of aggression over the past five years were being forced to work despite a high risk of COVID-19 contagion (19.8 percent); insults or hate speech (19.2 percent); public ridicule (16.6 percent). espionage (11.7 percent); digital hacking (7.3 percent); harassment while on the job (7.2 percent); threats (7.1 percent); and stalking (5.1 percent).

According to the World Press Freedom Index published by Reporters Without Borders, Mexico was ranked 128th in 2023. This rank is alarmingly high for a middle-income country. This position is very close to those ones in 2020 and 2021: 143rd. The above may be associated with a more complex context in which an inertia of antipress violence that clearly has not been successfully stopped remains visible; and yet there have been some very tenuous advances on this topic. That is to say, we are currently experiencing a situation with certain chiaroscuros.

As in the past, public officials and local politicians on the state and municipal levels are still the main culprits of aggression against the media. According to 2023 data furnished by the Mecanismo de Protección para Personas Defensoras de Derechos Humanos y Periodistas, a division of the Ministry of the Interior, local public officials, often in collusion with organized crime, perpetrate more than 40 percent of aggressions against the press.[27] Additionally, according to reports from civic society, manipulation continues to prevail on a local level, including denial of information requests, discretional control of official advertising budgets, the use of legal loopholes against the press, and other violent forms of control and intimidation, especially during times when political tensions run high, such as during election periods.

It is clear little has changed in the relationship between power and the press on a local level, where local journalists are more exposed to politicians and government officials' arbitrariness, abuse, and intolerance. Perhaps this is a major deficiency of Mexican public life. Dedicated as they are to coverage of their immediate surroundings, local reporters run greater risks, such as reporting on problems in community life (land regulations and exploitation of natural resources), citizens' reports, municipal politics, local crime, and regional influential groups or powerful factions. Indeed, how could it be otherwise? Journalism is conditioned by the local social, economic, and criminal structures in which it operates. This is especially true at the country's territorial and social peripheries, where precariousness prevails in tandem with reduced editorial and economic independence and greater levels of censorship, where the democratic rules of the game enjoyed by major media outlets and journalists in the capital and other major metropolitan areas do not apply. In other words, freedom of the press is not present in some regions.

Mexico has one of the highest indices of homicide in Latin America. However, in recent years there have been some changes worth noting. From 2018 to date, the federal administration, in conjunction with state agencies, has stopped the increasing rise in premeditated homicides that began in 2008. It has even managed to reduce it. According to INEGI, from 2018 to 2023, the homicide rate fell from twenty-nine to twenty-five per every hundred thousand inhabitants. Moreover, during this period, there was also a reduction in felonies, federal crimes—such as crimes against public health and those related to arms—and kidnappings. Despite all this, Mexico remains the most violent democracy in the Western Hemisphere.

For observers like analyst Eduardo Guerrero, an influential Mexican specialist in public security and violence, organized crime syndicates have

CONCLUSION

proven far too resilient and are "stronger than ever."[28] According to Guerrero, local criminal cells expanded from 250 in 2018 to over 350 in 2022. These criminal organizations have not only multiplied but also diversified, increasingly turning to new illicit activities. In 2023, *Science* magazine reported that organized crime syndicates employ over 170,000 people nationwide.[29] If cartels were a single business, the article suggests, it would be the fifth-largest employer in the country.[30] Crime cells still have the capacity to shock and remain one of the bloodiest censors of the press. According to Artículo 19 Mexico, these criminal cells were responsible for only 6 percent of aggressions against journalists in 2022, but their presence inhibits investigative journalism and spreads fear and censorship in civil society and the media profession.

Since 2007, nongovernmental organizations such as Artículo 19 Mexico and Reporters Without Borders have consistently documented that the aggressions of organized crime represent only a small percentage of all aggressions against the press. Still, public insecurity, corruption, institutional weakness, and the fear instilled by these criminal cells have deeply undermined the social fabric and civic life necessary for journalism to flourish. So, journalism is no longer practiced in zones of the country that lack well-rooted, critical journalistic institutions and where rumors, disinformation, or silence prevail.

On a federal level, there are few guarantees of the free practice of journalism. Pedro Vacca, the special rapporteur for freedom of expression at the Inter-American Commission on Human Rights, said the daily morning press conferences known as *mañaneras* held by President Andrés Manuel López Obrador may foster a climate hostile to journalists.[31] In 2022, Artículo 19 Mexico registered 176 occasions at which the president made stigmatizing comments about the media, journalists, and NGOs. The London-based organization has said that such a climate could encourage a breeding ground for attacks on the press in countries like Mexico, where there is a deeply rooted culture of intolerance of journalistic criticism at all levels of government.

Yet verbal attacks are only one element of the cocktail of hostility journalists face. Where verbally assaulting journalists does not do the job, there

CONCLUSION

is always spycraft. In 2023, the *New York Times* revealed that the Mexican army under the current administration continues to surveil human rights defenders and journalists, despite having promised to abandon the practice.[32] This revelation, which followed a leak on army intelligence in 2022, allows us to infer that the spy program Pegasus is still in use. This is not an isolated case. According to a poll by Worlds of Journalism Mexico, one in ten journalists has been spied on or surveilled over the past five years.

At first glance, under the current administration, the insecurity journalists face has continued, and there is still an ocean to be crossed in terms of freedom of the press. But closer scrutiny of the topic also suggests that freedom of the press on the federal level in Mexico has made small advances in recent years. That progress is related to the reduction in funds distributed to the press for propaganda purposes, the strengthening of the Mecanismo para la Protección de Periodistas y Defensores de Derechos Humanos, and advances in how justice is meted out. Of course, all of these are insufficient changes for warranting a robust exercise of freedom of expression and freedom of the press.

Under the current administration, the federal government has reduced the budget assigned to public advertising by over 80 percent in comparison to its predecessors. According to some observers, the vast majority of those funds were used to reward or punish the press. They also pointed out that the diminished funding has had great impact on communications because in Mexico, official resources comprise a considerable part of media outlets' annual income. This is a significant advance since from the start of political alternance in the first decade of the twenty-first century, federal government administrations have increased these resources exponentially. Nevertheless, this recent transformation is insufficient because clearer, more just, and more transparent ground rules for access to public advertising are still needed. In fact, the allocation of public advertisement in the media is still very opaque and it is still used as a government manipulation tool in the news industry. This, of course, has remained as a national trend among all levels of government and within all political parties.

The government has also succeeded in increasing the capacities of the Mecanismo para la Protección de Periodistas y Defensores de Derechos

CONCLUSION

Humanos. From 2018 to 2023, the number of people benefiting from the Mecanismo increased 172 percent, reaching over 2,000 persons, 604 of whom are journalists. Among the main measures of protection granted are the relocation and assignment of panic buttons. The budget allocation to the Mecanismo's budget has also increased consistently, growing from 250 million Mexican pesos (US$13.0 million) in 2018 to 643 million Mexican pesos (US$31.9 million) in 2022. The Mecanismo's staff also grew from forty to eighty public officials in five years, allowing them to take on more cases. However, some civic observers and journalists say that there is a stubborn case backlog and lack of coordination between local and federal officials. For example, in recent years, local mechanisms have been created for the protection of journalists and human rights defenders in seventeen out of thirty-two states. However, they suffer from limitations similar to those that characterize the Mecanismo on a federal level.

In a country where the safety of citizens and journalists is guaranteed, there would be no need for individual protection mechanisms. But Mexico is still far from attaining that goal. Sixteen years after the creation of the Mecanismo and two thousand beneficiaries later, it is clear this agency remains essential. In the future, it would be advantageous if this Mechanism were supported by regulations that standardize its performance with regard to local agencies; moreover, a broad national strategy is required, one that privileges a preventative focus rather than a reactive one.

Deficient journalist protections are not the greatest obstacle to guaranteeing the practice of critical journalism in Mexico. As this book makes clear, government inefficiency in securing that guarantee adds to a general perception that aggressions against the press go unpunished. Impunity is the state's most egregious assault on the sector.

In Mexico today, attacking a journalist is relatively easy and also free of consequences. According to Artículo 19 Mexico, impunity for crimes against the press is close to 100 percent (99.1 percent of crimes against freedom of expression committed from 2010 to 2018 went unpunished).[33] Hence, the judicial system's failure to act is overwhelming, and after five years of a presidential administration begun in 2018, structural limitations persist. To be fair, there have been tentative, albeit grossly insufficient, advances in access to justice.

During the present administration, the Fiscalía and federal authorities have followed through on certain emblematic cases. In December 2021, Undersecretary of Human Rights, Population, and Migration Alejandro Encinas of the Secretaría de Gobernación apologized to family members of the journalist Alfredo Jiménez Mota for state participation in his disappearance, which occurred in April 2005. At the time he went missing, Jiménez Mota was a police reporter for Sonora's *El Imparcial.* The official commented, "I come here to offer a public apology, because the Mexican state was unable to guarantee and protect the integrity of Alfredo, who, through the practice of his profession as a journalist, contributed to the strengthening of the press, freedom of expression, and liberty in Sonora." The family accepted the apology as long as the government pledged to close the case, which has gone unsolved for eighteen years.

This was the first time the Mexican state had offered a public apology of this kind, showing a desire on the part of the federal government to recognize and vindicate the press and acknowledge the grave crisis of violence. Of course, an apology does not mean the case is closed, the loss of life compensated, or the family healed. State recognition of its responsibility does help prevent similar acts of violence and foster a sense of justice.

Not all efforts have been purely symbolic. There have also been some tangible consequences, notably in two other emblematic cases that arose under the current administration, both under the jurisdiction of the Fiscalía Especial para la Atención de Delitos cometidos en contra de la Libertad de Expresión (FEADLE) (Special District Attorney's Office for Attention to Crimes Committed Against Freedom of Expression). One was the arrest and sentencing, between 2020 and 2021, of former PAN party mayor Hugo Schultz, a coconspirator and perpetrator of the murder of investigative journalist Miroslava Breach, which took place in 2017.[34] Also in 2021, a thirty-two-year sentence was handed down against Juan Francisco "P," el Quillo, for the murder of long-form journalist Javier Valdez Cárdenas, killed in 2017. However, two cases in an ocean of impunity are a drop in the bucket.[35]

CONCLUSION

Beyond these stories, FEADLE has made few advances during this period. A report on the Fiscalía said that 85 percent of all sentences it handed down were issued between 2018 and 2021. The most common crimes to receive sentencing were homicide, abuse of authority, threats, torture, and personal injuries. However, a considerable backlog of cases remains. Over thirteen years, FEADLE has brought to trial only 21 percent of the aggressions currently under investigation, resulting in thirty-five prison sentences. Observers like Sara Mendiola, an activist and director of the civil journalist defense organization Propuesta Cívica, have pointed out that loopholes in the Fiscalía's jurisdiction remain. As stated in this book's second chapter, continues to be its most potent weapon in solving crimes against freedom of expression in a country where every state acts as a stronghold of power for elected officials. Moreover, since 2000, FEADLE has had reports of only 101 journalist homicides, one-third less than those registered by official agencies such as the Ministry of the Interior. Of those 101, the Fiscalía has found a relationship between the crime and the victim's profession in only 45 cases; in the rest, it declared incompetence.

Impunity is the main issue still pending nationwide regarding freedom of expression. The existence of special agencies dedicated to solving crimes against freedom of expression is relevant. Still, fifteen years after its creation, the Fiscalía has proven that it does not function efficiently outside of the system it forms part of. And, of course, it could hardly be otherwise. As lawyers say, the accessory follows the principal. That said, solving emblematic crimes and painting red lines regarding specific crimes such as murder may bring about favorable results, as was the case in the first decade of the twenty-first century in Colombia. Punishing the worst crimes, like murders and forced disappearances, elevates the perception of risk and sends a message of state intolerance for such crimes. Otherwise, the message is that attacking journalists has no consequences.

For all these reasons, seeking government support is not the first option for journalists who encounter aggression while on the job. According to the Worlds of Journalism Mexico poll, only 14 percent seek such support from government officials. Journalists do not expect empathy from investigative officials and do not trust them. Instead, they seek out members of their

CONCLUSION

profession when they are victims of aggression. The poll estimates that eight out of ten turn to colleagues at their own media outlet for help, and three in ten to networks that protect journalists. These figures illustrate the vital nature of social capital and professional solidarity, a point this book makes repeatedly.

We must conclude then that Mexican journalists are thwarted by an environment in which little changes, fostering professional precariousness, intolerance of a critical press, and criminal violence.

Nevertheless, in recent years, we have witnessed signs associated with our model of resilient newsmakers among a small fraction inside the journalistic community. These individual, organizational, and collective mechanisms adapt to adversities and the continued practice of journalism by privileging security at all times. According to the study cited above, among journalists' most frequently used protective measures are: "being more careful with information verification" (89.3 percent), "training in security measures" (57 percent), and "establishing contact networks with colleagues" (56.6 percent). Over the years, these journalistic practices have become more deeply rooted. Critical journalism always finds a way. These practices' prevalence demonstrates in-depth change among those critical journalists in Mexico who increasingly collaborate to report and publish stories of great value and impact and to create a united front against a wild, lawless Mexico.

The outlook for a critical press is dark but not desolate. Wherever journalism is committed to its public and community vocation, resources may be found to join forces against arbitrary and authoritarian constructs. Practicing critical journalism in Mexico, as in many other places, implies resilience, adapting to adversity, and committing to accountability and transparency without losing sight of personal safety or one's immediate surroundings.

Given the violence, corruption, and impunity in Mexico, some sectors of critical journalism have found it efficacious to focus on professional resilience as a means to move forward. Personal and professional values play an indispensable role; they are the motor that drives journalists. But that is not the only thing fostering a critical press. The guarantees, support, and protection of media outlets also play a fundamental role in the profession.

CONCLUSION

When they turn a blind eye to aggression as a sin of omission or because of proximity to power, networks of resistance and support arise. Defying a violent and hostile environment, social capital, collective resources cemented in trust, and shared values, ideals, and practices catalyze journalistic endeavors of great impact and caliber. Social capital is key to resistance, for no one can bear the brunt of power and aggression alone.

APPENDIX I
GLOSSARY OF TRANSLATED TERMS

GOVERNMENT AGENCIES, INITIATIVES, MINISTRIES, AND FORCES

SPANISH	ENGLISH
Centro Nacional de Inteligencia (CNI, prev., Centro de Investigación y Seguridad Nacional [CISEN])	National Intelligence Center (predecessor to Center for Research and National Security)
Comisión Nacional de los Derechos Humanos (CNDH)	National Human Rights Commission
Ejército Mexicano	Mexican army
Fiscalía Especial para la Atención de Delitos cometidos contra la Libertad de Expresión (FEADLE)	Special District Attorney's Office for Attention to Crimes Committed Against Freedom of Expression
Fiscalía Especial para la Atención de Delitos cometidos contra Periodistas	Special District Attorney's Office for Crimes Committed Against Journalists
Fiscalía General de la República (FGR)	Office of the Attorney General of the Republic
"Gobierno Espía"	"Government Spies" (political strategy)
Guardia Nacional (GN)	National Guard

(*continued*)

APPENDIX I

GOVERNMENT AGENCIES, INITIATIVES, MINISTRIES, AND FORCES (continued)

SPANISH	ENGLISH
Instituto Nacional de Estadística y Geografía (INEGI)	National Institute of Statistics and Geography
Mecanismo de Protección para Personas Defensoras de Derechos Humanos y Periodistas (El Mecanismo)	Mechanism to Protect Human Rights Defenders and Journalists (The Mechanism)
Policía Federal	Federal Police
Programa de Agravios a Periodistas y Defensores de Derechos Humanos de la Comisión Nacional de los Derechos Humanos	Program of Attacks on Journalists and Human Rights Defenders, National Human Rights Commission
Secretaría de Gobernación (SEGOB)	Ministry of the Interior
Secretaría de Hacienda y Crédito Público (SHCP)	Ministry of Finance
Secretaría de la Defensa Nacional (SEDENA)	National Defense Ministry
Suprema Corte de Justicia de la Nación (SCJN)	Supreme Court of Justice of the Nation

NGOS, CIVIC AND HUMAN RIGHTS ORGANIZATIONS, AND MEDIA PLATFORMS

SPANISH	ENGLISH
Agenda de Periodistas	Journalists' Agenda
<I>Blog del Narco</I>	<I>Narcotics Blog</I>
Casa de los Derechos de Periodistas	Journalists' Rights House
Centro de Derechos Humanos Miguel Agustín Pro Juárez	Miguel Agustín Pro Juárez Human Rights Center
Colectivo de Análisis de Seguridad con Democracia (CASEDE)	Security Analysis with Democracy Collective
Consejo de Periodistas del Papaloapan	Papaloapan Journalists' Council
Grupo Prensa Oaxaca	Oaxaca Press Group
Hub de Periodismo de Investigación de la Frontera Norte	Hub of Investigative Journalism on the Northern Border

GLOSSARY OF TRANSLATED TERMS

SPANISH	ENGLISH
Los queremos vivos	We Want Them Back Alive
Periodistas de a Pie	Journalists on Foot
Prensa, no disparen	Press, Don't Shoot!
Propuesta Cívica	Civic Proposal
Proyecto Fénix	Phoenix Project
Red de Periodistas Noreste	Northeastern Network of Journalists
Red periodistas de Juárez	Juárez Network of Journalists
Relatoría Especial para la Libertad de Expresión (RELE)	Special Rapporteurship for Freedom of Expression
Reporteros sin Fronteras México (RSF)	Reporters Without Borders in Mexico
Sociedad Interamericana de Prensa en México	Inter-American Press Society in Mexico
Tú y yo coincidimos en la noche terrible	You and I Met That Terrible Night
Unidad de Respuesta Rápida de la Sociedad Interamericana de Prensa en México	Quick Response Unit of the Inter-American Press Society in Mexico
Voces Irritilas	Irritating Voices
Voz Alterna	Alternative Voice

ACADEMIC INSTITUTIONS

SPANISH	ENGLISH
El Colegio de México (COLMEX)	College of Mexico
Real Academia Española (RAE)	Royal Spanish Academy
Universidad Nacional Autónoma de México (UNAM)	National Autonomous University of Mexico

APPENDIX I

POLITICAL MOVEMENTS AND PARTIES, LABOR UNIONS

SPANISH	ENGLISH
Antorcha Campesina o el Movimiento Antorchista	Farmers' Torch, or the Torchbearing Movement
Movimiento de Regeneración Nacional (MORENA)	National Regeneration Movement
Movimiento de Unificación y Lucha Triqui (MULT)	Triqui Movement of Unification and Struggle
Partido Acción Nacional (PAN)	National Action Party
Partido Revolucionario Institucional (PRI)	Revolutionary Institutional Party
Sindicato Nacional de Trabajadores de la Educación (SNTE)	National Union of Education Workers
Sindicato Nacional de Trabajadores de la Prensa (SNTP)	National Union of Press Workers

TERMINOLOGY

SPANISH	ENGLISH
cacique	Local strongman
crónica	New Journalism
cronista	Long-form journalist or chronicler

GLOSSARY OF TRANSLATED TERMS

CARTELS

SPANISH	ENGLISH
Cartel del Golfo	Gulf [of Mexico] Cartel
Cartel de Sinaloa	Sinaloa Cartel
Cartel Jalisco Nueva Generación	Jalisco New Generation Cartel
Familia Michoacana	Michoacán Family
Los Zetas	The Zs

APPENDIX II
STUDY DESIGN

Over the past two decades, a series of major social transformations took place in Mexico. These included the early decades of the democratic experience, the consolidation of an open and liberal economy, the boom in all-powerful governors, and the criminal insurgency. My investigation was designed to understand how such social changes have impacted the field of journalism, especially between 2006 and 2018, a period that encompassed two presidential administrations. Hence, this study seeks to contribute to a wave of recent investigations that have focused on analyzing this issue from the standpoint of journalism and academia.[1] Unlike these investigations, this book presents a polyphonic version of this reality, offering a set of conceptual propositions for understanding this phenomenon and at the same time registering the voices of dozens of journalists, activists, and public officials scattered across the country.

Likewise, as my investigation advanced, I chose to channel my energy into unraveling, with an analysis centered on individuals, how journalists who reported this reality were able to continue to do so, despite multiple obstacles and limitations around them. How is agency possible in such adverse situations? What resources are within reach to achieve this? How

APPENDIX II

extended are these practices, and what are their main limitations? This wave of studies has included very little analysis of these questions; this book seeks to contribute modestly to answering them. Shedding light on them also helps explain the resilience of journalistic autonomy within other repressive and hostile contexts.

Therefore, as in other, similar investigations, this investigative labor centers far more on news and information production than on consumption, placing special emphasis on factors that either limit or enable journalistic routines.[2] This book has benefited from a detailed analysis of documents, data, and dozens of journalistic studies. And yet, at its foundation is the comparison of the individual experiences of a group of journalists I interviewed who are dedicated to covering high-risk stories in Mexico, especially between the first decade of the twenty-first century and 2018.

In keeping with this concept, the main investigation tool I relied on for this book was qualitative, in-depth interviewing, a very fruitful technique in analyzing actors facing situations that involve risk or violence.[3] From 2014 to 2016, I carried out fieldwork across the country, ranging from periods of two weeks to six months, and interviewed seventy-nine people, using a strategic sample that benefited from the snowball technique, in which participants assisted me in identifying other potential subjects. It is important to mention that by using this technique, it is very likely that these informants possess stronger "social capital" because they are connected.

Thirty-five percent of these interviews were carried out in person, while the rest took place over the telephone. The vast majority of those interviewed (85 percent) were journalists, especially reporters who cover some of the most sensitive issues in the country, including corruption scandals, abuse of power, criminal confrontations, in-depth reporting on the world of drug trafficking, or serious human rights violations such as massacres or forced displacements. The remainder of the interviews were with a strategic set of key informants, who helped me understand the professional environment of journalists, such as freedom of the press activists (seven) and public officials in key positions (four). The journalists I interviewed held different positions: copy editors, general directors, editors, reporters (on public safety, politics, and general issues), columnists, investigative

STUDY DESIGN

journalists, and long-form journalists. These interviews lasted from twenty minutes to four hours, or fifty minutes on average. In total, I compiled thirty-nine hours of recorded audio material. The interviews were transcribed verbatim and codified thematically; later on, patterns were identified that guided and informed this book.

Because of the sensitive nature of the material my subjects shared with me, a great many of these interviews are referred to anonymously in this book. The confidentiality of my sources has been maintained at all times.

As seen in detail in the appendix, the interviews may be divided into two major groups. The first consists of interviews with permanent residents of Mexico City. This group, which comprises thirty people, is composed of journalists, activists, and public officials selected for their professional work. A group of seven activists I interviewed in 2014 includes representatives of the most important associations defending freedom of the press in the country, such as Artículo 19 Mexico, Reporters Without Borders, la Sociedad Interamericana de Prensa, Casa de los Derechos de los Periodistas, Colectivo de Análisis de Seguridad con Democracia, and Centro de Derechos Humanos Miguel Agustín Pro Juárez.

The public servants interviewed are high-level officials at agencies such as the Fiscalía Especial para la Atención de Delitos Cometidos contra de la Libertad de Expresión, Mecanismo de Protección para Personas Defensoras de Derechos Humanos y Periodistas, and Programa de Agravios a Periodistas y Defensores de Derechos Humanos of the Comisión Nacional de los Derechos Humanos.

The twenty journalists in the first category include prominent journalists, columnists, and chroniclers with nationwide impact who commonly cover sensitive topics in the most inhospitable regions of the country. Although these journalists are based in the nation's capital, they travel frequently to the interior to report on issues and events that take place there. Among them are members of journalistic organizations like Periodistas de a Pie and long-form journalists who publish in magazines like *Gatopardo*. Also in this category, we find some directors of the principal Mexican periodicals, such as *Proceso*, *Reforma*, and *La Jornada*, and local periodicals like *El Siglo de Torreón* who are recognized for their critical and independent vocation. I also included two foreign investigative journalists and two journalists with long and distinguished academic careers at prestigious universities, such as the Universidad Nacional Autónoma de México and El Colegio de México.

The other group of subjects encompasses those living permanently outside of the capital and consists of forty-eight journalists from ten different states. Following a preliminary selection, the states chosen possessed two criteria: (1) those that had higher rates of criminal violence, including instances of first-degree, premeditated homicide, and (2) journalists based in all five regions of Mexico.[4] From each state, I selected five journalists. I contacted twenty-nine of them through CASEDE, the local NGO that has worked with them while backing local protection protocols; the remainder were contacted using the snowball technique. Journalists from this sample live and work in twenty cities across the nation, including some considered the most dangerous, such as Chihuahua and Ciudad Juárez (Chihuahua), Mazatlán and Culiacán (Sinaloa), Ciudad Victoria and Tampico (Tamaulipas), Morelia (Michoacán), Ecatepec (Estado de México), and Acapulco (Guerrero). They also operate in high-risk areas such as Tierra Caliente (Michoacán) and La Montaña (Guerrero).

In each of these ten states, I attempted to contact three local journalists and two national correspondents. The total number was thirty and eighteen, respectively. The thirty local journalists live outside the capital and work (or have worked) for local media outlets on stories related to security, organized crime, corruption, abuse of power, and serious human rights violations. Some of them have also led broader investigations and written opinion columns or chronicles. This group works (or has worked) for the most prominent media outlets in their state, such as *El Diario de Juárez* (Chihuahua), *Ríodoce, El Debate*, and *Noroeste* (Sinaloa); *El Sur* and *La Jornada Guerrero* (Guerrero); *Expreso* and a legacy newspaper in Nuevo Laredo (Tamaulipas); and *Proceso Jalisco* and *El Informador* (Jalisco). Others are employed by digital initiatives that offer them greater editorial freedom and flexibility as contributors, such as *Revista Espejo* (Sinaloa) and *Página 3* (Oaxaca). The eighteen national correspondents are journalists based outside the capital who work or regularly contribute to a major national media

STUDY DESIGN

outlet, such as *Proceso, Reforma, La Jornada, El Universal, Milenio, Radio Acir, Enfoque Noticias, Vice News*, AFP, and AP. All commonly cover themes relevant to their states, especially politics, security, and economics. Notably, national correspondents for print media almost always conduct far-reaching investigations.[5]

To each one of these forty-eight journalists from outside the capital, I presented an open questionnaire of twenty questions. They covered topics including the status of freedom of the press and levels of risk in their states; their perception of violence against the press; strategies of publication; attacks on them owing to their journalistic practice; relationships with other colleagues and civic allies seeking protection; and comments regarding impunity.

The vast majority of the journalists I conversed with—nearly three-fourths of them—had faced aggression derived from their journalistic practice during their professional careers. These attacks, which targeted some journalists multiple times, include direct and remote threats (via telephone or digitally), intimidations, beatings and thefts, public slander, cybernetic espionage, physical attacks on their media facilities, torture, illegal abductions, and aggressions requiring exile.

Paralyzed by fear, one investigative journalist went into exile with their partner outside the country after being threatened for investigating the brutal homicide of a reporter colleague. Municipal police officers, acting on orders from the city mayor, brutally assaulted a community journalist who was covering a protest. Another reporter fled their home state after being threatened by the governor. One editor sheltered the outlet's news team inside the building as gunmen hired by organized crime cells riddled the façade with bullets. State authorities bothered by critical coverage spied on, harassed, and libeled another young reporter.

Given the sensitive nature of these incidents, at all times I followed the ethical protocol of British academics from Sheffield and Leeds Universities, where this book took shape as doctoral research. My research benefited greatly from the time these journalists devoted to me to discuss their work and their openness and confidence in me in describing the traumatic, painful episodes they have endured.

APPENDIX II

Finally, in writing this book, I also relied on my own experience and knowledge in the field of Mexican journalism and communications. Over the past decade, I have carried out different roles that range from professor of communications and journalism to public official and spokesperson for the minister of finance (2020–2021) and the National Institute of Statistics and Geography (since 2022). These roles allowed me to get to know different facets of the "rules of the game" followed by critical journalists. Moreover, my experience as a researcher for two projects focusing on issues of freedom of the press and the security of journalists guided my research and writing. The first, in 2016, was under the aegis of UNESCO and the Centre for Freedom of the Media of the University of Sheffield. The second, in 2018, was commissioned by CASEDE and the United States Agency for International Development.

APPENDIX III
LISTS OF INTERVIEWS

1. Javier Garza Ramos, chief editor/director, *El Siglo de Torreón*, September 24, 2015.
2. Julio Hernández, columnist, *La Jornada San Luis*, September 10, 2015.
3. Rafael Rodríguez, director, *Proceso*, December 16, 2014.
4. Anonymous, top executive, press, November 30, 2015.
5. Jorge Carrasco, investigative reporter, national magazine, November 30, 2015.
6. Guillermo Osorno, editor, press, November 29, 2021.
7. Anonymous, investigative journalist and editor, press, December 8, 2015.
8. Anonymous, veteran journalist, Casa de los Derechos de los Periodistas, September 28, 2015.
9. Víctor Hugo Reyna, journalist, El Colegio de Sonora, September 14, 2015.
10. Ioan Grillo, freelance journalist, September 10, 2015.
11. Marco Lara Klahr, freelance journalist, December 22, 2015.
12. Emiliano Ruiz Parra, journalist, December 22, 2014.
13. Daniela Pastrana, journalist, Periodistas de a Pie, December 30, 2014.
14. Anonymous, journalist, *Wall Street Journal*, September 15, 2015.
15. Anonymous, journalist from Durango, November 20, 2015.
16. Emilio Lugo, journalist, press, September 19, 2015.

APPENDIX III

17. Diego Enrique Osorno, freelance journalist, March 2, 2018.
18. Norma Trujillo, journalist, *La Jornada/Voz Alterna*, November 27, 2021.
19. Anonymous, journalist, Agence France-Presse (AFP), December 2, 2015.
20. Rodrigo González, Artículo 19 (NGO), México, November 28, 2014.
21. Armando Rodríguez, CASEDE (NGO), December 14, 2014.
22. Darío Fritz, NGO, December 9, 2015.
23. Justine Dupuy, Fundar (NGO), November 25, 2014.
24. Balbina Flores, RSF (NGO), November 18, 2014.
25. Victor Ruiz Arrazola, RSF (NGO), November 17, 2015.
26. Edgar Cortez, NGO, September 23, 2015.
27. Sergio Aguayo, NGO/academic, El Colegio de México, November 17, 2015.
28. Anonymous, public official, Secretaría de Gobernación, November 27, 2015.
29. Anonymous, public official, Secretaría de Gobernación, November 27, 2015.
30. Anonymous, high-ranking official, CNDH, October 2, 2015.
31. Anonymous, public official, PGR, December 9, 2015.

Chihuahua

1. Anonymous, multimedia reporter, radio/TV, December 11, 2015.
2. Anonymous, political journalist, *El Diario de Juárez*, December 11, 2015.
3. Anonymous, reporter, *El Diario de Juárez*, December 16, 2015.
4. Anonymous, investigative journalist, *El Diario de Juárez*, January 16, 2016.
5. Anonymous, deputy director, press, January 22, 2016.

Estado de México

1. Anonymous, reporter, press, January 14, 2016.
2. Anonymous, police beat reporter, *Hoy*/UNO TV, January 21, 2016.
3. Anonymous, reporter, UNO TV, February 27, 2016.
4. Anonymous, correspondent, *La Jornada*, March 20, 2016.

Guerrero

1. Anonymous, investigative journalist, Radio Universidad Guerrero, September 20, 2015.

LISTS OF INTERVIEWS

2. Anonymous, reporter, newspaper, December 11, 2015.
3. Anonymous, reporter, *El regional de la Costa*, December 12, 2015.
4. Anonymous, correspondent, *La Jornada*, January 7, 2016.
5. Anonymous, correspondent, *Reforma*, January 8, 2016.

Jalisco
1. Anonymous, political journalist, *Milenio*, January 16, 2016.
2. Anonymous, investigative journalist, *VICE News*, January 19, 2016.
3. Anonymous, police beat reporter, *El Informador*, January 26, 2016.
4. Anonymous, correspondent, *Proceso*, January 27, 2016.
5. Anonymous, journalist, January 28, 2016.

Michoacán
1. Francisco Castellanos, investigative journalist, *Proceso*, December 14, 2015.
2. Anonymous, freelance reporter, December 16, 2015.
3. Antonio Ramos, reporter, *Cambio*, December 22, 2015.
4. Anonymous, correspondent, national newspaper, January 8, 2016.
5. Anonymous, multimedia reporter, radio, January 18, 2016.

Nuevo León
1. Anonymous, freelance reporter, January 12, 2016.
2. Anonymous, freelance reporter, January 22, 2016.
3. Anonymous, investigative journalist, national magazine, January 27, 2016.
4. Anonymous, correspondent, *La Jornada*, January 27, 2016.
5. Erick Muñiz, national correspondent, January 28, 2016.

Oaxaca
1. Anonymous, reporter, *El Imparcial*, December 8, 2015.
2. Anonymous, investigative journalist, *El Imparcial/Página 3/La Jornada*, December 11, 2015.
3. Anonymous, national correspondent, *Proceso*, December 14, 2015.
4. Anonymous, reporter, magazine, January 7, 2016.
5. Anonymous, investigative journalist, *Reforma*, January 9, 2016.

APPENDIX III

Sinaloa
1. Anonymous, freelance reporter, Asociación 7 de Julio (NGO), December 7, 2015.
2. Anonymous, deputy director, radio station, December 9, 2015.
3. Anonymous, journalist and cofounder, *Espejo/Ríodoce*, December 10, 2015.
4. Anonymous, freelance reporter, December 16, 2015.
5. Anonymous, deputy director, *Noroeste*, January 8, 2016.

Tamaulipas
1. Anonymous, political journalist, *Milenio*, December 4, 2015.
2. Anonymous, reporter, *Expreso*, December 5, 2015.
3. Anonymous, rreporter, newspaper, December 10, 2015.
4. Anonymous, journalist, *Expreso*, December 22, 2015.
5. Anonymous, news editor, *Expreso/La Razón*, January 12, 2016.

Veracruz
1. Noé Zavaleta, correspondent, *Proceso*, September 19, 2015.
2. Anonymous, reporter, Grupo Imagen, December 10, 2015
3. Anonymous, reporter, *Ver Veracruz*, January 12, 2016.
4. Anonymous, freelance reporter, January 29, 2016.

MAP 1 States in Mexico.

APPENDIX IV

TIME LINE

2000—First democratically elected administration, led by President Vicente Fox Quezada of the Partido Acción Nacional (PAN).

2004 (June)—Killing of Francisco Ortiz Franco, Tijuana investigative reporter and editor at *Zeta* magazine.

2005 (April)—Disappearance of journalist Alfredo Jiménez Mota in Sonora.

2005 (June)—Launch of anti-drug military operation México Seguro (Safe Mexico)

2006 (February)—Creation of the Office of the Special Prosecutor for the Attention of Crimes Committed Against Journalists (FEADLE predecessor).

2006 (December)—Start of second democratically elected administration, led by President Felipe Calderón Hinojosa of PAN.

2006 (December)—Launch of joint Operation Michoacán by Mexican government.

2007—Founding of Periodistas de a Pie, an independent journalists' network.

APPENDIX IV

2008 (March)—Launch of joint Operation Chihuahua by Mexican government.

2008 (November)—Killing of journalist Armando Rodríguez Carreón "El Choco" in Ciudad Juárez, Chihuahua.

2010 (July)—Launch of "Los queremos vivos" protest.

2010 (July)—Creation of FEADLE.

2012 (June)—Creation of the Mechanism for the Protection of Journalists.

2012 (April)—Killing of investigative journalist Regina Martínez in Xalapa, Veracruz.

2012 (December)—Start of third democratically elected administration, led by President Enrique Peña Nieto of the Partido de la Revolución Institucional (PRI).

2014 (February)—Killing of local journalist Gregorio Jiménez de la Cruz in Veracruz and launch of collective "Prensa, no disparen."

2014 (November)—Report by leading Mexican journalist Carmen Aristegui on a media scandal concerning Enrique Peña Nieto's "Casa Blanca" (White House), a mansion owned by the Mexican president.

2015 (July)—Killing of photojournalist Ruben Espinoza and activist Nadia Vera in Mexico City.

2017 (March)—Killing of investigative reporter Miroslava Breach in Chihuahua city

2017 (May)—Killing of investigative reporter and cronista Javier Valdez Cárdenas in Culiacán, Sinaloa.

2017 (June)—Launch of "Agenda de Periodistas," a national mobilization of independent journalists.

2018 (December)—Start of the fourth democratically elected administration, led by Andrés Manuel López Obrador of the Movimiento de Regeneración Nacional (MORENA) party.

NOTES

INTRODUCTION: "OUTRAGE BROUGHT US TOGETHER"

1. Author interview with long-form journalist Emiliano Ruiz Parra, December 22, 2014.
2. Author interview with investigative journalist and editor, December 8, 2015.
3. Committee to Protect Journalists, "Gregorio Martínez de la Cruz," 2014, https://cpj.org/data/people/gregorio-jimenez-de-la-cruz/.
4. Author interview with journalist Daniela Pastrana, December 30, 2014.
5. Emiliano Ruiz Parra, "Goyo, en la boca del lobo," *Cosecha roja*, February 7, 2015, https://cosecharoja.org/goyo-en-la-boca-del-lobo/.
6. Author interview with journalist Daniela Pastrana.
7. Ruiz Parra, "Goyo, en la boca del lobo."
8. Author interview with long-form journalist Emiliano Ruiz Parra.
9. Author interview with long-form journalist Diego Enrique Osorno, March 2, 2018.
10. See Alan Knight, "México bronco, México manso: Una reflexión sobre la cultura cívica mexicana," *Política y gobierno* 3, no. 1 (1996): 5–30.
11. Author interview with long-form journalist Diego Enrique Osorno.
12. John Nerone, *Violence Against the Press: Policing the Public Sphere in U.S. History* (New York: Oxford University Press, 1994), 214.
13. Julieta Alejandra Brambila and Sallie L. Hughes, "Violence Against Journalists," in *The International Encyclopedia of Journalism Studies*, ed. Tim. P. Vos and Folker Hanusch (Hoboken, NJ: Wiley-Blackwell, 2019), 1–9.
14. Stathis N. Kalyvas, *The Logic of Violence in Civil War* (Cambridge: Cambridge University Press, 2006).

INTRODUCTION

15. Ruiz Parra, "Goyo, en la boca del lobo."
16. Nerone, *Violence Against the Press*, 111–27.
17. Silvio Waisbord, "Antipress Violence and the Crisis of the State," *Harvard International Journal of Press/Politics* 7, no. 3 (2002): 90–109.
18. Author interview with a veteran journalist, September 28, 2015.
19. Anita R. Gohdes and Sabine C. Carey, "Canaries in a Coal-Mine? What the Killings of Journalists Tell Us About Future Repression," *Journal of Peace Research* 54, no. 2 (2017): 157–74.
20. Author interview with Michoacán journalist, December 16, 2015.
21. Sallie L. Hughes et al., "Expanding Influences Research to Insecure Democracies: How Violence, Public Insecurity, Economic Inequality, and Uneven Democratic Performance Shape Journalists' Perceived Work Environments," *Journalism Studies* 18, no. 5 (2017): 645–65.
22. "The consolidation of investigative reporting in Colombia in the 1970s earlier than elsewhere in the region suggests that the most violent democracy offers better conditions than authoritarian regimes, even when the latter reach their gentler, kinder, and final days." Silvio Waisbord, *Watchdog Journalism in South America: News, Accountability, and Democracy* (New York: Columbia University Press, 2000).
23. Barbie Zelizer, "Terms of Choice: Uncertainty, Journalism, and Crisis," *Journal of Communication* 65, no. 5 (2015): 888–908.
24. Author interview with Ciudad Juárez, Chihuahua, political journalist, December 11, 2015.
25. Rosemary J. Novak and Sarah Davidson, "Journalists Reporting on Hazardous Events: Constructing Protective Factors within the Professional Role," *Traumatology* 19, no. 4 (2013): 313–22.
26. Other investigators have also encountered similar findings: Mark Pearson et al., "Building Journalists' Resilience Through Mindfulness Strategies," *Journalism* 22, no. 7 (2021): 1647–64; Marína Urbániková and Lenka Haniková, "Coping with the Murder: The Impact of Ján Kuciak's Assassination on Slovak Investigative Journalists," *Journalism Practice* 16, no. 9 (2022): 1927–47; Sallie L. Hughes et al., "Coping with Occupational Stress in Journalism: Professional Identities and Advocacy as Resources," *Journalism Studies* 22, no. 8 (2021): 971–91.
27. Sallie L. Hughes, *Newsrooms in Conflict: Journalism and the Democratization of Mexico* (Pittsburgh: University of Pittsburgh Press, 2006), 5.
28. Maria Repnikova, *Media Politics in China: Improvising Power Under Authoritarianism* (Cambridge: Cambridge University Press, 2017).
29. Frida Viridiana Rodelo, "Periodismo en entornos violentos: el caso de los periodistas de Culiacán, Sinaloa," *Comunicación y sociedad*, no. 12 (2009): 101–18.
30. Pierre Bourdieu, "The Political Field, the Social Science Field, and the Journalistic Field," in *Bourdieu and the Journalistic Field*, ed. Rodney Benson and Erik Neveu, (Cambridge: Polity Press, 2005), 29–47.
31. Claudia Mellado et al., "Comparing Journalism Cultures in Latin America: The Case of Chile, Brazil, and Mexico," *International Communication Gazette* 74, no. 1 (2012): 60–77.

INTRODUCTION

32. Author interview with Oaxaca national correspondent, December 14, 2015.
33. Author interview with Ciudad Juárez, Chihuahua, newspaper deputy director, January 22, 2016.
34. Author interview with Monterrey, Nuevo León, freelance reporter, January 22, 2016.
35. Mireya Márquez Ramírez and Sallie Hughes, "Panorama de los perfiles demográficos, laborales y profesionales de los periodistas en México: Reporte de investigación," *Global Media Journal México* 14, no. 26 (2017): 91–152.
36. Pablo Piccato, *A History of Infamy: Crime, Truth, and Justice in Mexico* (Berkeley: University of California Press, 2017).
37. Daniel C. Hallin, "Nota Roja: Popular Journalism and the Transition to Democracy in Mexico," in *Tabloid Tales: Global Debates Over Media Standards*, ed. Collin Sparks and John Tulloch (Lanham, MD: Rowman & Littlefield, 2000), 267–84.
38. Waisbord, *Watchdog Journalism*; Ella McPherson, "Spot News Versus Reportage: Newspaper Models, the Distribution of Newsroom Credibility, and Implications for Democratic Journalism in Mexico," *International Journal of Communication* 6, (2012): 2301–17; Magdalena Saldaña and Rachel R. Mourão, "Reporting in Latin America: Issues and Perspectives on Investigative Journalism in the Region," *International Journal of Press/Politics* 23, no. 3 (2018): 299–323.
39. Lydia Cacho et al., *La ira de México: Siete voces contra la impunidad* (Mexico City: Penguin Random House, 2016).
40. Author interview with long-form journalist Diego Enrique Osorno.
41. Gabriela Polit Dueñas, *Unwanted Witnesses: Journalists and Conflict in Contemporary Latin America* (Pittsburgh: University of Pittsburgh Press, 2019).
42. Pierre Bourdieu, "The Forms of Capital," in *Handbook of Theory and Research for the Sociology of Education*, ed. John Richardson (Westport, CT: Greenwood, 1986), 241–58.
43. Julie Battilana and Thomas D'Aunno, "Institutional Work and the Paradox of Embedded Agency," in *Institutional Work: Actors and Agency in Institutional Studies of Organizations*, ed. Thomas B. Lawrence, Roy Suddaby, and Bernard Leca (Cambridge: Cambridge University Press, 2009), 31–58.
44. Robin Vandevoordt, "Why Journalists Covered Syria the Way They Did: On the Role of Economic, Social, and Cultural Capital," *Journalism* 18, no. 5 (2017): 609–25.
45. Matthew Powers and Sandra Vera Zambrano, "Explaining the Formation of Online News Startups in France and the United States: A Field Analysis," *Journal of Communication* 66, no. 5 (2016): 857–77, https://doi.org/10.1111/jcom.12253.
46. In this book, I follow an approach very similar to those used by the sociologist Robin Vandevoordt in his study of journalists in Syria. Robin Vandevoordt, "Covering the Syrian Conflict: How Middle East Reporters Deal with Challenging Situations," *Media, War & Conflict* 9 (2016): 306–24.
47. Michael Schudson, "Autonomy from What?" in *Bourdieu and the Journalistic Field*, ed. Rodney Benson and Erik Neveu (Cambridge: Polity Press, 2005), 214–23.
48. Throughout this book, the concept of organizational capital is used not as a mere substitute for economic capital but rather as a dimension to which I am paying special

INTRODUCTION

attention. The economic dimension underlies the analysis presented here, for example, in the continuous analysis made between the unequal access to material resources possessed by local journalists who cover daily news, correspondents who carry out investigations, and long-form journalists, among others.
49. María Soledad Segura and Silvio Waisbord, *Media Movements: Civil Society and Media Policy Reform in Latin America* (London: Zed Books, 2016).

1. WHY HAS IT BECOME SO EASY TO KILL JOURNALISTS?

1. Author interview with Morelia, Michoacán, investigative journalist Francisco Castellanos, December 14, 2015.
2. Vulnerability in the field of journalism is not a phenomenon limited to Mexico but rather a worldwide trend with similar origins and consequences. Silvio Waisbord, "The Vulnerabilities of Journalism," *Journalism* 20, no. 1 (2019): 210–13.
3. Author interview with activist Balbina Flores, November 18, 2014.
4. Sallie L. Hughes et al., "Expanding Influences Research to Insecure Democracies: How Violence, Public Insecurity, Economic Inequality, and Uneven Democratic Performance Shape Journalists' Perceived Work Environments," *Journalism Studies* 18, no. 5 (2017): 645–65.
5. Mireya Márquez Ramírez, "Post-Authoritarian Politics in a Neoliberal Era: Revising Media and Journalism Transition in Mexico," in *Media Systems and Communication Policies in Latin America*, ed. Manuel Alejandro Guerrero and Mireya Márquez Ramírez (London: Palgrave Macmillan, 2014), 272–92.
6. While it is true that this kind of journalism is not the rule but, rather, the exception nationwide, it also means that the practice of journalism has transitioned from a predominantly authoritarian culture to a hybrid one where different models coexist, such as adaptive, militant, responsive, and community authoritarianism, among others. See Sallie L. Hughes, *Newsrooms in Conflict: Journalism and the Democratization of Mexico* (Pittsburgh: University of Pittsburgh Press, 2006).
7. Chappell Lawson, "Mexico's Unfinished Transition: Democratization and Authoritarian Enclaves in Mexico," *Mexican Studies/Estudios Mexicanos* 16, no. 2 (2000): 267–87.
8. Author interview with analyst and academic researcher Sergio Aguayo, November 17, 2015.
9. Hughes, *Newsrooms in Conflict*; Manuel Alejandro Guerrero, "Sistemas mediáticos en democracias no consolidadas: El caso de México," *Pangea: Revista de Red Académica Iberoamericana de Comunicación* 11, no. 1 (2020): 5–23.
10. Larry Diamond, "Elections Without Democracy: Thinking About Hybrid Regimes," *Journal of Democracy* 13, no. 2 (2002): 21–35.
11. Christian Bjørnskov and Andreas Freytag, "An Offer You Can't Refuse: Murdering Journalists as an Enforcement Mechanism of Corrupt Deals," *Public Choice* 167, no. 3 (2016): 221–43.

1. WHY HAS IT BECOME SO EASY TO KILL JOURNALISTS?

12. Victor Asal et al., "Killing the Messenger: Regime Type as a Determinant of Journalist Killing, 1992–2008," *Foreign Policy Analysis* 14, no. 1 (2018): 24–43.
13. Sallie L. Hughes and Yulia Vorobyeva, "Explaining the Killing of Journalists in the Contemporary Era: The Importance of Hybrid Regimes and Subnational Variations," *Journalism* 22, no. 8 (2021): 1873–91.
14. Author interview with columnist Julio Hernández López, September 10, 2015.
15. Rogelio Hernández Rodríguez, *El centro dividido: La nueva autonomía de los gobernadores* (Mexico City: El Colegio de México, 2008).
16. Leo Zuckermann, "Los nuevos virreyes," *Proceso*, April 28, 2004.
17. Author interview with columnist Julio Hernández López.
18. Author interview with activist Justine Dupuy, November 25, 2014.
19. José Luis Benavides, "Gacetilla: A Keyword for a Revisionist Approach to the Political Economy of Mexico's Print News Media," *Media, Culture & Society* 22, no. 1 (2000): 85–104.
20. Guillermo O'Donnell, "On the State, Democratization, and Some Conceptual Problems: A Latin American View with Glances at Some Postcommunist Countries," *World Development* 21, no. 8 (1993): 1355–69; Jacqueline Behrend and Laurence Whitehead, eds., *Illiberal Practices: Territorial Variance Within Large Federal Democracies* (Baltimore, MD: Johns Hopkins University Press, 2016).
21. Edward L. Gibson, *Boundary Control: Subnational Authoritarianism in Federal Democracies* (Cambridge University Press, 2013).
22. Elisabeth Malkin, "Mexico's Attorney General Resigns Under Pressure," *New York Times*, October 16, 2017, https://www.nytimes.com/2017/10/16/world/americas/mexico-attorney-general-resigns.html.
23. Author interview with *Proceso* director Rafael Rodríguez, December 16, 2014.
24. See Gibson, *Boundary Control*.
25. Julián Durazo Herrmann, "Media and Subnational Democracy: The Case of Bahia, Brazil," *Democratization* 24, no. 1 (2017): 81–99; Celia del Palacio Montiel, "Periodismo impreso, poderes y violencia en Veracruz 2010–2014: Estrategias de control de la información," *Comunicación y Sociedad*, no. 24 (2015): 19–46, http://www.scielo.org.mx/pdf/comso/n24/n24a2.pdf.
26. Andreas Schedler, "The Menu of Manipulation," *Journal of Democracy* 13, no. 2 (2002): 36–50.
27. Benjamin T. Smith, *The Dope: The Real History of the Mexican Drug Trade* (New York: Norton, 2021).
28. Piero Stanig, "Regulation of Speech and Media Coverage of Corruption: An Empirical Analysis of the Mexican Press," *American Journal of Political Science* 59, no. 1 (2015): 175–93, https://doi.org/10.1111/ajps.12110; María Grisel Salazar Rebolledo, "Aliados estratégicos y los límites de la censura: El poder de las leyes para silenciar a la prensa," *Revista Mexicana de ciencias políticas y sociales* 64, no. 235 (2018): 495–522, http://www.scielo.org.mx/pdf/rmcps/v64n235/0185-1918-rmcps-64-235-495.pdf.

1. WHY HAS IT BECOME SO EASY TO KILL JOURNALISTS?

29. María Grisel Salazar Rebolledo, "¿Cooptar o reprimir? Intervenciones autoritarias sobre la prensa local mexicana," *América Latina hoy: Revista de ciencias sociales* 84 (2020): 117–36.
30. Marisa Kellam and Elizabeth A. Stein, "Silencing Critics: Why and How Presidents Restrict Media Freedom in Democracies," *Comparative Political Studies* 49, no. 1 (2016): 36–77.
31. Sallie L. Hughes and Mireya Márquez Ramírez, "Local-Level Authoritarianism, Democratic Normative Aspirations, and Antipress Harassment: Predictors of Threats to Journalists in Mexico," *International Journal of Press/Politics* 23, no. 4 (2018): 539–60.
32. Author interview with Ciudad Juárez Chihuahua, newspaper deputy director, January 22, 2016.
33. Author interview with journalist Ioan Grillo, September 10, 2015.
34. Andreas Schedler, *En la niebla de la guerra: Los ciudadanos ante la violencia criminal organizada* (Mexico City: CIDE, 2018).
35. Mary Kaldor, *New and Old Wars: Organised Violence in a Global Era* (Hoboken, NJ: John Wiley & Sons, 2013).
36. See Smith, *The Dope*.
37. Luis Astorga, *El siglo de las drogas: Del Porfiriato al nuevo milenio* (Mexico City: Debolsillo, 2016); Guillermo Valdés Castellanos, *Historia del narcotráfico en México* (Mexico City: Aguilar, 2013).
38. Guillermo Trejo and Sandra Ley, *Votes, Drugs, and Violence: The Political Logic of Criminal Wars in Mexico* (Cambridge: Cambridge University Press, 2020).
39. Richard Snyder and Angélica Durán Martínez, "Drugs, violence, and state-sponsored protection rackets in Mexico and Colombia," *Colombia Internacional*, no. 70 (2009): 61–91.
40. David Pérez Esparza, Carlos A. Perez Ricart, and Eugenio Weigend Vargas, *Gun Trafficking and Violence: From the Global Network to the Local Security Challenge* (London: Palgrave Macmillan, 2021).
41. Interview with Guadalajara, Jalisco, political journalist, January 16, 2016.
42. Eduardo Guerrero Gutiérrez, "Epidemias de violencia," *Nexos*, July 1, 2012, https://www.nexos.com.mx/?p=14884.
43. Eduardo Guerrero Gutiérrez, "La raíz de la violencia," *Nexos*, June 1, 2011, https://www.nexos.com.mx/?p=14318.
44. Author interview with a top executive, Mexico City, November 30, 2015.
45. Schedler, *En la niebla de la guerra*.
46. Shannan Mattiace and Sandra Ley, "Yucatán as an Exception to Rising Criminal Violence in México," *Journal of Politics in Latin America* 14, no. 1 (2022): 103–19.
47. Eduardo Guerrero Gutiérrez, "La segunda ola de violencia," *Nexos*, April 1, 2018, https://www.nexos.com.mx/?p=36947.
48. Saúl Hernández, "Las 5 cosas que no sabías y tienes que saber de la guerra en el periodo de Felipe Calderón," *Animal Político*, January 28, 2017, https://www.animalpolitico.com/2017/01/guerra-narco-calderon/.
49. Author interview with Sinaloa freelance reporter, December 16, 2015.

1. WHY HAS IT BECOME SO EASY TO KILL JOURNALISTS?

50. Julian Matthews and Kelechi Onyemaobi, "Precarious Professionalism: Journalism and the Fragility of Professional Practice in the Global South," *Journalism Studies* 21, no. 13 (2020): 1836–51.
51. Brian Creech, "Bearing the Cost to Witness: The Political Economy of Risk in Contemporary Conflict and War Reporting," *Media, Culture & Society* 40, no. 4 (2018): 567–83; Sallie L. Hughes et al., "Coping with Occupational Stress in Journalism: Professional Identities and Advocacy as Resources," *Journalism Studies* 22, no. 8 (2021): 971–91; Anthony Feinstein, "Mexican Journalists: An Investigation of Their Emotional Health," *Journal of Traumatic Stress* 25, no. 4 (2012): 480–83; Anthony Feinstein, "Mexican Journalists and Journalists Covering War: A Comparison of Psychological Wellbeing," *Journal of Aggression, Conflict, and Peace Research* 5, no. 2 (2013): 77–85, doi: http://dx.doi.org/10.1108/17596591311313672; Rogelio Flores Morales, Verónica Reyes Pérez, and Lucy María Reidl Martínez, "El impacto psicológico de la guerra contra el narcotráfico en periodistas mexicanos," *Revista Colombiana de psicología* 23, no. 1 (2014): 177–92.
52. Víctor Hugo Reyna García, "Más allá de la violencia: La incertidumbre laboral en el periodismo mexicano," *Sur le journalisme, About journalism, Sobre jornalismo* 7, no. 1 (2018): 98–113.
53. Arne L. Kalleberg, "Precarious Work, Insecure Workers: Employment Relations in Transition," *American Sociological Review* 74, no. 1 (2009): 1–22.
54. Matthews and Onyemaobi, "Precarious Professionalism," 1836–38.
55. Márquez Ramírez and Hughes, "Panorama de los perfiles demográficos."
56. Author interview with Michoacán local multimedia reporter, January 18, 2016.
57. Author interview with Estado de México police beat reporter, January 21, 2016.
58. Author interview with Guadalajara, Jalisco, correspondent January 27, 2016.
59. Author interview with Monterrey, Nuevo León, investigative journalist, January 27, 2016.
60. Author interview with investigative journalist and editor, December 8, 2015.
61. Author interview with Veracruz freelance journalist, January 29, 2016.
62. Jeannine E. Relly and Celeste González de Bustamante, "Global and Domestic Networks Advancing Prospects for Institutional and Social Change: The Collective Action Response to Violence Against Journalists," *Journalism & Communication Monographs* 19, no. 2 (2017): 84–152, https://doi.org/10.1177/1522637917702618.
63. Author interview with journalist Daniela Pastrana, December 30, 2014.
64. Author interview with journalist Daniela Pastrana.
65. Author interview with journalist from Durango, November 20, 2015.
66. Author interview with journalist from Durango.
67. Author interview with Sinaloa freelance journalist, December 16, 2015.
68. Author interview with Michoacán local multimedia reporter, January 18, 2016.
69. Daniel C. Hallin and Stylianos Papathanassopoulos, "Political Clientelism and the Media: Southern Europe and Latin America in Comparative Perspective," *Media, Culture & Society* 24, no. 2 (2002): 175–95.
70. Emily Edmonds-Poli, "The Effects of Drug-War Related Violence on Mexico's Press and Democracy," Wilson Center, April 2013, https://www.wilsoncenter.org/sites/default

1. WHY HAS IT BECOME SO EASY TO KILL JOURNALISTS?

/files/media/documents/publication/edmonds_violence_press.pdf; Jeannine E. Relly and Celeste González de Bustamante, "Silencing Mexico: A Study of Influences on Journalists in the Northern States," *International Journal of Press/Politics* 19, no. 1 (2014): 119.

71. Hallin and Papathanassopoulos, "Political Clientelism and the Media," 188–90; Natalia Roudakova, "Media—Political Clientelism: Lessons from Anthropology," *Media, Culture & Society* 30, no. 1 (2008): 41–59.
72. Author interview with columnist Julio Hernández López.
73. Author interview with editor Guillermo Osorno, November 29, 2021.
74. Author interview with Ciudad Juárez, Chihuahua, political journalist.
75. Andreas Schedler, "The Collapse of Solidarity in Criminal Civil War: Citizen Indifference Towards the Victims of Organized Violence in Mexico (2014)," APSA 2014 Annual Meeting Paper, available at SSRN: https://ssrn.com/abstract=2454202.
76. Author interview with Michoacán national correspondent, January 8, 2016.
77. Author interview with Oaxaca journalist, December 14, 2015.
78. Schedler, *En la niebla de la guerra*.
79. Celeste González de Bustamante and Jeannine E. Relly, "Professionalism Under Threat of Violence: Journalism, Reflexivity, and the Potential for Collective Professional Autonomy in Northern Mexico," *Journalism Studies* 17, no. 6 (2016): 684–702.
80. Katherine Fink, "The Biggest Challenge Facing Journalism: A Lack of Trust," *Journalism* 20, no. 1 (2019): 40–43.

2. THE WAVE OF VIOLENCE AGAINST THE PRESS

1. Author interview national correspondent Erick Muñiz in Nuevo León, January 28, 2016.
2. Julieta Alejandra Brambila and Sallie L. Hughes, "Violence Against Journalists," in *The International Encyclopedia of Journalism Studies*, ed. Tim. P. Vos and Folker Hanusch (Hoboken, NJ: Wiley-Blackwell, 2019), 1–9.
3. Silvio Waisbord, "Mob Censorship: Online Harassment of U.S. Journalists in Times of Digital Hate and Populism," *Digital Journalism* 8, no. 8 (2020): 1030–46.
4. John Nerone, *Violence Against the Press: Policing the Public Sphere in U.S. History* (New York: Oxford University Press, 1994), 215.
5. Author interview with investigative journalist Marco Lara Klahr, December 22, 2015.
6. Laura Y. Calderón, "An Analysis of Mayoral Assassinations in Mexico, 2000–17," Global Initiative Against Transnational Organized Crime, January 15, 2018, https://globalinitiative.net/analysis/an-analysis-of-mayoral-assassinations-in-mexico-2000-17/.
7. Patricia Bartley, Erick Monterrosas, and Paola Pacheco Ruiz, "Resisting a Hostile and Insecure Environment for Defending Rights in Mexico," in *Protecting Human Rights Defenders at Risk*, ed. Alice M. Nah (London: Routledge, 2020), 104–29.
8. Although many journalists who cover armed conflicts have lost their lives in the crossfire as the result of their work in the field, researchers like Professor Chris Paterson from

2. THE WAVE OF VIOLENCE AGAINST THE PRESS

the University of Leeds argue that during the Iraq invasion, some journalists and media outlets, such as the Qatar television broadcaster Al Jazeera, have become military targets themselves because they are perceived as "the enemy." Chris Paterson, *War Reporters Under Threat: The United States and Media Freedom* (London: Pluto Press, 2014).

9. Jos Midas Bartman, "Murder in Mexico: Are Journalists Victims of General Violence or Targeted Political Violence?," *Democratization* 25, no. 7 (2018): 1093–1113; Terry Gould, *Matar a un periodista: El peligroso oficio de informar* (Barcelona: Los libros del Lince, 2010).

10. Reporteros Sin Fronteras, "Un periodista dado por desaparecido," January 20, 2016, https://rsf.org/es/un-periodista-dado-por-desaparecido.

11. "Tamaulipas: Qué es la 'zona silenciada' de México y por qué la ONU exige la atención del gobierno," *BBC*, June 2, 2018, https://www.bbc.com/mundo/noticias-america-latina-44338586.

12. "Ataques contra medios con explosivos o armas de fuego," Artículo 19, August 4, 2015, https://articulo19.org/ataques-contra-medios-con-explosivos-o-armas-de-fuego/.

13. "Lanzan Granada a Instalaciones de Periódico en Coahuila," Artículo 19, July 21, 2011, https://articulo19.org/lanzan-granada-a-instalaciones-de-periodico-en-coahuila/.

14. "En México, 24 periodistas permanecen desaparecidos," Artículo 19, January 23, 2018, https://articulo19.org/periodistasdesaparecidos/.

15. Agencia de los Estados Unidos para el Desarrollo Internacional, "Desplazamiento Forzado de periodistas en la Ciudad de México," Comisión de Derechos Humanos de la Ciudad de México, January 13, 2021, https://cdhcm.org.mx/wp-content/uploads/2021/01/13.-Diagnostico-CDMX-Digital.pdf.

16. Sallie L. Hughes and Mireya Márquez Ramírez, "Examining the Practices that Mexican Journalists Employ to Reduce Risk in a Context of Violence," *International Journal of Communication*, no. 11 (2017): 499–521.

17. Anthony Feinstein, "Mexican Journalists: An Investigation of Their Emotional Health," *Journal of Traumatic Stress* 25, no. 4 (2012): 480–83; Rogelio Flores Morales, Verónica Reyes Pérez, and Lucy María Reidl Martínez, "El impacto psicológico de la guerra contra el narcotráfico en periodistas mexicanos," *Revista Colombiana de psicología* 23, no. 1 (2014): 177–92; Sallie L. Hughes et al., "Coping with Occupational Stress in Journalism: Professional Identities and Advocacy as Resources," *Journalism Studies* 22, no. 8 (2021): 971–91.

18. Hughes et al., "Coping with Occupational Stress in Journalism," 972–80.

19. Flores Morales, Reyes Pérez, and Reidl Martínez, "El impacto psicológico," 183–88.

20. Anthony Feinstein, "Mexican Journalists and Journalists Covering War: A Comparison of Psychological Wellbeing," *Journal of Aggression, Conflict, and Peace Research* 5, no. 2 (2013): 77–85, http://dx.doi.org/10.1108/17596591311313672.

21. Feinstein, "Mexican Journalists: An Investigation of Their Emotional Health," 482.

22. Author interview with attorney and activist Víctor Ruiz Arrazola, November 17, 2015.

23. Silvio Waisbord, "Democratic Journalism and 'Statelessness,'" *Political Communication* 24, no. 2 (2007): 115–29.

24. Author interview with Veracruz journalist, January 12, 2016.

2. THE WAVE OF VIOLENCE AGAINST THE PRESS

25. Parametría, "Estudio completo sobre Libertad de Prensa y Periodismo en México," February 7, 2018, http://www.parametria.com.mx/estudios/estudio-completo-sobre-libertad-de-prensa-y-periodismo-en-mexico/.
26. Author interview with human rights defense attorney Edgar Cortez, September 23, 2015.
27. Andreas Schedler, *En la niebla de la guerra. Los ciudadanos ante la violencia criminal organizada* (Mexico City: CIDE, 2018).
28. Author interview with journalist, January 28, 2016.
29. Author interview with analyst and academic researcher Sergio Aguayo, November 17, 2015.
30. Julieta Alejandra Brambila and Jairo Alfonso Lugo-Ocando, "Lobbying for Life: Violence Against the Press and the Public Interest," in *Public Interest Communication Critical Debates and Global Contexts*, ed. Jane Johnston and Magda Pieczka (Routledge, 2018), 192–209.
31. Salvador de León Vázquez and Rubén Arnoldo González Macías, "Reportear en el desamparo: Análisis de las medidas de protección a periodistas en México desde el contexto local," *Revista de comunicación* 19, no. 2 (2020): 87–109, http://www.scielo.org.pe/pdf/rcudep/v19n2/2227-1465-rcudep-19-02-87.pdf.
32. Author interview with analyst and academic researcher Sergio Aguayo.
33. Julieta Alejandra Brambila, "Informe 2018, Avances y tareas pendientes para el fortalecimiento de la libertad de expresión en México," CASEDE, September 2018, https://www.casede.org/index.php/biblioteca-casede-2-0/periodismo-y-libertad-de-expresion/70-informe-libertad-de-expresion-2018/file
34. Author interview with high-ranking Secretaría de Gobernación official, November 27, 2015.
35. Author interview with high-ranking Secretaría de Gobernación official.
36. Celeste González de Bustamante and Jeannine E. Relly, "Global Domestic Networks Advancing Prospects for Institutional and Social Change: The Collective Action Response to Violence Against Journalists," *Journalism & Communication Monographs* 19, no. 2 (2017): 84–152, https://doi.org/10.1177/1522637917702618.
37. Brambila, "Informe 2018."
38. Author interview with high-ranking Secretaría de Gobernación official.
39. Brambila, "Informe 2018."
40. Author interview with Edgar Cortez.
41. Brambila, "Informe 2018."
42. Author interview with national correspondent Erick Muñiz in Nuevo León, January 28, 2016.
43. Author interview with an investigative journalist from Monterrey, Nuevo León, January 27, 2016.
44. Author interview with an investigative journalist from Monterrey, Nuevo León.
45. Author interview with Emilio Lugo, displaced investigative journalist, September 19, 2015.
46. Author interview with high-ranking Secretaría de Gobernación official.
47. Author interview with Emilio Lugo.

2. THE WAVE OF VIOLENCE AGAINST THE PRESS

48. Author interview with high-ranking Secretaría de Gobernación official.
49. Reporteros Sin Fronteras, "Asesinato de Rubén Pat: 'Las autoridades mexicanas no protegieron lo suficiente al periodista,'" July 24, 2018, https://rsf.org/es/asesinato-de-rubén-pat-las-autoridades-mexicanas-no-protegieron-lo-suficiente-al-periodista.
50. Author interview with Edgar Cortez.
51. "El caso Narvarte, la verdad como 'exquisitez,'" Artículo 19, July 2019, https://articulo19.org/wp-content/uploads/2019/07/A19-La_verdad_como_exquisitez-04-v3-WEB.pdf.
52. "Protocolo de la Impunidad en Delitos contra Periodistas," Artículo 19, February 25, 2019, https://articulo19.org/informeimpunidad/.
53. Edward L. Gibson, *Boundary Control: Subnational Authoritarianism in Federal Democracies* (Cambridge: Cambridge University Press, 2013).
54. Author interview with activist Balbina Flores, November 18, 2014.
55. Brambila and Lugo-Ocando, "Lobbying for Life."
56. "Por qué en México es tan fácil matar y nunca pisar la cárcel," *BBC*, July 4, 2018, https://www.bbc.com/mundo/noticias-america-latina-44681164.
57. Author interview with high-ranking PGR official, December 9, 2015.
58. Author interview with attorney and activist Víctor Ruiz Arrazola.
59. Artículo 19, "9 años de impunidad para Moisés Sánchez y su familia: ¡Basta ya!" Artículo 19, January 24, 2024, https://articulo19.org/9-anos-de-impunidad-para-moises-sanchez-y-su-familia-basta-ya/.
60. Author interview with high-ranking official from the CNDH, October 2, 2015.
61. Author interview with investigative journalist Marco Lara Klahr.
62. Artículo 19, "Protocolo de la Impunidad."
63. Brambila, "Informe 2018."
64. Brambila, "Informe 2018."
65. Author interview with Monterrey, Nuevo León, freelance reporter, January 22, 2016.
66. Author interview with *Proceso* director Rafael Rodríguez, December 16, 2014.
67. Author interview with *Proceso* director Rafael Rodríguez.
68. Celeste González de Bustamante and Jeannine E. Relly, *Surviving Mexico: Resistance and Resilience Among Journalists in the Twenty-First Century* (Austin: University of Texas Press, 2021).
69. Author interview with Veracruz crime-beat reporter, December 10, 2015.
70. Benjamin T. Smith, "The Paradoxes of the Public Sphere: Journalism, Gender, and Corruption in Mexico, 1940–70," *Journal of Social History* 52, no. 4 (2019): 1330–54.
71. Anabel Hernández, *El Traidor: El diario secreto del hijo del Mayo* (Mexico City: Penguin Random House, 2019); "La casa blanca de Enrique Peña Nieto (investigación especial)," *Aristegui Noticias*, November 9, 2014, https://aristeguinoticias.com/0911/mexico/la-casa-blanca-de-enrique-pena-nieto/; Daniela Rea, *Nadie les pidió perdón: Historias de impunidad y resistencia* (Barcelona: Ediciones Urano, 2019); Lydia Cacho, *Los demonios del Edén. El poder que protege a la pornografía infantil* (Mexico City: Debolsillo, 2017); Marcela Turati, *Fuego cruzado: Las víctimas atrapadas en la guerra del narco* (Mexico City: Grijalbo, 2011).

2. THE WAVE OF VIOLENCE AGAINST THE PRESS

72. Comunicación e Información de la Mujer A. C., "Informe: Violencia contra Mujeres Periodistas 2012–2018," CIMAC, November 2019, https://cimac.org.mx/wp-content/uploads/2019/11/Herenciadeunsexenio-1.pdf.
73. According to data from Artículo 19 Mexico, from 2006 to 2016, 105 homicides were registered, of which 8 were women and 97 were men. "Periodistas asesinadas/os en México, en relación con su labor informativa," Artículo 19, https://articulo19.org/periodistasasesinados/.
74. Such was the case of the murder of journalist Anabel Flores, who after her death in 2016 was smeared by allegations that she was in a romantic relationship with "a drug lord." Leopoldo Maldonado, "El delito de ser víctima," *Horizontal*, February 23, 2016.
75. Natalia Roudakova, "Journalism as 'Prostitution': Understanding Russia's Reactions to Anna Politkovskaya's Murder," *Political Communication* 26, no. 4 (2009): 412–29.
76. Jenaro Villamil, "Filtran versión de que asesinato de Regina Martínez fue 'pasional,'" *Proceso*, June 23, 2012, https://www.proceso.com.mx/nacional/2012/6/23/filtran-version-de-que-asesinato-de-regina-martinez-fue-pasional-104649.html.
77. Dana Priest et al., "A Murder in Veracruz: Slain Journalist's Story a Portrait of a Violent, Corrupt Era in Mexico," *Washington Post*, December 6, 2020, https://www.washingtonpost.com/graphics/2020/investigations/regina-martinez-mexican-journalist-murdered-veracruz/.
78. Lydia Cacho, *Memorias de una infamia* (Mexico City: Debolsillo, 2010), 91.
79. Comunicación e Información de la Mujer A. C., "Informe: Violencia contra mujeres periodistas."
80. Comunicación e Información de la Mujer A. C., "Informe: Violencia contra mujeres periodistas."
81. Azucena Rangel, "Incorporando la perspectiva de género en los mecanismos de protección a periodistas en México, Irán, y Afganistán," *Milenio*, May 3, 2021, https://www.milenio.com/politica/mujeres-periodistas-victimas-7-tipos-violencia-unesco.
82. Brambila and Hughes, "Violence Against Journalists."
83. Laura Iesue et al., "Risk, Victimization, and Coping Strategies of Journalists in Mexico and Brazil," *Sur le journalisme, About Journalism, Sobre jornalismo* 10, no. 1 (2021): 62.
84. Laurel Miranda, "Feminismo transfóbico + psicología = 'terapias de conversión,'" *Homosensual*, March 4, 2021, https://www.homosensual.com/lgbt/trans/feminismo-transfobico-psicologia-terapias-de-conversion/.
85. Instituto Nacional de Estadística y Geografía, "Estadísticas a propósito del día internacional de la eliminación de la discriminación racial," press release, March 19, 2020, https://www.inegi.org.mx/contenidos/saladeprensa/aproposito/2020/DISCRIMINAC_NAL.pdf.
86. Author interview with journalist Ioan Grillo, September 10, 2015.
87. Committee to Protect Journalists, "Pedro Canché: 272 Days in Prison," CPJ, https://cpj.org/campaigns/pressuncuffed/pedro-canche/.
88. Guadalupe Lizárraga, "Policías de Tlapa golpean a periodista de *Los Ángeles Press*," *Zapateando*, May 15, 2013, https://zapateando.wordpress.com/2013/05/15/policias-de-tlapa-golpean-a-periodista-de-los-angeles-press/.

2. THE WAVE OF VIOLENCE AGAINST THE PRESS

89. Author interview with Michoacán journalist Antonio Ramos, December 22, 2015.
90. Author interview with Michoacán journalist Antonio Ramos.
91. Raúl Zepeda Gil, "Violencia en Tierra Caliente: Desigualdad, desarrollo y escolaridad en la guerra contra el narcotráfico," *Estudios sociológicos* 36, no. 106 (2018): 125–59.
92. Author interview with Michoacán journalist Antonio Ramos.
93. Nuestra aparente rendición, "José Antonio García Apac," 2012, http://www.nuestraaparenterendicion.com/tuyyocoincidimosenlanocheterrible/index.php/component/k2/item/60-jose-antonio-garcia-apac#.YVUa_2aA4-Q.
94. Author interview with Michoacán local multimedia reporter, January 18, 2016.
95. Author interview with investigative journalist Marco Lara Klahr.
96. Hughes and Márquez Ramírez, "Examining the Practices"; Frida Viridiana Rodelo, "Periodismo en entornos violentos: El caso de los periodistas de Culiacán, Sinaloa," *Comunicación y sociedad*, no. 12 (2009): 101–18.
97. Violeta Alejandra Santiago Hernández, "Análisis del impacto de la violencia en la situación económica y el ejercicio de la libertad de expresión en un grupo de periodistas veracruzanos," *Anuario de Investigación CONEICC* 1, no. 27 (2020): 22–37; Norma Trujillo Báez, "El crimen de Regina Martínez: El teatro de la justicia," IPYS, https://impunidad.ipys.org/pages/historias/regina-martinez.html; Paloma Dupont de Dinechin, "Regina Martínez: Tras los pasos de una verdad enterrada," *Forbidden Stories*, https://forbiddenstories.org/es/regina-martinez-sur-les-traces-dune-verite-enterree/.
98. Celeste González de Bustamante and Jeannine E. Relly, "Professionalism Under Threat of Violence: Journalism, Reflexivity, and the Potential for Collective Professional Autonomy in Northern Mexico," *Journalism Studies* 17, no. 6 (2016): 684–702.
99. Author interview with Guerrero investigative journalist, September 20, 2015.
100. Daniel C. Hallin and Paolo Mancini, *Comparing Media Systems: Three Models of Media and Politics* (Cambridge: Cambridge University Press, 2004).
101. Robert David Sack, *Human Territoriality: Its Theory and History* (Cambridge: Cambridge University Press, 1986).
102. Nerone, *Violence Against the Press*, 213.
103. Julieta Alejandra Brambila, "Forced Silence: Determinants of Journalist Killings in Mexico's States, 2010–2015," *Journal of Information Policy*, no. 7 (2017): 297–326.
104. Brambila, "Forced Silence," 299–307.
105. Javier Garza Ramos, "Violencia contra periodistas en México: De norte a sur," *El País*, July 6, 2015, https://elpais.com/internacional/2015/07/07/actualidad/1436232886_933931.html
106. "Informe 2009: Entre la Violencia y la Indiferencia," Artículo 19, July 3, 2012, https://articulo19.org/informe-2009-entre-la-violencia-y-la-indiferencia/.
107. Author interview with Rodrigo González, Artículo 19, November 28, 2014.
108. Francisco Goldman, "Who Killed Rubén Espinosa and Nadia Vera?," *New Yorker*, August 14, 2015, https://www.newyorker.com/news/news-desk/who-killed-ruben-espinosa-and-nadia-vera.
109. Author interview with investigative journalist and editor, December 8, 2015.

3. VIOLENT CENSORS

1. Author interview with a journalist and cofounder of *Revista Ríodoce* in Sinaloa, December 10, 2015.
2. John Nerone, *Violence Against the Press: Policing the Public Sphere in U.S. History* (New York: Oxford University Press, 1994), 214.
3. Robert Darnton, "Censorship, A Comparative View: France, 1789–East Germany, 1989," *Representations*, no. 49 (1995): 40–60.
4. Chappel Lawson, *Building the Fourth Estate: Democratization and Media Opening in Mexico* (Stanford University, 1999); Sallie L. Hughes, *Newsrooms in Conflict: Journalism and the Democratization of Mexico* (Pittsburgh: University of Pittsburgh Press, 2006).
5. Miguel Ángel Granados, *Examen de la comunicación en México* (Mexico City: El Caballito, 1981).
6. Benjamin T. Smith, *The Mexican Press and Civil Society, 1940–1976: Stories from the Newsroom, Stories from the Street* (University of North Carolina Press, 2018), 281.
7. Nerone, *Violence Against the Press*, 214.
8. Author interview with Morelia, Michoacán, investigative journalist Francisco Castellanos, December 14, 2015.
9. María Grisel Salazar Rebolledo, "Ejercer el periodismo en entornos violentos: Análisis empírico de las zonas de silencio en México," *Perfiles Latinoamericanos* 29, no. 58 (2021), dx.doi.org/10.18504/pl2958-001-2021.
10. Author interview with Ciudad Juárez, Chihuahua, newspaper deputy director, January 22, 2016; Luz del Carmen Sosa, "Nadie investiga el asesinato de fotógrafo de *El Diario*," *El Diario*, September 16, 2012, https://diario.mx/Local/2012-09-16_ac5b8680/nadie-investiga-el-asesinato—de-fotografo-de-el-diario/.
11. Author interview with Secretaría de Gobernación analyst, November 2015.
12. Stathis N. Kalyvas, *The Logic of Violence in Civil War* (Cambridge: Cambridge University Press, 2006), 24.
13. Christian Bjørnskov and Andreas Freytag, "An Offer You Can't Refuse: Murdering Journalists as an Enforcement Mechanism of Corrupt Deals," *Public Choice* 167, no. 3 (2016): 221–43; Marisa Kellam and Elizabeth A. Stein, "Silencing Critics: Why and How Presidents Restrict Media Freedom in Democracies," *Comparative Political Studies* 49, no. 1 (2016): 36–77.
14. Bradley E. Holland and Viridiana Ríos, "Informally Governing Information: How Criminal Rivalry Leads to Violence Against the Press in Mexico," *Journal of Conflict Resolution* 61, no. 5 (2017): 1095–1119; Edgar Guerra, "Crueldad y brutalidad en las formas de morir de los periodistas en México: Una aproximación desde la microsociología," *Sociológica* 34, no. 97 (2019): 215–47.
15. Holland and Ríos, "Informally Governing Information."
16. Smith, *The Mexican Press and Civil Society*; Kevin G. Barnhurst, "Contemporary Terrorism in Peru: Sendero Luminous and the Media," *Journal of Communication* 41, no. 4

3. VIOLENT CENSORS

(1991): 75–89. If we make a historical comparison between the period of electoral authoritarianism and contemporary Mexico, the main censors of the press are very similar. The British historian Benjamin Smith documented the murders of around 20 journalists from 1940 to 1960 and 189 violent attacks against journalists and local communications media. The perpetrators of these attacks, in over half of the cases, as we find today, were politicians and public servants. Moreover, during those years, regional actors wielding power constantly attacked the press as criminal cells and radical social groups do today. The main motive of these aggressions then and now was to exclude from the public arena information that would harm the personal reputation or indicate acts of corruption and abuse of power. Smith, *The Mexican Press and Civil Society*.

17. Waisbord, "Mob Censorship."
18. "Democracia Simulada: Nada que aplaudir. Informe 2017," Artículo 19, March 20, 2018, https://articulo19.org/wp-content/uploads/2018/03/INFORME-A19-2017_v04.pdf.
19. José Luis Ortiz Garza, "Mercenary Writers of British Propaganda in Mexico During the Second World War" (5th International Conference for Literary Journalism, Roehampton University, London, May 21, 2009).
20. They are also known as community police. Antonio Fuentes Díaz and Guillermo Paleta Pérez, "Violencia y autodefensas comunitarias en Michoacán, México," *Iconos: Revista de ciencias sociales*, no. 53 (2015): 171–86.
21. Author interview with Michoacán journalist Antonio Ramos, December 22, 2015.
22. Author interview with *Noroeste* newspaper deputy director, January 8, 2016.
23. Author interview with *Noroeste* newspaper deputy director.
24. Author interview with attorney and activist Víctor Ruiz Arrazola, November 17, 2015.
25. Artículo 19 and Justice for Journalists and Fundación para la Libertad de Prensa, "Leyes del silencio: Acoso judicial contra la libertad de expresión en México y Colombia," Artículo 19, May 3, 2021, https://articulo19.org/wp-content/uploads/2021/05/INFORME-LEYES-DEL-SILENCIO.pdf.
26. Piero Stanig, "Regulation of Speech and Media Coverage of Corruption: An Empirical Analysis of the Mexican Press," *American Journal of Political Science* 59, no. 1 (2015): 175–93, https://doi.org/10.1111/ajps.12110.
27. "Así te espía el gobierno en internet," Artículo 19, July 23, 2015, https://articulo19.org/asi-te-espia-el-gobierno-en-internet/.
28. Artículo 19, Red en Defensa de los Derechos Digitales, and Social TIC, "Gobierno Espía: Vigilancia sistemática a periodistas y defensores de derechos humanos en México," R3D, June 2017, https://r3d.mx/wp-content/uploads/GOBIERNO-ESPIA-2017.pdf.
29. Author interview with Oaxaca national newspaper investigative journalist, January 9, 2016.
30. Author interview with investigative journalist from Monterrey, Nuevo León, January 27, 2016.
31. Author interview with Sinaloa freelance journalist, December 7, 2015.
32. Interview with local journalist from Guerrero, December 11, 2015.

3. VIOLENT CENSORS

33. Reporteros Sin Fronteras, "Elecciones en México, manchadas por la violencia contra periodistas," January 20, 2016, https://rsf.org/es/noticias/elecciones-en-mexico-manchadas-por-la-violencia-contra-periodistas.
34. Bjørnskov and Freytag, "An Offer You Can't Refuse"; Silvio Waisbord, *Watchdog Journalism in South America: News, Accountability, and Democracy* (New York: Columbia University Press, 2000); Smith, *The Mexican Press and Civil Society*; Victor Asal et al., "Killing the Messenger: Regime Type as a Determinant of Journalist Killing, 1992–2008," *Foreign Policy Analysis* 14, no. 1 (2018): 24–43.
35. Salazar Rebolledo, "Ejercer el periodismo en entornos violentos."
36. Author interview with Estado de México journalist, January 14, 2016.
37. This is commonly accomplished by journalists of a certain prestige through books and feature articles; well-established independent reporters and columnists in traditional media outlets (such as *Reforma, El Universal, Proceso, El País, Zeta*); digital initiatives with a public, critical vocation, such as *Aristegui Noticias, Sin Embargo, Animal Político,* and *Ríodoce*; or civic collectives with a journalistic vocation, such as Quinto Elemento, Pie de Página, and others. As in other countries, the role of leaks and inter-elite conflicts, as well as editorial backing and group work, are crucial to these publications.
38. Author interview with Guadalajara, Jalisco, political journalist, January 16, 2016.
39. Salazar, "Ejercer el periodismo en entornos violentos"; Sallie L. Hughes and Yulia Vorobyeva, "Explaining the Killing of Journalists in the Contemporary Era: The Importance of Hybrid Regimes and Subnational Variations," *Journalism* 22, no. 8 (2021): 1873–91.
40. Author interview with local multimedia reporter in Michoacán, January 18, 2016.
41. Author interview with local multimedia reporter in Michoacán.
42. Author interview with Ciudad Victoria, Tamaulipas, police reporter, December 10, 2015.
43. Author interview with Ciudad Victoria, Tamaulipas, newspaper information chief January 12, 2016.
44. Guerra, "Crueldad y brutalidad," 234, 238–39.
45. Author interview with U.S. investigative journalist in Mexico City, September 15, 2015.
46. Holland and Ríos, "Informally Governing Information," 1112–1115.
47. Julieta Alejandra Brambila, "Forced Silence: Determinants of Journalist Killings in Mexico's States, 2010–2015," *Journal of Information Policy*, no. 7 (2017): 297–326.
48. Frida Viridiana Rodelo, "Periodismo en entornos violentos: El caso de los periodistas de Culiacán, Sinaloa," *Comunicación y sociedad*, no. 12 (2009): 101–18; Jeannine E. Relly and Celeste González de Bustamante, "Silencing Mexico: A Study of Influences on Journalists in the Northern States," *International Journal of Press/Politics* 19, no. 1 (2014): 119.
49. Author interview with Ciudad Juárez, Chihuahua, multimedia reporter, December 11, 2015.
50. Author interview with Ciudad Victoria, Tamaulipas, newspaper information chief, January 12, 2016.
51. Author interview with *El Siglo de Torreón* editorial director Javier Garza Ramos, September 24, 2015.

4. STRATEGIES FOR AUTONOMOUS SAFETY

52. "El narco calla a los periódicos del norte," *Proceso*, March 19, 2013, https://www.proceso.com.mx/reportajes/2013/3/19/el-narco-calla-los-periodicos-del-norte-115840.html.
53. Author interview with *El Siglo de Torreón* editorial director Javier Garza Ramos.
54. Author interview with Tampico, Tamaulipas, political reporter, December 4, 2015.
55. Author interview with columnist Julio Hernández López, September 10, 2015.
56. Author interview with Tampico, Tamaulipas, political reporter.
57. Interview with Ciudad Juárez, Chihuahua, investigative journalist, January 16, 2016.
58. Sin Embargo, "Agrupaciones de periodistas en Juárez denuncian ataques sistemáticos de la policía de Julián Leyzaola," February 12, 2012, https://www.sinembargo.mx/12-02-2012/148078.
59. Gloria Leticia Díaz, "Las víctimas de Leyzaola claman justicia," *Proceso*, June 1, 2019, https://www.proceso.com.mx/reportajes/2019/6/1/las-victimas-de-leyzaola-claman-justicia-225756.html.
60. Author interview with Veracruz freelance journalist, January 29, 2016.
61. Smith, *The Mexican Press and Civil Society*; Pablo A. Piccato, "Murders of Nota Roja: Truth and Justice in Mexican Crime News," *Past and Present* 223, no. 1 (2014): 195–231; Daniel C. Hallin, "Nota Roja," in *Tabloid Tales: Global Debates Over Media Standards*, ed. Collin Sparks and John Tulloch (Lanham, MD: Rowman & Littlefield, 2000).
62. Author interview with journalist and activist Dario Fritz, December 9, 2015.
63. Author interview with journalist in Jalisco, January 28, 2016.
64. Author interview with Estado de México crime-beat journalist, January 21, 2016.
65. World Justice Project, "Cuánta tortura: Prevalencia de violencia ilegal en el proceso penal mexicano 2006–2016," 2019, https://worldjusticeproject.mx/wp-content/uploads/2019/11/GIZ-Reporte_Cuánta-Tortura.pdf.
66. Brambila, "Forced Silence," 317.
67. Author interview with Guerrero investigative journalist, September 20, 2015.
68. Author interview with Oaxaca national newspaper investigative journalist, January 9, 2016.
69. Fernando I. Salmerón Castro, "Caciques: Una revisión teórica sobre el control político local," *Revista Mexicana de ciencias políticas y sociales* 30, nos. 117–18 (1984).
70. Will G. Pansters, "Drug Trafficking, the Informal Order, and Caciques: Reflections on the Crime-Governance Nexus in Mexico," *Global Crime* 19, nos. 3–4 (2018): 315–38.
71. Author interview with Estado de México journalist, January 14, 2016.
72. Author interview with Michoacán correspondent, January 8, 2016.
73. Author interview with Michoacán correspondent, January 8, 2016.
74. Author interview with Michoacán correspondent, January 8, 2016.

4. STRATEGIES FOR AUTONOMOUS SAFETY

1. Author interview with Monterrey, Nuevo León, investigative journalist, January 27, 2016.
2. Author interview with Monterrey, Nuevo León, investigative journalist.

4. STRATEGIES FOR AUTONOMOUS SAFETY

3. Melva Frutos, "Cómo hacer coberturas de alto riesgo en la frontera," Border Center for Journalist and Bloggers, September 1, 2021, https://www.bordercenter.net/es/blog/entrevista-juan-cedillo/.
4. Author interview with Monterrey, Nuevo León, investigative journalist.
5. Séverine Durin, "Periodismo bajo fuego. Métodos letales de coacción de la prensa durante la guerra contra el narcotráfico," Encartes 2, no. 3, (2019): 82–111, https://encartes.mx/coaccion-prensa-narcotrafico/.
6. Author interview with Monterrey, Nuevo León, investigative journalist.
7. Robin Vandevoordt, "Why Journalists Covered Syria the Way They Did: On the Role of Economic, Social, and Cultural Capital," *Journalism* 18, no. 5 (2017): 609–25.
8. Author interview with former Sinaloa deputy director of radio station, December 9, 2015.
9. This is a pattern that different researchers have discovered among journalists who work under conditions of extreme risk, including Rosemary J. Novak and Sarah Davidson, "Journalists Reporting on Hazardous Events: Constructing Protective Factors Within the Professional Role," *Traumatology* 19, no. 4 (2013): 313–22; Magdalena Obermaier, Michaela Hofbauer and Carsten Reinemann, "Journalists as Targets of Hate Speech: How German Journalists Perceive the Consequences for Themselves and How They Cope with It," *SCM Studies in Communication and Media* 7, no. 4 (2018): 499–524; Mark Pearson et al., "Building Journalists' Resilience Through Mindfulness Strategies," *Journalism* 22, no. 7 (2021): 1647–64; and Sallie L. Hughes et al., "Coping with Occupational Stress in Journalism: Professional Identities and Advocacy as Resources," *Journalism Studies* 22, no. 8 (2021): 971–91. In this sense, the strategies for autonomous safety analyzed here are very similar to the counterstrategies to resist self-censorship that researchers Marta Milena and Toby Miller found among a group of Colombian journalists. Marta Milena Barrios and Toby Miller, "Voices of Resilience: Colombian Journalists and Self-Censorship in the Post-Conflict Period," *Journalism Practice* 15, no. 10 (2021): 1423–40.
10. Noha Mellor, "Strategies for Autonomy: Arab Journalists Reflecting on Their Roles," *Journalism Studies* 10, no. 3 (2009): 307–21.
11. Vera Slavtcheva-Petkova et al., "Conceptualizing Journalists' Safety Around the Globe," *Digital Journalism* 11, no. 7 (2023): 1211–29.
12. Piers Robinson et al., *Pockets of Resistance: British News Media, War, and Theory in the 2003 Invasion of Iraq* (Manchester: Manchester University Press, 2010).
13. Joao Ozawa et al., "Attacks Against Journalists in Brazil: Catalyzing Effects and Resilience During Jair Bolsonaro's Government," *International Journal of Press/Politics*, July 6, 2023, https://doi.org/10.1177/19401612231182618.
14. Thomas F. Gieryn, "Boundary-Work and the Demarcation of Science from Non-Science: Strains and Interests in Professional Ideologies of Scientists," *American Sociological Review* 48, no. 6 (1983): 781–95.
15. Jeannine Relly and Celeste González de Bustamante, "Global and Domestic Networks Advancing Prospects for Institutional and Social Change: The Collective Action Response to Violence Against Journalists," *Journalism & Communication Monographs*

4. STRATEGIES FOR AUTONOMOUS SAFETY

19, no. 2 (2017): 84–152, https://doi.org/10.1177/1522637917702618; Julieta Alejandra Brambila and Jairo Alfonso Lugo-Ocando, "Lobbying for Life: Violence Against the Press and the Public Interest," in *Public Interest Communication Critical Debates and Global Contexts*, ed. Jane Johnston and Magda Pieczka (London: Routledge, 2018), 192–209.
16. Author interview with national correspondent based in Michoacán, January 8, 2016.
17. Author interview with Michoacán national correspondent.
18. Author interview with Michoacán national correspondent.
19. A broad catalog of these is compiled in Celeste González de Bustamante and Jeannine E. Relly, *Surviving Mexico: Resistance and Resilience Among Journalists in the Twenty-First Century* (Austin: University of Texas Press, 2021).
20. Author interview with police reporter, Ciudad Victoria, Tamaulipas, December 10, 2015.
21. Author interview with Ciudad Victoria, Tamaulipas, police reporter.
22. Janet Harris and Kevin Williams, *Reporting War and Conflict* (London: Routledge, 2018).
23. Sallie L. Hughes and Mireya Márquez Ramírez, "How Unsafe Contexts and Overlapping Risks Influence Journalism Practice. Evidence from a Survey of Mexican journalists," in *The Assault on Journalism: Building Knowledge to Protect Freedom of Expression*, ed. Ulla Carlsson and Reeta Pöyhtäri (Gothenburg, Sweden: Nordicom, Gothenburg University, 2017), 311, http://www.unesco.se/wp-content/uploads/2017/04/The-Assault-on-Journalism.pdf.
24. Author interview with Sinaloa journalist and digital magazine director, December 10, 2015.
25. Author interview with Sinaloa journalist and digital magazine director.
26. Author interview with Ciudad Juárez, Chihuahua, investigative journalist, January 16, 2016.
27. Author interview with *Noroeste* newspaper deputy director, January 8, 2016.
28. Hughes and Márquez Ramírez, "How Unsafe Contexts," 307.
29. Author interview with Guadalajara, Jalisco, national newspaper crime-beat journalist, January 26, 2016.
30. Author interview with Guadalajara, Jalisco, national newspaper crime-beat journalist.
31. Author interview with local Guerrero journalist, December 11, 2015.
32. Author interview with Morelia, Michoacán, investigative journalist Francisco Castellanos, December 14, 2015.
33. Author interview with Oaxaca national newspaper investigative journalist, January 9, 2016.
34. Author interview with U.S. investigative journalist in Mexico City, September 15, 2015.
35. Ioan Grillo is the author of several books on this topic: *Blood Gun Money: How America Arms Gangs and Cartels* (New York: Bloomsbury, 2021); *El Narco: Inside Mexico's Criminal Insurgency* (New York: Bloomsbury, 2011); *Gangster Warlords: Drug Dollars, Killing Fields, and the New Politics of Latin America* (New York: Bloomsbury Press, 2016).
36. Author interview with journalist Ioan Grillo.
37. Author interview with Oaxaca investigative journalist, December 11, 2015.

4. STRATEGIES FOR AUTONOMOUS SAFETY

38. Author interview with Sinaloa journalist and digital magazine director, December 10, 2015.
39. Author interview with Ciudad Juárez, Chihuahua, investigative journalist, January 16, 2016.
40. A book by Gabriela Polit Dueñas is particularly useful in understanding this phenomenon. Gabriela Polit Dueñas, *Unwanted Witnesses: Journalists and Conflict in Contemporary Latin America* (Pittsburgh: University of Pittsburgh Press, 2019).
41. Pablo Ferri and Daniela Rea, *La Tropa: Por qué mata un soldado* (Mexico City: Aguilar, 2019).
42. Author interview with long-form journalist Diego Enrique Osorno.
43. Author interview with Diego Enrique Osorno.
44. Javier Garza Ramos, "Balazos en el estadio," *El País*, August 20, 2021, https://elpais.com/mexico/opinion/2021-08-20/balazos-en-el-estadio.html.
45. Javier Garza Ramos, "*El Siglo de Torreón*: La violencia ya no es novedad," *Nexos*, August 1, 2013, https://nexos.com.mx/?p=15421.
46. Garza, "*El Siglo de Torreón*."
47. Some owners of critical communications media (such as *Reforma*) have moved out of Mexico.
48. Author interview with Javier Garza Ramos.
49. Paul DiMaggio, "Interest and Agency in Institutional Theory," in *Research on Institutional Patterns: Environment and Culture*, ed. Lynne G. Zucker (Cambridge: Ballinger, 1988), 3–21.
50. Author interview with Javier Garza Ramos.
51. Author interview with Javier Garza Ramos.
52. Author interview with Javier Garza Ramos.
53. María Verza, "¿Cómo informar sobre un México corrupto, violento, en guerra? Ríodoce da pasos de resistencia," Sociedad Interamericana de Prensa, August 4, 2017, https://www.sipiapa.org/notas/1211623-como-informar-un-mexico-corrupto-violento-guerra.
54. Author interview with a former Sinaloa deputy director, December 9, 2015.
55. Author interview with Guadalajara, Jalisco, national newspaper crime-beat journalist.
56. Author interview with journalist and scholar Víctor Hugo Reyna, September 14, 2015. He explores this subject in detail himself in an academic article: Víctor Hugo Reyna García, "Journalists as Mobility Agents: Labor Mobilities, Individualized Identities, and Emerging Organizational Forms," *Journalism* 24, no. 2 (2021).
57. Author interview with Mexico City newspaper top executive, November 30, 2015.
58. Author interview with Ciudad Juárez, Chihuahua, newspaper deputy director, January 22, 2016.
59. Author interview with Ciudad Juárez, Chihuahua, newspaper deputy director.
60. Author interview with Francisco Castellanos.
61. Author interview with Veracruz crime-beat reporter, December 10, 2015.
62. Hughes and Márquez Ramírez, "How Unsafe Contexts," 303.
63. Author interview with *Noroeste* newspaper deputy director.
64. Author interview with Ciudad Juárez, Chihuahua, newspaper deputy director.

4. STRATEGIES FOR AUTONOMOUS SAFETY

65. Author interview with *Noroeste* newspaper deputy director.
66. Óscar Medina, "Zeta: El periodismo suicida," *Prodavinci*, July 19, 2010, https://historico.prodavinci.com/2010/07/19/actualidad/zeta-el-periodismo-suicida/.
67. Author interview with Javier Garza Ramos.
68. Author interview with Javier Garza Ramos.
69. "Drug Hitmen Kidnap Four Mexican Journalists: Report," Reuters, July 28, 2010, https://www.reuters.com/article/us-mexico-drugs-idUSTRE66R5VC20100729.
70. Javier Garza Ramos, "Under Fire in Mexico: 'They Hit Us,'" *ReVista*, June 22, 2011, https://revista.drclas.harvard.edu/under-fire-in-mexico/.
71. Author interview with *Noroeste* newspaper deputy director.
72. Daniela Pastrana, "*Voz Alterna*: La rebelión del miedo," *Pie de Página*, June 12, 2019, https://piedepagina.mx/voz-alterna-la-rebelion-del-miedo/.
73. Norma Trujillo Báez, "La geografía de los desaparecidos en Veracruz," *Pie de Página*, June 13, 2019, https://piedepagina.mx/la-geografia-de-los-desaparecidos-en-veracruz/.
74. Author interview with Veracruz journalist Norma Trujillo.
75. Matthew Powers and Sandra Vera Zambrano, "Explaining the Formation of Online News Startups in France and the United States: A Field Analysis," *Journal of Communication* 66, no. 5 (2016): 857–77, https://doi.org/10.1111/jcom.12253.
76. The digital startups analyzed here were *Lado B*, *Chiapas Paralelo*, *Página 3*, *Colectivo Voz Alterna*, *InnDaga*, *La Verdad*, *Raichali*, *Zona Docs*, *Amapola*, *Trinchera*, and *Pie de Página*. Sarelly Martínez Mendoza and Diego Noel Ramos Rojas, "Periodismo colaborativo: Tejiendo redes en disputa por la palabra y la agenda informativa," *Comunicación y Sociedad* (2020): 1–22, https://doi.org/10.32870/cys.v2020.7608.
77. José Luis Requejo-Alemán and Jairo Lugo-Ocando, "Assessing the Sustainability of Latin American Investigative Non-Profit Journalism," *Journalism Studies* 15, no. 5 (2014): 522–32, https://doi.org/10.1080/1461670X.2014.885269.
78. Lucas Graves and Magda Konieczna, "Qualitative Political Communication:| Sharing the News: Journalistic Collaboration as Field Repair," *International Journal of Communication* 9 (2015): 1966–84.
79. Mark Deuze, "Collaboration, Participation, and the Media," *New Media & Society* 8, no. 4 (2006): 691–98, https://doi.org/10.1177/1461444806065665.
80. Seth C. Lewis, "The Tension Between Professional Control and Open Participation: Journalism and Its Boundaries," *Information, Communication, & Society* 15, no. 6 (2012): 836–66, https://doi.org/10.1080/1369118X.2012.674150.
81. Matthew Powers, *NGOs as Newsmakers: The Changing Landscape of International News* (New York: Columbia University Press, 2018); Richard Sambrook, ed., *Global Teamwork: The Rise of Collaboration in Investigative Journalism* (Oxford: Reuters Institute for the Study of Journalism, 2018).
82. Lourdes M. Cueva Chacón and Magdalena Saldaña, "Stronger and Safer Together: Motivations for and Challenges of (Trans)National Collaboration in Investigative Reporting in Latin America," *Digital Journalism* 9, no. 2 (2021): 196–214, https://doi.org/10.1080/21670811.2020.1775103.

4. STRATEGIES FOR AUTONOMOUS SAFETY

83. Bregtje Van der Haak, Michael Parks and Manuel Castells, "The Future of Journalism: Networked Journalism," *International Journal of Communication* 6, no. 16 (2012): 2923–38.
84. Author interview with Guadalajara, Jalisco, political journalist, January 16, 2016.
85. Author interview with Michoacán journalist Antonio Ramos, December 22, 2015.
86. Author interview with Jalisco journalist, January 28, 2016.
87. Author interview with Monterrey, Nuevo León, investigative journalist.
88. Author interview with journalist Ioan Grillo.
89. Author interview with Estado de México police beat reporter, January 21, 2016.
90. Author interview with Guadalajara, Jalisco, political journalist.
91. Interview with Tamaulipas newspaper journalist, December 22, 2015.
92. Sallie L. Hughes and Mireya Márquez Ramírez, "Examining the Practices that Mexican Journalists Employ to Reduce Risk in a Context of Violence," *International Journal of Communication*, no. 11 (2017): 509.
93. Author interview with Veracruz national correspondent Noé Zavaleta, September 19, 2015.
94. Author interview with Tampico, Tamaulipas, political reporter, December 4, 2015.

5. STRATEGIES FOR RESISTANCE

1. Froylán Enciso, "Lamento por mi compa, Javier Valdez," *Horizontal*, May 17, 2017.
2. The media that joined the strike were the Mexican edition of *Vice News* and the websites *Pie de Página, Cultura Colectiva News, Zona Franca, Lado B de Puebla, Página 3*, and *Horizontal*, among others. There were also printed media, such as *Luces del Siglo, El Popular de Puebla*, and *El Siglo de Durango*.
3. Alberto Nájar, "Medios en paro, portadas en negro: La inédita protesta de los periodistas mexicanos al asesinato de Javier Valdez," *BBC Mundo*, May 16, 2017, https://www.bbc.com/mundo/noticias-america-latina-39944188.
4. Interview with journalist Guillermo Osorno.
5. Sidney Tarrow, *Power in Movement: Social Movements and Contentious Politics* (Cambridge: Cambridge University Press, 2012).
6. Andreas Schedler, *En la niebla de la guerra: Los ciudadanos ante la violencia criminal organizada* (Mexico: CIDE, 2018).
7. Michel Foucault, "El ojo del poder: Entrevista con Michel Foucault," in *El Panóptico*, ed. Jeremías Benthan (Barcelona: La Piqueta, 1980).
8. Manuel Castells, *Communication Power* (Oxford: Oxford University Press, 2013).
9. George A. Bonanno, "The Resilience Paradox," *European Journal of Psychotraumatology* 12, no. 1 (2021): 1–8.
10. David A. Snow, "Grievances, Individual and Mobilizing," in *The Wiley-Blackwell Encyclopedia of Social and Political Movements*, ed. David A. Snow et al. (Hoboken, NJ: John Wiley & Sons, 2013).

5. STRATEGIES FOR RESISTANCE

11. Rosemary J. Novak and Sarah Davidson, "Journalists Reporting on Hazardous Events: Constructing Protective Factors within the Professional Role," *Traumatology* 19, no. 4 (2013): 313–22.
12. Sallie L. Hughes et al., "Coping with Occupational Stress in Journalism: Professional Identities and Advocacy as Resources," *Journalism Studies* 22, no. 8 (2021): 971–91.
13. Violeta Alejandra Santiago Hernández, "Análisis del impacto de la violencia en la situación económica y el ejercicio de la libertad de expresión en un grupo de periodistas veracruzanos," *Anuario de Investigación CONEICC* 1, no. 27 (2020): 22–37.
14. Foucault, "El ojo del poder."
15. Marta Milena Barrios and Toby Miller, "Voices of Resilience: Colombian Journalists and Self-Censorship in the Post-Conflict Period," *Journalism Practice* 15, no. 10 (2021): 1423–40.
16. Interview with Emilio Lugo, displaced investigative journalist, September 19, 2015.
17. Interview with Emilio Lugo.
18. Homero Campa Butrón, "Cuando el mecanismo falla" (master's thesis, Centro de Investigación y Docencia Económicas, 2014), http://repositorio-digital.cide.edu/bitstream/handle/11651/452/127777.pdf?sequence=1&isAllowed=y.
19. Interview with Emilio Lugo.
20. Barrios and Miller, "Voices of Resilience."
21. Celia Del Palacio Montiel, "Resistencia, resiliencia, y luchas por la memoria de la violencia: Los periodistas en Veracruz, México," *Chasqui: Revista Latinoamericana de comunicación*, no. 143 (2020): 199–214; Barrios and Miller, "Voices of Resilience"; Violeta Alejandra Santiago Hernández, "Periodismo resiliente: El ideal del rol social para ejercer el periodismo en contexto de violencia macrocriminal en México," in *Ecossistema jornalístico*, ed. Liliane Ito and Rita Paulino (Aveiro, Portugal: Ria Editorial, 2021), 277–98.
22. Novak and Davidson, "Journalists Reporting on Hazardous Events"; Hughes et al., "Coping with Occupational Stress."
23. Bonanno, "The Resilience Paradox," 5.
24. Laura Iesue et al., "Risk, Victimization, and Coping Strategies of Journalists in Mexico and Brazil," *Sur le journalisme, About Journalism, Sobre jornalismo* 10, no. 1 (2021): 62–81.
25. Hughes et al., "Coping with Occupational Stress."
26. Interview with Veracruz freelance journalist, January 29, 2016.
27. Hughes et al., "Coping with Occupational Stress."
28. Interview with Oaxaca reporter, January 7, 2016.
29. Hughes et al., "Coping with Occupational Stress."
30. Novak and Davidson, "Journalists Reporting on Hazardous Events."
31. Interview with *Noroeste* deputy director, January 8, 2016.
32. Interview with Oaxaca national correspondent, December 14, 2015.
33. Interview with former Sinaloa deputy director, December 9, 2015.
34. Interview with Michoacán national correspondent, January 8, 2016.

5. STRATEGIES FOR RESISTANCE

35. Interview with Oaxaca investigative journalist, December 11, 2015.
36. One of the more insightful works about Regina Martínez's killing is Katherine Corcoran, *In the Mouth of the Wolf: A Murder, a Cover-Up, and the True Cost of Silencing the Press* (London: Bloomsbury, 2022).
37. Interview with Jorge Carrasco, investigative reporter, national magazine, November 30, 2015.
38. Jorge Carrasco Araizaga, "'Es inútil, señor gobernador, no le creemos': CRÓNICA del encuentro entre Julio Scherer y Javier Duarte," *Sin Embargo*, May 6, 2012, https://www.sinembargo.mx/06-05-2012/225442.
39. Julio Scherer García, *Vivir* (Mexico: Grijalbo, 2012).
40. "Proceso ante el crimen de Regina Martínez," *Proceso*, April 29, 2012, https://www.proceso.com.mx/regina-martinez/2012/4/29/proceso-ante-el-crimen-de-regina-martinez-101979.html.
41. Interview with Rafael Rodríguez Castañeda.
42. Interview with Jorge Carrasco.
43. Interview with Jorge Carrasco.
44. Interview with Jorge Carrasco.
45. Scherer García, *Vivir*.
46. Interview with Veracruz national correspondent Noé Zavaleta, September 19, 2015.
47. Interview with columnist Julio Hernández López, September 10, 2015.
48. Interview with Veracruz national correspondent Noé Zavaleta.
49. Nina Lakhani, Dana Priest, and Paloma Dupont de Dinechin, "Murder in Mexico: Journalists Caught in the Crosshairs," *The Guardian*, December 6, 2020, https://www.theguardian.com/world/2020/dec/06/murder-in-mexico-journalists-caught-in-the-crosshairs-regina-martinez-cartel-project.
50. Márquez Ramírez and Hughes, "Panorama de los perfiles demográficos."
51. "Ataques contra medios con explosivos o armas de fuego," Artículo 19, August 4, 2015, https://articulo19.org/ataques-contra-medios-con-explosivos-o-armas-de-fuego/.
52. In some cases, such as *El Siglo de Torreón*'s, these measures were reinforced by other forms of government protection, such as stationing public security personnel at building entrances. Interview with *El Siglo de Torreón* editorial director Javier Garza Ramos.
53. Interview with *Noroeste* deputy director, January 8, 2016.
54. Interview with Armando Rodríguez, December 14, 2014.
55. Interview with local Sinaloa journalist, December 16, 2015.
56. Interview with Javier Garza Ramos.
57. Interview with Javier Garza Ramos.
58. Interview with Michoacán national correspondent.
59. Interview with Erick Muñiz, correspondent in Nuevo León, January 28, 2016.
60. Interview with top executive, Mexico City, November 30, 2015.
61. Interview with Oaxaca national newspaper investigative journalist, January 9, 2016.
62. Interview with *Noroeste* deputy director.

5. STRATEGIES FOR RESISTANCE

63. Interview with *Noroeste* deputy director.
64. Interview with *Noroeste* deputy director.
65. Artículo 19, "Ataques contra medios con explosivos o armas de fuego."
66. Interview with Tamaulipas journalist, December 22, 2015.
67. Interview with Tamaulipas journalist, December 22, 2015.
68. Mayra Zepeda, "Atacan instalaciones de Grupo Reforma y *El Mañana*," *Animal Político*, July 11, 2012, https://www.animalpolitico.com/2012/07/atacan-instalaciones-de-grupo-reforma-y-el-manana/.
69. Mireya Márquez Ramírez, "Valores normativos y prácticas de reporteo en tensión: Percepciones profesionales de periodistas en México," *Cuadernos de información*, no. 30 (2012): 97–110.
70. Interview with Mexico City national newspaper director.
71. Periodistas de a Pie, "Quiénes somos," PdP, https://periodistasdeapie.org.mx/quienes-somos/.
72. Interview with journalist Daniela Pastrana.
73. Interview with journalist Daniela Pastrana.
74. Centro de Investigación Periodística, "Periodistas mexicanos: Ni uno más," *CIPER*, August 9, 2010, https://www.ciperchile.cl/2010/08/09/periodistas-mexicanos-%e2%80%9cni-uno-mas%e2%80%9d/.
75. "Periodistas marchan en el DF: Los queremos vivos (2010)," Nefimanson, August 10, 2010, video, 14:42, https://www.youtube.com/watch?v=5g72tm5DleY.
76. Julieta Alejandra Brambila, "Journalists' Resistance Movements: A Subnational Comparative Approach in Mexico's Most Violent States" (paper presented at the Reuters Institute Summer School on Comparative Qualitative Research on Journalism and News Media, Oxford University, September 2017).
77. María Soledad Segura and Silvio Waisbord, *Media Movements: Civil Society and Media Policy Reform in Latin America* (London: Zed Books, 2016).
78. Márquez Ramírez and Hughes, "Panorama de los perfiles demográficos."
79. Interview with Oaxaca reporter, January 7, 2016.
80. Interview with Estado de México journalist, January 21, 2016.
81. Interview with Sinaloa journalist and digital magazine cofounder, December 10, 2015.
82. Interview with Ciudad Juárez, Chihuahua, political journalist, December 11, 2015.
83. Interview with Oaxaca national correspondent.
84. Periodistas de a Pie, "Quiénes somos."
85. Interview with Daniela Pastrana.
86. Interview with Ciudad Juárez, Chihuahua, political journalist.
87. Robert Putnam, Robert Leonardi, and Raffaella Nanetti, *Making Democracy Work: Civic Traditions in Modern Italy* (Princeton, NJ: Princeton University Press, 1994).
88. Elinor Ostrom and T. K. Ahn, "The Meaning of Social Capital and Its Link to Collective Action," in *Handbook on Social Capital: The Troika of Sociology, Political Science, and Economics*, ed. Gert T. Svendsen and Gunnar L. Svendsen (Northampton, MA: Edward Elgar, 2009), 17–35.

5. STRATEGIES FOR RESISTANCE

89. Andreas Schedler, "The Criminal Community of Victims and Perpetrators: Cognitive Foundations of Citizen Detachment from Organized Violence in Mexico," *Human Rights Quarterly* 38, no. 4 (2016): 1038–69.
90. Interview with Tamaulipas newspaper journalist, December 22, 2015.
91. Sidney Tarrow, "Cycles of Collective Action: Between Moments of Madness and the Repertoire of Contention," *Social Science History* 17, no. 2 (1993): 281–307.
92. Celeste González de Bustamante and Jeannine E. Relly, "Global Domestic Networks Advancing Prospects for Institutional and Social Change: The Collective Action Response to Violence Against Journalists," *Journalism & Communication Monographs* 19, no. 2 (2017): 84–152, https://doi.org/10.1177/1522637917702618; Julieta Alejandra Brambila and Jairo Alfonso Lugo-Ocando, "Lobbying for Life: Violence Against the Press and the Public Interest," in *Public Interest Communication Critical Debates and Global Contexts*, ed. Jane Johnston and Magda Pieczka (Routledge, 2018), 192–209.
93. González de Bustamante and Relly, "Professionalism Under Threat of Violence"; María Grisel Salazar Rebolledo, "Strategic Allies and the Survival of Critical Media Under Repressive Conditions: An Empirical Analysis of Local Mexican Press," *International Journal of Press/Politics* 24, no. 3 (2019): 341–62.
94. Salvador de León Vázquez, "Profesionalización autogestiva de los periodistas mexicanos organizados," *Global Media Journal* 15, no. 28 (2018): 78–99.
95. Interview with Darío Fritz.
96. Interview with journalist Daniela Pastrana.
97. Celeste González de Bustamante and Jeannine E. Relly, "Professionalism Under Threat of Violence."
98. Interview with Ciudad Juárez, Chihuahua, investigative journalist.
99. De León Vázquez, "Profesionalización autogestiva."
100. Jeannine E. Relly and Celeste González de Bustamante, "Global and Domestic Networks Advancing Prospects for Institutional and Social Change: The Collective Action Response to Violence Against Journalists," *Journalism & Communication Monographs* 19, no. 2 (2017): 84–152, https://doi.org/10.1177/1522637917702618.
101. Interview with a veteran journalist, September 28, 2015.
102. Thirty of the fifty journalists who answered my questionnaire had had some form of collective training.
103. Mirjam Gollmitzer, "Precariously Employed Watchdogs? Perceptions of Working Conditions Among Freelancers and Interns," *Journalism Practice* 8, no. 6 (2014): 826–84; Mohammad Yousuf and Maureen Taylor, "Helping Syrians Tell Their Story to the World: Training Syrian Citizen Journalists Through Connective Journalism," *Journalism Practice* 11, nos. 2–3 (2017): 302–18.
104. Interview with journalist Daniela Pastrana.
105. Interview with Ciudad Juárez, Chihuahua, multimedia reporter, December 11, 2015.
106. Interview with Ciudad Juárez, Chihuahua, political journalist.
107. Interview with Oaxaca journalist, December 8, 2015.
108. Interview with Guadalajara, Jalisco, correspondent, January 27, 2016.

CONCLUSION

109. This has been a growing process. Some of the first mass protest acts may be traced further back. However, one of journalism's first mass protests was the 2012 Los queremos vivos march, mentioned at the start of this section. Other episodes discussed here took place following the murders of Regina Martínez (2012), Gregorio Jiménez de la Cruz (2014), Rubén Espinoza (2015), Miroslava Breach (2017), and Javier Valdez Cárdenas (2017).
110. Interview with Nuevo León freelance journalist, January 12, 2016.
111. Interview with AFP special affairs journalist in Mexico City, December 2, 2015.
112. Interview with Jalisco journalist, January 28, 2016.
113. Interview with Guerrero national correspondent, January 8, 2016.
114. Interview with AFP special affairs journalist in Mexico City.
115. Segura and Waisbord, *Media Movements*, 64–69.
116. Jairo Lugo-Ocando, ed., *The Media in Latin America* (London: McGraw-Hill Education, 2008); Silvio Waisbord, "Between Support and Confrontation: Civic Society, Media Reform, and Populism in Latin America," *Communication, Culture & Critique* 4, no. 1 (2011): 97–117.
117. Brambila and Lugo-Ocando, "Lobbying for Life," 192.
118. Interview with Oaxaca reporter, January 7, 2016.
119. Interview with journalist Guillermo Osorno.

CONCLUSION

1. Stephen Reese, *The Crisis of the Institutional Press* (Cambridge: Polity Press, 2021).
2. Jackie Harrison and Stefanie Pukallus, "The Politics of Impunity: A Study of Journalists' Experiential Accounts of Impunity in Bulgaria, Democratic Republic of Congo, India, Mexico and Pakistan," *Journalism* 22, no. 2 (2021): 303–19, https://doi.org/10.1177 /1464884918778248.
3. Peter Berglez and Amanda Gearing, "The Panama and Paradise Papers: The Rise of a Global Fourth Estate," *International Journal of Communication* 12 (2018): 4573–92.
4. Celeste González de Bustamante and Jeannine Relly, *Surviving Mexico: Resistance and Resilience Among Journalists in Twenty-First Century* (Austin: University of Texas Press, 2021), 79.
5. María Grisel Salazar Rebolledo, *Más allá de la violencia* (Mexico City: CIDE, 2022).
6. Silvio Waisbord, "Center for Media at Risk Launch Symposium, Panel 4: Journalism," Annenberg School for Communication Annenberg School for Communication, May 23, 2018, video, 2:12:15, https://www.youtube.com/watch?v=TsnVBVMijVY&t=2878s.
7. Noha Mellor, "Strategies for Autonomy: Arab Journalists Reflecting on Their Roles," *Journalism Studies* 10, no. 3 (2009): 307–21.
8. Maria Repnikova, "Contesting the State Under Authoritarianism: Critical Journalists in China and Russia," *Comparative Politics* 51, no. 1 (2018): 41–60; Maria Repnikova, "Critical Journalists in China and Russia," in *Citizens and the State in Authoritarian Regimes:*

CONCLUSION

Comparing China and Russia, ed. Karrie Koesel, Valerie Bunce, and Jessica Weiss, (Oxford: Oxford University Press, 2020).
9. Repnikova, "Contesting the State"; Repnikova, "Critical Journalists in China and Russia."
10. Umaru A. Pate and Hamza Idris, "How Journalists Survived to Report: Professionalism and Risk Management in the Reporting of Terror Groups and Violent Extremism in North East Nigeria," in *The Assault on Journalism: Building Knowledge to Protect Freedom of Expression*, ed. Ulla Carlsson and Reeta Pöyhtäri (Gothenburg, Sweden: University of Gothenburg, Nordicom, 2017), 159, http://www.unesco.se/wp-content/uploads/2017/04/The-Assault-on-Journalism.pdf.
11. Gretchen Dworznik, "Journalism and Trauma: How Reporters and Photographers Make Sense of What They See," *Journalism Studies* 7, no. 4 (2006): 534–53.
12. Rosemary Novak and Sarah Davidson, "Journalists Reporting on Hazardous Events: Constructing Protective Factors Within the Professional Role," *Traumatology* 19, no. 4 (2013): 313–22.
13. Laura Lozano and Lucía Suescún Garay, "Significados que reflejan algunos periodistas colombianos tras vivir hechos violentos de censura" (bachelor's thesis, Pontificia Universidad Javeriana, 2020), https://repository.javeriana.edu.co/bitstream/handle/10554/52183/Trabajo%20de%20Grado.pdf?sequence=1&isAllowed=y.
14. Vera Slavtcheva-Petkova, *Russia's Liberal Media* (New York: Routledge, 2018).
15. "'El Faro' traslada a Costa Rica su estructura legal y administrativa ante el acoso del Gobierno de Nayib Bukele," *El País*, April 14, 2023, https://elpais.com/internacional/2023-04-14/el-faro-traslada-a-costa-rica-su-estructura-legal-y-administrativa-ante-el-acoso-del-gobierno-de-nayib-bukele.html.
16. Laura Oliver, "'Illuminate the Darkness': Creating an Independent News Site in Crisis-Hit Venezuela," Global Investigative Journalism Network, December 21, 2021, https://gijn.org/independent-news-venezuela/.
17. Lucia Mesquita and Mathias-Felipe de-Lima-Santos, "Blurred Boundaries of Journalism to Guarantee Safety: Approaches of Resistance and Resilience for Investigative Journalism in Latin America," *Journalism Studies* 24, no. 7 (2023): 916–35.
18. Elsebeth Frey, "Preparing for Risks and Building Resilience," *Journalism Studies* 24, no. 7 (2023): 1008–25.
19. Gisele Barão da Silva, Giulia Sbaraini Fontes, and Francisco Marques, "Risks and Resilience in the Case of Brazilian Female Journalists: How Women Perceive Violence Against Media Professionals and Cope with Its Effects," *Journalism Studies* 24, no. 7 (2023): 956–75.
20. Simon Cottle, Richard Sambrook, and Nick Mosdell, *Reporting Dangerously: Journalist Killings, Intimidation and Security* (London: Palgrave Macmillan, 2016).
21. Germán Rey, "Colombia, cuatro décadas de violencia," *Infoamérica*, no. 10 (2016): 27–37.
22. Marta Milena Barrios and Toby Miller, "Voices of Resilience: Colombian Journalists and Self-Censorship in the Post-Conflict Period," *Journalism Practice* 15, no. 10 (2021): 1423–40.

CONCLUSION

23. Sarah A. Ganter and Fernando O. Paulino, "Between Attack and Resilience: The Ongoing Institutionalization of Independent Digital Journalism in Brazil," *Digital Journalism* 9, no. 2 (2021): 235–54.
24. Marína Urbániková and Lenka Haniková, "Coping with the Murder: The Impact of Ján Kuciak's Assassination on Slovak Investigative Journalists," *Journalism Practice* 16, no. 9 (2022): 1927–47.
25. This poll was taken from a random sample of 486 journalists nationwide, estimating in a representative and probabilistic manner a pool of 25,000 journalists in Mexico, and was carried out from November 2021 to November 2022. The poll, which forms part of the global project Worlds of Journalism, delves into dimensions such as demographic, occupational, and professional variables; professional roles, forms of aggression, and security measures; and the impact of COVID. The author, in cooperation with a consortium of researchers, acted as regional coordinator of this poll.
26. Frida Rodelo et al., "Periodistas en México: Encuesta de sus perfiles demográficos, laborales y profesionales," *Global Media Journal México* 20, no. 39 (2023): 110–59, https://doi.org/10.29105/gmjmx20.39-512.
27. Cámara de Diputados, "Comisión conoce los avances del Mecanismo de Protección para Personas Defensoras de Derechos Humanos y Periodistas," Boletín 4799, August 16, 2023, https://comunicacionsocial.diputados.gob.mx/index.php/boletines/comision-conoce-los-avances-del-mecanismo-de-proteccion-para-personas-defensoras-de-derechos-humanos-y-periodistas.
28. Elena Reina, "Eduardo Guerrero: 'El narco mexicano no está debilitado, está más fuerte que nunca,'" *El País*, August 21, 2022, https://elpais.com/mexico/2022-08-21/eduardo-guerrero-el-narco-mexicano-no-esta-debilitado-esta-mas-fuerte-que-nunca.html.
29. Rafael Prieto-Curiel, Gian Maria Campedelli, and Alejandro Hope, "Reducing Cartel Recruitment Is the Only Way to Lower Violence in Mexico," *Science* 381, no. 6664 (2023): 1312–16, https://doi.org/10.1126/science.adh2888.
30. Thomas Graham, "Mexican Cartels Are Fifth-Largest Employers in the Country, Study Finds," *The Guardian*, September 21, 2023, https://www.theguardian.com/world/2023/sep/21/mexico-cartels-fifth-largest-employer-study.
31. Almudena Barragán, "El relator de la CIDH para la libertad de expresión pide a López Obrador suspender 'Quién es quién de las mentiras,'" *El País*, February 2, 2022, https://elpais.com/mexico/2022-02-03/el-relator-de-la-cidh-para-la-libertad-de-expresion-pide-a-lopez-obrador-suspender-quien-es-quien-de-las-mentiras.html.
32. Natalie Kitroeff and Ronen Bergman, "El espionaje del ejército mexicano genera temores de un 'Estado militar,'" *New York Times*, March 7, 2023, https://www.nytimes.com/es/2023/03/07/espanol/espionaje-ejercito-pegasus-mexico.html.
33. Emir Olivares, "La impunidad es de 99.13% en delitos contra periodistas," *La Jornada*, February 26, 2019, https://www.jornada.com.mx/2019/02/26/politica/008n2pol.
34. See Micaela Varela, "El exalcalde de Chihuahua Hugo Schultz, condenado a ocho años de prisión por ayudar a los asesinos de Miroslava Breach," *El País*, June 16, 2021,

CONCLUSION

https://elpais.com/mexico/2021-06-16/el-exalcalde-de-chihuahua-hugo-schultz-condenado-a-ocho-anos-de-prision-por-ayudar-a-los-asesinos-de-miroslava-breach.html.
35. Cristian Díaz, "Sentencian a 32 años a uno de los asesinos del periodista Javier Valdez," *La Jornada*, June 17, 2021, https://www.jornada.com.mx/notas/2021/06/17/estados/sentencian-a-32-anos-a-uno-de-los-asesinos-de-periodista-javier-valdez/.

APPENDIX II: STUDY DESIGN

1. Some relevant journalistic items on this topic are the book *Shooting the Messengers: The Dangerous World of Mexican Journalism* and the chronicle "Mexico: Risking Life for Truth." Special mention, because of the information provided and the elevated literary style, goes to *Narcoperiodismo*, published by Javier Valdez in 2016; Alma Guillermoprieto, "Mexico: Risking Life for Truth," *New York Review of Books*, November 22, 2012, https://www.nybooks.com/articles/2012/11/22/mexico-risking-life-truth/; Javier Valdez Cárdenas, *Narcoperiodismo: La prensa en medio del crimen y la denuncia* (Madrid: Aguilar, 2016); Témoris Grecko, *Shooting the Messengers: The Dangerous World of Mexican Journalism* (New York: Harper Collins, 2020).

In the academic field, the most extensive investigations on this topic published to date are the books Celeste González de Bustamante and Jeannine E. Relly, *Surviving Mexico: Resistance and Resilience Among Journalists in the Twenty-First Century* (Austin: University of Texas Press, 2021); Katherine Corcoran, *In the Mouth of the Wolf: A Murder, a Cover-Up, and the True Cost of Silencing the Press* (London: Bloomsbury, 2022); and María Grisel Salazar Rebolledo, *Más allá de la violencia* (Mexico City: CIDE, 2022). One of the first and most influential investigations on this topic is that of Frida Viridiana Rodelo, although other investigators have contributed relevant work as well: Rodelo, "Periodismo en entornos violentos"; Celia del Palacio Montiel, "Periodismo impreso, poderes y violencia en Veracruz, 2010–2014: Estrategias de control de la información," *Comunicación y Sociedad*, no. 24 (2015): 19–46, http://www.scielo.org.mx/pdf/comso/n24/n24a2.pdf; Bradley Holland and Viridiana Ríos, "Informally Governing Information: How Criminal Rivalry Leads to Violence Against the Press in Mexico," *Journal of Conflict Resolution* 61, no. 5 (2017): 1095–1119; Sallie L. Hughes and Mireya Márquez Ramírez, "Examining the Practices that Mexican Journalists Employ to Reduce Risk in a Context of Violence," *International Journal of Communication*, no. 11 (2017): 499–521; Salvador de León Vázquez, "Profesionalización autogestiva de los periodistas mexicanos organizados," *Global Media Journal* 15, no. 28 (2018): 78–99; María Grisel Salazar Rebolledo, "Strategic Allies and the Survival of Critical Media Under Repressive Conditions: An Empirical Analysis of Local Mexican Press," *International Journal of Press/Politics* 24, no. 3 (2019): 341–62.
2. Ulf Hannerz, *Foreign News* (Chicago: University of Chicago Press, 2012); Mark Pedelty, *War Stories: The Culture of Foreign Correspondents* (London: Routledge, 2013); Maria Repnikova, *Media Politics in China* (Cambridge: Cambridge University Press: 2017);

STUDY DESIGN

Lindsay Palmer, *The Fixers: Local News Workers and the Underground Labor of International Reporting* (New York: Oxford University Press, 2019).
3. Stefan Malthaner, *Fieldwork in the Context of Violent Conflict and Authoritarian Regimes* (New York: Oxford University Press, 2014).
4. Julieta Alejandra Brambila, "Forced Silence: Determinants of Journalist Killings in Mexico's States, 2010–2015," *Journal of Information Policy*, no. 7 (2017): 297–326.
5. Throughout this study, I also followed criteria for data verification to ensure reliability and validity, such as appropriate sampling (which refers to selecting participants that represent or have knowledge of the research topic at hand) and collecting and analyzing data concurrently (to integrate and contrast data from different sources, also known as the triangulation of qualitative data).

BIBLIOGRAPHY

Agencia de los Estados Unidos para el Desarrollo Internacional. "Desplazamiento Forzado de periodistas en la Ciudad de México." Comisión de Derechos Humanos de la Ciudad de México (CDHCM), January 13, 2021. https://cdhcm.org.mx/wp-content/uploads/2021/01/13.-Diagnostico-CDMX-Digital.pdf.
"Agrupaciones de periodistas en Juárez denuncian ataques sistemáticos de la policía de Julián Leyzaola." *Sin Embargo*, February 12, 2012. https://www.sinembargo.mx/12-02-2012/148078.
Artículo 19. "9 años de impunidad para Moisés Sánchez y su familia: ¡Basta ya!" Artículo 19, January 24, 2024. https://articulo19.org/9-anos-de-impunidad-para-moises-sanchez-y-su-familia-basta-ya/.
Artículo 19. "El caso Narvarte: La verdad como 'exquisitez.'" Artículo 19, July 2019. https://articulo19.org/wp-content/uploads/2019/07/A19-La_verdad_como_exquisitez-04-v3-WEB.pdf.
Artículo 19. "Democracia Simulada: Nada que aplaudir." Artículo 19, March 20, 2018. https://articulo19.org/wp-content/uploads/2018/03/INFORME-A19-2017_v04.pdf.
Artículo 19. "En México, 24 periodistas permanecen desaparecidos." Artículo 19, January 23, 2018. https://articulo19.org/periodistasdesaparecidos/.
Artículo 19. "Informe 2009: Entre La Violencia y La Indiferencia." Artículo 19, July 3, 2012. https://articulo19.org/informe-2009-entre-la-violencia-y-la-indiferencia/.
Artículo 19. "Periodistas asesinadas/os en México: En relación con su labor informativa." https://articulo19.org/periodistasasesinados/.
Artículo 19. "Protocolo de la Impunidad en Delitos contra Periodistas." Artículo 19, February 25, 2019. https://articulo19.org/informeimpunidad/.

BIBLIOGRAPHY

Artículo 19, Justice for Journalists, and Fundación para la Libertad de Prensa. "Leyes del silencio: Acoso judicial contra la libertad de expresión en México y Colombia." May 3, 2021. https://articulo19.org/wp-content/uploads/2021/05/INFORME-LEYES-DEL-SILENCIO.pdf.

Artículo 19, Red en Defensa de los Derechos Digitales, and Social TIC. "Gobierno Espía: Vigilancia sistemática a periodistas y defensores de derechos humanos en México." June 2017. https://r3d.mx/wp-content/uploads/GOBIERNO-ESPIA-2017.pdf.

Asal, Victor, Matthew Krain, Amanda Murdie, and Brandon Kennedy. "Killing the Messenger: Regime Type as a Determinant of Journalist Killing, 1992–2008." *Foreign Policy Analysis* 14, no. 1 (2018): 24–43.

Astorga, Luis. *El siglo de las drogas: Del Porfiriato al nuevo milenio*. Mexico City: Debolsillo, 2016.

Barão da Silva, Gisele, Giulia Sbaraini Fontes, and Francisco Marques. "Risks and Resilience in the Case of Brazilian Female Journalists: How Women Perceive Violence Against Media Professionals and Cope with Its Effects. *Journalism Studies* 24, no. 7 (2023): 956–75.

Barnhurst, Kevin G. "Contemporary Terrorism in Peru: Sendero Luminous and the Media." *Journal of Communication* 41, no. 4 (1991): 75–89.

Barragán, Almudena. "El relator de la CIDH para la libertad de expresión pide a López Obrador suspender 'Quién es quién de las mentiras.'" *El País*, February 2, 2022. https://elpais.com/mexico/2022-02-03/el-relator-de-la-cidh-para-la-libertad-de-expresion-pide-a-lopez-obrador-suspender-quien-es-quien-de-las-mentiras.html.

Barrios, Marta Milena, and Toby Miller. "Voices of Resilience: Colombian Journalists and Self-Censorship in the Post-Conflict Period." *Journalism Practice* 15, no. 10 (2021): 1423–40.

Bartley, Patricia, Erick Monterrosas, and Paola Pacheco Ruiz. "Resisting a Hostile and Insecure Environment for Defending Rights in Mexico." In *Protecting Human Rights Defenders at Risk*, ed. Alice M. Nah, 104–29. London: Routledge, 2020.

Bartman, Jos Midas. "Murder in Mexico: Are Journalists Victims of General Violence or Targeted Political Violence?" *Democratization* 25, no. 7 (2018): 1093–1113.

Battilana, Julie, and Thomas Aunno. "Institutional Work and the Paradox of Embedded Agency." In *Institutional Work: Actors and Agency in Institutional Studies of Organizations*, ed. Thomas B. Lawrence, Roy Suddaby, and Bernard Leca, 31–58. Cambridge: Cambridge University Press, 2009.

BBC News. "Por qué en México es tan fácil matar y nunca pisar la cárcel." July 4, 2018. https://www.bbc.com/mundo/noticias-america-latina-44681164.

BBC News. "Tamaulipas: qué es la 'zona silenciada' de México y por qué la ONU exige la atención del gobierno." June 2, 2018. https://www.bbc.com/mundo/noticias-america-latina-44338586.

Behrend, Jacqueline, and Laurence Whitehead, eds. *Illiberal Practices: Territorial Variance Within Large Federal Democracies*. Baltimore: Johns Hopkins University Press, 2016.

Benavides, José Luis. "Gacetilla: A Keyword for a Revisionist Approach to the Political Economy of Mexico's Print News Media." *Media, Culture & Society* 22, no. 1 (2000): 85–104.

BIBLIOGRAPHY

Benson, Rodney, and Erik Neveu, eds. *Bourdieu and the Journalistic Field*. London: Polity Press, 2005.

Berglez, Peter, and Amanda Gearing. "The Panama and Paradise Papers. The Rise of a Global Fourth Estate." *International Journal of Communication* 12 (2018): 4573–92.

Bjørnskov, Christian, and Andreas Freytag. "An Offer You Can't Refuse: Murdering Journalists as an Enforcement Mechanism of Corrupt Deals." *Public Choice* 167, no. 3 (2016): 221–43.

Bonanno, George A. "The Resilience Paradox." *European Journal of Psychotraumatology* 12, no. 1 (2021): 1–8.

Bourdieu, Pierre. "The Forms of Capital." In *Handbook of Theory and Research for the Sociology of Education*, ed. John Richardson, 241–58. Westport, CT: Greenwood, 1986.

Bourdieu, Pierre. "The Political Field, the Social Science Field, and the Journalistic Field." In *Bourdieu and the Journalistic Field*, ed. Rodney Benson and Erik Neveu, 29–47. London: Polity Press, 2005.

Brambila, Julieta Alejandra. "Forced Silence: Determinants of Journalist Killings in Mexico's States, 2010–2015." *Journal of Information Policy*, no. 7 (2017): 297–326.

Brambila, Julieta Alejandra. "Informe 2018: Avances y tareas pendientes para el fortalecimiento de la libertad de expresión en México." CASEDE, September 2018. https://www.casede.org/index.php/biblioteca-casede-2-o/periodismo-y-libertad-de-expresion/70-informe-libertad-de-expresion-2018/file.

Brambila, Julieta Alejandra. "Journalists' Resistance Movements: A Subnational Comparative Approach in Mexico's Most Violent States." Paper presented at the Reuters Institute Summer School on Comparative Qualitative Research on Journalism and News Media, September 2017.

Brambila, Julieta Alejandra. "Reporting Dangerously in Mexico: Capital, Risks, and Strategies Among Journalists." PhD diss. University of Leeds, 2018.

Brambila, Julieta Alejandra, and Sallie L. Hughes. "Violence Against Journalists." In *The International Encyclopedia of Journalism Studies*, ed. Tim. P. Vos and Folker Hanusch, 1–9. Hoboken, NJ: Wiley-Blackwell, 2019.

Brambila, Julieta Alejandra, and Jairo Alfonso Lugo-Ocando. "Lobbying for Life: Violence Against the Press and the Public Interest." In *Public Interest Communication: Critical Debates and Global Contexts*, ed. Jane Johnston and Magda Pieczka, 192–209. London: Routledge, 2018.

Cacho, Lydia. *Los demonios del Edén. El poder que protege a la pornografía infantil*. Mexico City: Debolsillo, 2017.

Cacho, Lydia. *Memorias de una infamia*. Mexico City: Debolsillo, 2014.

Cacho, Lydia, Sergio González Rodriguez, Anabel Hernandez, Diego Osorno, Emiliano Ruiz Parra. *La ira de México: Siete voces contra la impunidad*. Mexico City: Penguin Random House, 2016.

Calderón, Laura Y. "An Analysis of Mayoral Assassinations in Mexico, 2000–17." Global Initiative Against Transnational Organized Crime, January 15, 2018. https://globalinitiative.net/analysis/an-analysis-of-mayoral-assassinations-in-mexico-2000-17/.

BIBLIOGRAPHY

Cámara de Diputados. "Comisión conoce los avances del Mecanismo de Protección para Personas Defensoras de Derechos Humanos y Periodistas." Boletín 4799, August 16, 2023. https://comunicacionsocial.diputados.gob.mx/index.php/boletines/comision-conoce-los-avances-del-mecanismo-de-proteccion-para-personas-defensoras-de-derechos-humanos-y-periodistas.

Campa Butrón, Homero. "Cuando el mecanismo falla." Master's thesis. Centro de Investigación y Docencia Económicas, 2014. http://repositorio-digital.cide.edu/bitstream/handle/11651/452/127777.pdf?sequence=1&isAllowed=y

Carrasco Araizaga, Jorge. "'Es inútil, señor gobernador, no le creemos': CRÓNICA del encuentro entre Julio Scherer y Javier Duarte." *Sin Embargo*, May 6, 2012. https://www.sinembargo.mx/06-05-2012/225442.

Castells, Manuel. *Communication Power*. Oxford: Oxford University Press, 2013.

Centro de Investigación Periodística. "Periodistas mexicanos: Ni uno más." *CIPER*, August 9, 2010. https://www.ciperchile.cl/2010/08/09/periodistas-mexicanos-%e2%80%9cni-uno-mas%e2%80%9d/.

Committee to Protect Journalists. "Gregorio Martínez de la Cruz." 2014. https://cpj.org/data/people/gregorio-jimenez-de-la-cruz/.

Committee to Protect Journalists. "Pedro Canché: 272 Days in Prison." https://cpj.org/campaigns/pressuncuffed/pedro-canche/.

Comunicación e Información de la Mujer A. C. (CIMAC). "Informe: Violencia contra Mujeres Periodistas 2012–2018." November 2019. https://cimac.org.mx/wp-content/uploads/2019/11/Herenciadeunsexenio-1.pdf.

Corcoran, Katherine. *In the Mouth of the Wolf: A Murder, a Cover-Up, and the True Cost of Silencing the Press*. London: Bloomsbury Publishing, 2022.

Cottle, Simon, Richard Sambrook, and Nick Mosdell. *Reporting Dangerously: Journalist Killings, Intimidation, and Security*. London: Palgrave Macmillan, 2016.

Creech, Brian. "Bearing the Cost to Witness: The Political Economy of Risk in Contemporary Conflict and War Reporting." *Media, Culture & Society* 40, no. 4 (2018): 567–83.

Cueva Chacón, Lourdes M., and Magdalena Saldaña. "Stronger and Safer Together: Motivations for and Challenges of (Trans)National Collaboration in Investigative Reporting in Latin America." *Digital Journalism* 9, no. 2 (2021): 196–214. https://doi.org/10.1080/21670811.2020.1775103.

Darnton, Robert. "Censorship, a Comparative View: France, 1789–East Germany, 1989." *Representations*, no. 49 (1995): 40–60.

De León Vázquez, Salvador. "Profesionalización autogestiva de los periodistas mexicanos organizados." *Global Media Journal* 15, no. 28 (2018): 78–99.

De León Vázquez, Salvador, and Rubén Arnoldo González Macías. "Reportear en el desamparo: Análisis de las medidas de protección a periodistas en México desde el contexto local." *Revista de Comunicación* 19, no. 2 (2020): 87–109. http://www.scielo.org.pe/pdf/rcudep/v19n2/2227-1465-rcudep-19-02-87.pdf.

Del Palacio Montiel, Celia. "Periodismo impreso, poderes y violencia en Veracruz 2010–2014: Estrategias de control de la información." *Comunicación y Sociedad*, no. 24 (2015): 19–46. http://www.scielo.org.mx/pdf/comso/n24/n24a2.pdf.

BIBLIOGRAPHY

Del Palacio Montiel, Celia. "Resistencia, resiliencia y luchas por la memoria de la violencia: Los periodistas en Veracruz, México." *Chasqui: Revista Latinoamericana de Comunicación*, no. 143 (2020): 199–214.

Deuze, Mark. "Collaboration, Participation, and the Media." *New Media & Society* 8, no. 4 (2006): 691–98. https://doi.org/10.1177/1461444806065665.

Diamond, Larry. "Elections Without Democracy: Thinking About Hybrid Regimes." *Journal of Democracy* 13, no. 2 (2002): 21–35.

Díaz, Cristian. "Sentencian a 32 años a uno de los asesinos del periodista Javier Valdez." *La Jornada*, June 17, 2021. https://www.jornada.com.mx/notas/2021/06/17/estados/sentencian-a-32-anos-a-uno-de-los-asesinos-de-periodista-javier-valdez/.

Díaz, Gloria Leticia. "Las víctimas de Leyzaola claman justicia." *Proceso*, June 1, 2019. https://www.proceso.com.mx/reportajes/2019/6/1/las-victimas-de-leyzaola-claman-justicia-225756.html.

DiMaggio, Paul. "Interest and Agency in Institutional Theory." In *Research on Institutional Patterns: Environment and Culture*, ed. Lynne G. Zucker, 3–21. Cambridge: Ballinger Publishing, 1988.

Dupont de Dinechin, Paloma. "Regina Martínez: Tras los pasos de una verdad enterrada." *Forbidden Stories*. https://forbiddenstories.org/es/regina-martinez-sur-les-traces-dune-verite-enterree/.

Durazo Herrmann, Julián. "Media and Subnational Democracy: The Case of Bahia, Brazil." *Democratization* 24, no. 1 (2017): 81–99.

Durin, Séverine. "Periodismo bajo fuego: Métodos letales de coacción de la prensa durante la guerra contra el narcotráfico." *Encartes* 2, no. 3, (2019): 82–111. https://encartes.mx/coaccion-prensa-narcotrafico/.

Dworznik, Gretchen. "Journalism and Trauma: How Reporters and Photographers Make Sense of What They See." *Journalism Studies* 7, no. 4 (2006): 534–553.

Edmonds-Poli, Emily. "The Effects of Drug-War Related Violence on Mexico's Press and Democracy." Working Paper Series on Civic Engagement and Public Security in Mexico, Wilson Center, Washington, DC, April 2013. https://www.wilsoncenter.org/sites/default/files/media/documents/publication/edmonds_violence_press.pdf.

El Movimiento de Unificación y Lucha Triqui. "Movimiento de Unificación y Lucha Triqui." https://mult.mx.

"El narco calla a los periódicos del norte." *Proceso*, March 19, 2013. https://www.proceso.com.mx/reportajes/2013/3/19/el-narco-calla-los-periodicos-del-norte-115840.html.

El País. "'El Faro' traslada a Costa Rica su estructura legal y administrativa ante el acoso del Gobierno de Nayib Bukele." April 14, 2023. https://elpais.com/internacional/2023-04-14/el-faro-traslada-a-costa-rica-su-estructura-legal-y-administrativa-ante-el-acoso-del-gobierno-de-nayib-bukele.html.

Enciso, Froylan. "Lamento por mi compa, Javier Valdez." *Horizontal*, May 17, 2017.

Feinstein, Anthony. "Mexican Journalists: An Investigation of Their Emotional Health." *Journal of Traumatic Stress* 25, no. 4 (2012): 480–83.

BIBLIOGRAPHY

Feinstein, Anthony. "Mexican Journalists and Journalists Covering War: A Comparison of Psychological Wellbeing." *Journal of Aggression, Conflict, and Peace Research* 5, no. 2 (2013): 77–85. http://dx.doi.org/10.1108/17596591311313672.

Ferri, Pablo, and Daniela Rea. *La Tropa: Por qué mata un soldado*. Mexico City: Aguilar, 2019.

Fink, Katherine. "The Biggest Challenge Facing Journalism: A Lack of Trust." *Journalism* 20, no. 1 (2019): 40–43.

Flores Morales, Rogelio, Verónica Reyes Pérez, and Lucy María Reidl Martínez. "El impacto psicológico de la guerra contra el narcotráfico en periodistas mexicanos." *Revista Colombiana de Psicología* 23, no. 1 (2014): 177–92.

Foucault, Michel. "El ojo del poder: Entrevista con Michel Foucault." In *El Panóptico*, ed. Jeremías Benthan. Barcelona: La Piqueta, 1980.

Frey, Elsebeth. "Preparing for Risks and Building Resilience." *Journalism Studies* 24, no. 7 (2023): 1008–25.

Frutos, Melva. "Cómo hacer coberturas de alto riesgo en la frontera." Border Center for Journalists and Bloggers, September 1, 2021. https://www.bordercenter.net/es/blog/entrevista-juan-cedillo/.

Fuentes Díaz, Antonio, and Guillermo Paleta Pérez. "Violencia y autodefensas comunitarias en Michoacán, México." *Iconos: Revista de Ciencias Sociales*, no. 53 (2015): 171–86.

Ganter, Sarah A., and Fernando O. Paulino. "Between Attack and Resilience: The Ongoing Institutionalization of Independent Digital Journalism in Brazil." *Digital Journalism* 9, no. 2 (2021): 235–54.

Garza Ramos, Javier. "Balazos en el estadio." *El País*, August 20, 2021. https://elpais.com/mexico/opinion/2021-08-20/balazos-en-el-estadio.html.

Garza Ramos, Javier. *"El Siglo de Torreón*: La violencia ya no es novedad." *Nexos*, August 1, 2013. https://nexos.com.mx/?p=15421.

Garza Ramos, Javier. "Under Fire in Mexico: 'They Hit Us.'" *Revista*, June 22, 2011. https://revista.drclas.harvard.edu/under-fire-in-mexico/.

Garza Ramos, Javier. "Violencia contra periodistas en México: De norte a sur." *El País*, July 6, 2015. https://elpais.com/internacional/2015/07/07/actualidad/1436232886_933931.html.

Gibson, Edward L. *Boundary Control: Subnational Authoritarianism in Federal Democracies*. Cambridge: Cambridge University Press, 2013.

Gieryn, Thomas F. "Boundary-Work and the Demarcation of Science from Non-Science: Strains and Interests in Professional Ideologies of Scientists." *American Sociological Review* 48, no. 6 (1983): 781–95.

Gohdes, Anita R., and Sabine C. Carey. "Canaries in a Coal-Mine? What the Killings of Journalists Tell Us About Future Repression." *Journal of Peace Research* 54, no. 2 (2017): 157–74.

Goldman, Francisco. "Who Killed Rubén Espinosa and Nadia Vera?" *New Yorker*, August 14, 2015. https://www.newyorker.com/news/news-desk/who-killed-ruben-espinosa-and-nadia-vera.

Gollmitzer, Mirjam. "Precariously Employed Watchdogs? Perceptions of Working Conditions Among Freelancers and Interns." *Journalism Practice* 8, no. 6 (2014): 826–41.

González de Bustamante, Celeste, and Jeannine E. Relly. "Global Domestic Networks Advancing Prospects for Institutional and Social Change: The Collective Action Response to

BIBLIOGRAPHY

Violence Against Journalists." *Journalism & Communication Monographs* 19, no. 2 (2017): 84–152. https://doi.org/10.1177/1522637917702618.

González de Bustamante, Celeste, and Jeannine E. Relly. "Professionalism Under Threat of Violence: Journalism, Reflexivity, and the Potential for Collective Professional Autonomy in Northern Mexico." *Journalism Studies* 17, no. 6 (2016): 684–702.

González de Bustamante, Celeste, and Jeannine E. Relly. *Surviving Mexico: Resistance and Resilience Among Journalists in the Twenty-First Century*. Austin: University of Texas Press, 2021.

Gould, Terry. *Matar a un periodista: El peligroso oficio de informar*. Barcelona: Los libros del Lince, 2010.

Graham, Thomas. "Mexican Cartels Are Fifth-Largest Employers in the Country, Study Finds." *Guardian*, September 21, 2023. https://www.theguardian.com/world/2023/sep/21/mexico-cartels-fifth-largest-employer-study.

Granados, Miguel Ángel. *Examen de la comunicación en México*. Mexico City: El Caballito, 1981.

Graves, Lucas, and Magda Konieczna. "Qualitative Political Communication| Sharing the News: Journalistic Collaboration as Field Repair." *International Journal of Communication*, no. 9 (2015): 1966–84.

Grecko, Témoris. *Shooting the Messengers: The Dangerous World of Mexican Journalism*. New York: Harper Collins, 2020.

Grillo, Ioan. *Blood Gun Money: How America Arms Gangs and Cartels*. New York: Bloomsbury Publishing, 2021.

Grillo, Ioan. *El Narco: Inside Mexico's Criminal Insurgency*. New York: Bloomsbury Press, 2011.

Grillo, Ioan. *Gangster Warlords: Drug Dollars, Killing Fields, and the New Politics of Latin America*. New York: Bloomsbury Press, 2016.

Guerra, Edgar. "Crueldad y brutalidad en las formas de morir de los periodistas en México: Una aproximación desde la microsociología." *Sociológica* 34, no. 97 (2019): 215–47.

Guerrero, Manuel Alejandro. "Sistemas mediáticos en democracias no consolidadas: El caso de México." *Pangea: Revista de Red Académica Iberoamericana de Comunicación* 11, no. 1 (2020): 5–23.

Guerrero Gutiérrez, Eduardo. "Epidemias de violencia." *Nexos*, July 1, 2012. https://www.nexos.com.mx/?p=14884.

Guerrero Gutiérrez, Eduardo. "La raíz de la violencia." *Nexos*, June 1, 2011. https://www.nexos.com.mx/?p=14318.

Guerrero Gutiérrez, Eduardo. "La segunda ola de violencia." *Nexos*, April 1, 2018. https://www.nexos.com.mx/?p=36947.

Guillermoprieto, Alma. "Mexico: Risking Life for Truth." *New York Review of Books*, November 22, 2012. https://www.nybooks.com/articles/2012/11/22/mexico-risking-life-truth/.

Hallin, Daniel C. "Nota Roja: Popular Journalism and the Transition to Democracy in Mexico." In *Tabloid Tales: Global Debates over Media Standards*, ed. Collin Sparks and John Tulloch, 267–84. Lanham, MD: Rowman & Littlefield, 2000.

Hallin, Daniel C., and Paolo Mancini. *Comparing Media Systems: Three Models of Media and Politics*. Cambridge: Cambridge University Press, 2004.

BIBLIOGRAPHY

Hallin, Daniel C., and Stylianos Papathanassopoulos. "Political Clientelism and the Media: Southern Europe and Latin America in Comparative Perspective." *Media, Culture & Society* 24, no. 2 (2002): 175–95.

Hannerz, Ulf. *Foreign News*. Chicago: University of Chicago Press, 2012.

Harris, Janet, and Kevin Williams. *Reporting War and Conflict*. London: Routledge, 2018.

Harrison, Jackie, and Stefanie Pukallus. "The Politics of Impunity: A Study of Journalists' Experiential Accounts of Impunity in Bulgaria, Democratic Republic of Congo, India, Mexico, and Pakistan." *Journalism* 22, no. 2 (2021): 303–19.

Hernández, Anabel. *El Traidor: El diario secreto del hijo del Mayo*. Mexico City: Penguin Random House, 2019.

Hernández, Saúl. "Las 5 cosas que no sabías y tienes que saber de la guerra en el periodo de Felipe Calderón." *Animal Político*, January 28, 2017. https://www.animalpolitico.com/2017/01/guerra-narco-calderon/.

Hernández Rodriguez, Rogelio. *El centro dividido: La nueva autonomía de los gobernadores*. Mexico City: El Colegio de México, 2008.

Holland, Bradley E., and Viridiana Ríos. "Informally Governing Information: How Criminal Rivalry Leads to Violence Against the Press in Mexico." *Journal of Conflict Resolution* 61, no. 5 (2017): 1095–1119.

Hughes, Sallie L. *Newsrooms in Conflict: Journalism and the Democratization of Mexico*. Pittsburgh: University of Pittsburgh Press, 2006.

Hughes, Sallie L., Laura Iesue, Hilda Fernández de Ortega, Judith Cruz, and José Carlos Lozano. "Coping with Occupational Stress in Journalism: Professional Identities and Advocacy as Resources." *Journalism Studies* 22, no. 8 (2021): 971–91.

Hughes, Sallie L., and Mireya Márquez Ramírez. "Examining the Practices that Mexican Journalists Employ to Reduce Risk in a Context of Violence." *International Journal of Communication*, no. 11 (2017): 499–521.

Hughes, Sallie L., and Mireya Márquez Ramírez. "How Unsafe Contexts and Overlapping Risks Influence Journalism Practice: Evidence from a Survey of Mexican Journalists." In *The Assault on Journalism: Building Knowledge to Protect Freedom of Expression*, ed. Ulla Carlsson and Reeta Pöyhtäri, 303–16. Gothenburg, Sweden: University of Gothenburg, Nordicom, 2017. http://www.unesco.se/wp-content/uploads/2017/04/The-Assault-on-Journalism.pdf.

Hughes, Sallie L., and Mireya Márquez Ramírez. "Local-Level Authoritarianism, Democratic Normative Aspirations, and Antipress Harassment: Predictors of Threats to Journalists in Mexico." *International Journal of Press/Politics* 23, no. 4 (2018): 539–60.

Hughes, Sallie L., Claudia Mellado, Jesús Arroyave, José Luis Benitez, Arnold de Beer, Miguel Garcés, Katharina Lang, and Mireya Márquez Ramírez. "Expanding Influences Research to Insecure Democracies: How Violence, Insecurity, Economic Inequality and Uneven Democratic Performance Shape Journalists' Perceived Work Environments." *Journalism Studies* 18, no. 5 (2017): 645–65.

Hughes, Sallie L., and Yulia Vorobyeva. "Explaining the Killing of Journalists in the Contemporary Era: The Importance of Hybrid Regimes and Subnational Variations." *Journalism* 22, no. 8 (2021): 1873–91.

BIBLIOGRAPHY

Iesue, Laura, Sallie L. Hughes, Sonia Virgina Moreira, and Monica Sousa. "Risk, Victimization and Coping Strategies of Journalists in Mexico and Brazil." *Sur le journalisme, About journalism, Sobre jornalismo* 10, no. 1 (2021): 62–81.

Instituto Nacional de Estadística y Geografía (INEGI). "Estadísticas a propósito del día internacional de la eliminación de la discriminación racial." Press release, March 19, 2020. https://www.inegi.org.mx/contenidos/saladeprensa/aproposito/2020/DISCRIMINAC_NAL.pdf.

Kaldor, Mary. *New and Old Wars: Organized Violence in a Global Era*. Hoboken, NJ: Wiley, 2013.

Kalleberg, Arne L. "Precarious Work, Insecure Workers: Employment Relations in Transition." *American Sociological Review* 74, no. 1 (2009): 1–22.

Kalyvas, Stathis N. *The Logic of Violence in Civil War*. New York: Cambridge University Press, 2006.

Kellam, Marisa, and Elizabeth A. Stein. "Silencing Critics: Why and How Presidents Restrict Media Freedom in Democracies." *Comparative Political Studies* 49, no. 1 (2016): 36–77.

Kitroeff, Natalie, and Ronen Bergman. "El espionaje del ejército mexicano genera temores de un 'Estado militar.'" *New York Times*, March 7, 2023. https://www.nytimes.com/es/2023/03/07/espanol/espionaje-ejercito-pegasus-mexico.html.

Knight, Alan. "México bronco, México manso: Una reflexión sobre la cultura cívica mexicana." *Política y gobierno* 3, no. 1 (1996): 5–30.

"La casa blanca de Enrique Peña Nieto (investigación especial)." *Aristegui Noticias*, November 9, 2014.

Lakhani, Nina, Dana Priest, and Paloma Dupont de Dinechin. "Murder in Mexico: Caught in the Crosshairs." *The Guardian*, December 6, 2020. https://www.theguardian.com/world/2020/dec/06/murder-in-mexico-journalists-caught-in-the-crosshairs-regina-martinez-cartel-project.

Lawson, Chappell. Building the Fourth Estate: Democratization and Media Opening in Mexico. Berkeley: University of California Press, 1999.

Lawson, Chappell. "Mexico's Unfinished Transition: Democratization and Authoritarian Enclaves in Mexico." *Mexican Studies/Estudios Mexicanos* 16, no. 2 (2000): 267–87.

Lewis, Seth C. "The Tension Between Professional Control and Open Participation: Journalism and Its Boundaries." *Information, Communication & Society* 15, no. 6 (2012): 836–66. https://doi.org/10.1080/1369118X.2012.674150.

Lizárraga, Guadalupe. "Policías de Tlapa golpean a periodista de Los Ángeles Press." *Zapateando*, May 15, 2013. https://zapateando.wordpress.com/2013/05/15/policias-de-tlapa-golpean-a-periodista-de-los-angeles-press/.

Lozano, Laura Carolina, and Lucía Suescún Garay. "Significados que reflejan algunos periodistas colombianos tras vivir hechos violentos de censura." Bachelor's thesis. Pontificia Universidad Javeriana, 2020. https://repository.javeriana.edu.co/bitstream/handle/10554/52183/Trabajo%20de%20Grado.pdf?sequence=1&isAllowed=y.

Lugo-Ocando, Jairo, ed. *The Media in Latin America*. London: McGraw-Hill Education, 2008.

Maldonado, Leopoldo. "El delito de ser víctima." *Horizontal*, February 23, 2016.

BIBLIOGRAPHY

Malkin, Elisabeth. "Mexico's Attorney General Resigns Under Pressure." *New York Times*, October 16, 2017. https://www.nytimes.com/2017/10/16/world/americas/mexico-attorney-general-resigns.html.

Malthaner, Stefan. *Fieldwork in the Context of Violent Conflict and Authoritarian Regimes*. New York: Oxford University Press, 2014.

Márquez Ramírez, Mireya. "Post-Authoritarian Politics in a Neoliberal Era: Revising Media and Journalism Transition in Mexico." In *Media Systems and Communication Policies in Latin America*, ed. Manuel Alejandro Guerrero and Mireya Márquez Ramírez, 272–92. London: Palgrave Macmillan, 2014.

Márquez Ramírez, Mireya. "Valores normativos y prácticas de reporteo en tensión: Percepciones profesionales de periodistas en México." *Cuadernos de Información*, no. 30 (2012): 97–110.

Márquez Ramírez, Mireya, and Sallie Hughes. "Panorama de los perfiles demográficos, laborales y profesionales de los periodistas en México: Reporte de Investigación." *Global Media Journal México* 14, no. 26 (2017): 91–152.

Martínez Mendoza, Sarelly, and Diego Noel Ramos Rojas. "Periodismo colaborativo: Tejiendo redes en disputa por la palabra y la agenda informativa." *Comunicación y Sociedad* (2020): 1–22. https://doi.org/10.32870/cys.v2020.7608.

Matthews, Julian, and Kelechi Onyemaobi. "Precarious Professionalism: Journalism and the Fragility of Professional Practice in the Global South." *Journalism Studies* 21, no. 13 (2020): 1836–51.

Mattiace, Shannan, and Sandra Ley. "Yucatán as an Exception to Rising Criminal Violence in México." *Journal of Politics in Latin America* 14, no. 1 (2022): 103–19.

McPherson, Ella. "Spot News Reportage: Newspaper Models, the Distribution of Newsroom Credibility, and Implications for Democratic Journalism in Mexico." *International Journal of Communication* 6, (2012): 2301–17.

Medina, Óscar. "*Zeta*: El periodismo suicida." *Prodavinci*, July 19, 2010. https://historico.prodavinci.com/2010/07/19/actualidad/zeta-el-periodismo-suicida/.

Mellado, Claudia, Sonia Moreira, Claudia Lagos, and María Hernández. "Comparing Cultures in Latin America: The Case of Chile, Brazil, and Mexico." *International Communication Gazette* 74, no. 1 (2012): 60–77.

Mellor, Noha. "Strategies for Autonomy: Arab Journalists Reflecting on Their Roles." *Journalism Studies* 10, no. 3 (2009): 307–21.

Mesquita, Lucia, and Mathias-Felipe de-Lima-Santos. "Blurred Boundaries of Journalism to Guarantee Safety: Approaches of Resistance and Resilience for Investigative Journalism in Latin America." *Journalism Studies* 24, no. 7 (2023): 916–35.

Miranda, Laurel. "Feminismo transfóbico + psicología = 'terapias de conversión.'" *Homosensual*, March 4, 2021. https://www.homosensual.com/lgbt/trans/feminismo-transfobico-psicologia-terapias-de-conversion/.

Nájar, Alberto. "Medios en paro, portadas en negro: La inédita protesta de los periodistas mexicanos al asesinato de Javier Valdez." *BBC Mundo*, May 16, 2017. https://www.bbc.com/mundo/noticias-america-latina-39944188.

BIBLIOGRAPHY

Nerone, John. *Violence Against the Press: Policing the Public Sphere in U.S. History.* New York: Oxford University Press, 1994.

Novak, Rosemary J., and Sarah Davidson. "Journalists Reporting on Hazardous Events: Constructing Protective Factors Within the Professional Role." *Traumatology* 19, no. 4 (2013): 313–22.

Nuestra aparente rendición. "José Antonio García Apac." 2012. http://www.nuestraaparenterendicion.com/tuyyocoincidimosenlanocheterrible/index.php/component/k2/item/60-jose-antonio-garcia-apac#.YVUa_2aA4-Q.

Nuestra aparente rendición. "Tú y yo coincidimos en la noche terrible." 2012. http://www.nuestraaparenterendicion.com/tuyyocoincidimosenlanocheterrible/.

Obermaier, Magdalena, Michaela Hofbauer, and Carsten Reinemann. "Journalists as Targets of Hate: How German Journalists Perceive the Consequences for How They Cope with It." *SCM Studies in Communication and Media* 7, no. 4 (2018): 499–524.

O'Donnell, Guillermo. "On the State, Democratization, and Some Conceptual Problems: A Latin American View with Glances at Some Postcommunist Countries." *World Development* 21, no. 8 (1993): 1355–69.

Olivares, Emir. "La impunidad es de 99.13% en delitos contra periodistas." *La Jornada*, February 26, 2019. https://www.jornada.com.mx/2019/02/26/politica/008n2pol.

Oliver, Laura. "'Illuminate the Darkness': Creating an Independent News Site in Crisis-Hit Venezuela." *Global Investigative Journalism Network*, December 21, 2021. https://gijn.org/independent-news-venezuela/.

Ortiz Garza, José Luis. "Mercenary Writers of British Propaganda in Mexico During the Second World War." Paper presented at the 5th International Conference for Literary Journalism, Roehampton University, London, May 21, 2009.

Osorno, Diego Enrique. "Archivo *VICE*: A cinco años del manantial masacrado." *Vice*, July 17, 2016. https://www.vice.com/es/article/qbqdpq/el-manantial-masacrado.

Osorno, Diego Enrique. "'La masacre de Allende (I),' por @diegoeosorno." *Más por más*, July 7, 2014. https://www.maspormas.com/opinion/la-masacre-de-allende-i-por-diegoeosorno/.

Ostrom, Elinor, and T. K. Ahn. "The Meaning of Social Capital and Its Link to Collective Action." In *Handbook on Social Capital: The Troika of Sociology, Political Science and Economics*, ed. Gert T. Svendsen and Gunnar L. Svendsen, 17–35. Northampton, MA: Edward Elgar, 2009.

Ozawa, Joao, Josephine Lukito, Taeyoung Lee, Anita Varma, and Rosental Alves. "Attacks Against Journalists in Brazil: Catalyzing Effects and Resilience During Jair Bolsonaro's Government." *International Journal of Press/Politics*, July 6, 2023. https://doi.org/10.1177/19401612231182618.

Palmer, Lindsay. *The Fixers: Local News Workers and the Underground Labor of International Reporting.* New York: Oxford University Press, 2019.

Pansters, Will G. "Drug Trafficking, the Informal Order, and Caciques: Reflections on the Crime-Governance Nexus in Mexico." *Global Crime* 19, nos. 3–4 (2018): 315–38.

Parametría. "Estudio completo sobre Libertad de Prensa y Periodismo en México." February 7, 2018. http://www.parametria.com.mx/estudios/estudio-completo-sobre-libertad-de-prensa-y-periodismo-en-mexico/

BIBLIOGRAPHY

Pastrana, Daniela. "*Voz Alterna*: La rebellion del miedo." *Pie de Página*, June 12, 2019. https://piedepagina.mx/voz-alterna-la-rebellion-del-miedo/.

Pate, Umaru A., and Hamza Idris. "How Journalists Survived to Report: Professionalism and Risk Management in the Reporting of Terror Groups and Violent Extremism in North East Nigeria." In *The Assault on Journalism: Building Knowledge to Protect Freedom of Expression*, ed. Ulla Carlsson and Reeta Pöyhtäri, 159–70. Gothenburg, Sweden: University of Gothenburg, Nordicom, 2017. http://www.unesco.se/wp-content/uploads/2017/04/The-Assault-on-Journalism.pdf.

Paterson, Chris. *War Reporters Under Threat: The United States and Media Freedom*. London: Pluto Press, 2014.

Pearson, Mark, Cait McMahon, Analise O'Donovan, and Dustin O'Shannessy. "Building Journalists' Resilience Through Mindfulness Strategies." *Journalism* 22, no. 7 (2021): 1647–64.

Pedelty, Mark. *War Stories: The Culture of Foreign Correspondents*. London: Routledge, 2013.

Pérez Esparza, David, Carlos A. Perez Ricart, and Eugenio Weigend Vargas. *Gun Trafficking and Violence: From the Global Network to the Local Security Challenge*. London: Palgrave Macmillan, 2021.

Periodistas de a Pie. "Quiénes somos." https://periodistasdeapie.org.mx/quienes-somes/.

"Periodistas marchan en el DF: Los queremos vivos (2010)." Nefimanson, August 10, 2010, video, 14:42. https://www.youtube.com/watch?v=5g72tm5DleY.

Piccato, Pablo A. *History of Infamy: Crime, Truth, and Justice in Mexico*. Violence in Latin America in History, 4. Berkeley: University of California Press, 2017.

Piccato, Pablo A. "Murders of Nota Roja: Truth and Justice in Mexican Crime News." *Past and Present* 223, no. 1 (2014): 195–231.

Polit Dueñas, Gabriela. *Unwanted Witnesses: Journalists and Conflict in Contemporary Latin America*. Pittsburgh: University of Pittsburgh Press, 2019.

Powers, Matthew. *NGOs as Newsmakers: The Changing Landscape of International News*. New York: Columbia University Press, 2018.

Powers, Matthew, and Sandra Vera Zambrano. "Explaining the Formation of Online News Startups in France and the United States: A Field Analysis." *Journal of Communication* 66, no. 5 (2016): 857–77. https://doi.org/10.1111/jcom.12253.

Priest, Dana, Paloma de Dinechin, Nina Lakhani, and Veronica Espinosa. "A Murder in Veracruz: Slain Journalist's Story a Portrait of a Violent, Corrupt Era in Mexico." *Washington Post*, December 6, 2020. https://www.washingtonpost.com/graphics/2020/investigations/regina-martinez-mexican-journalist-murdered-veracruz/.

Prieto-Curiel, Rafael, Gian Maria Campedelli, and Alejandro Hope. "Reducing Cartel Recruitment Is the Only Way to Lower Violence in Mexico." *Science* 381, no. 6664 (2023): 1312–16. https://doi.org/10.1126/science.adh2888.

"*Proceso* ante el crimen de Regina Martínez." *Proceso*, April 29, 2012. https://www.proceso.com.mx/regina-martinez/2012/4/29/proceso-ante-el-crimen-de-regina-martinez-101979.html.

Putnam, Robert, Robert Leonardi, and Raffaella Nanetti. *Making Democracy Work: Civic Traditions in Modern Italy*. Princeton: Princeton University Press, 1994.

BIBLIOGRAPHY

Rangel, Azucena. "Incorporando la perspectiva de género en los mecanismos de protección a periodistas en México, Irán y Afganistán." *Milenio*, May 3, 2021. https://www.milenio.com/politica/mujeres-periodistas-victimas-7-tipos-violencia-unesco.

Rea, Daniela. *Nadie les pidió perdón: Historias de impunidad y resistencia.* Barcelona: Ediciones Urano, 2019.

Reese, Stephen. *The Crisis of the Institutional Press.* Cambridge: Polity Press, 2021.

Reina, Elena. "Eduardo Guerrero: 'El narco mexicano no está debilitado, está más fuerte que nunca.'" *El País*, August 21, 2022. https://elpais.com/mexico/2022-08-21/eduardo-guerrero-el-narco-mexicano-no-esta-debilitado-esta-mas-fuerte-que-nunca.html.

Relly, Jeannine E., and Celeste González de Bustamante. "Global and Domestic Networks Advancing Prospects for Institutional and Social Change: The Collective Action Response to Violence Against Journalists." *Journalism & Communication Monographs* 19, no. 2 (2017): 84–152. https://doi.org/10.1177/1522637917702618.

Relly, Jeannine E., and Celeste González de Bustamante. "Silencing Mexico: A Study of Influences on Journalists in the Northern States." *International Journal of Press/Politics* 19, no. 1 (2014): 108–31.

Repnikova, Maria. "Contesting the State Under Authoritarianism: Critical Journalists in China and Russia." *Comparative Politics* 51, no. 1 (2018): 41–60.

Repnikova, Maria. "Critical Journalists in China and Russia." In *Citizens and the State in Authoritarian Regimes: Comparing China and Russia*, ed. Karrie Koesel, Valerie Bunce, and Jessica Weiss. Oxford: Oxford University Press, 2020.

Repnikova, Maria. *Media Politics in China: Improvising Under Authoritarianism.* Cambridge: Cambridge University Press, 2017.

Reporteros Sin Fronteras. "Asesinato de Rubén Pat: 'Las autoridades mexicanas no de-rubén-pat-las-autoridades-mexicanas-no-protegieron-lo-suficiente-al-periodista.

Reporteros Sin Fronteras. "Elecciones en México, manchadas por la violencia contra periodistas." January 20, 2016. https://rsf.org/es/noticias/elecciones-en-mexico-manchadas-por-la-violencia-contra-periodistas.

Reporteros Sin Fronteras. "Un periodista dado por desaparecido." January 20, 2016. https://rsf.org/es/un-periodista-dado-por-desaparecido.

Requejo-Alemán, José Luis, and Jairo Lugo-Ocando. "Assessing the Sustainability of Latin American Investigative Non-Profit Journalism." *Journalism Studies* 15, no. 5 (2014): 522–32. https://doi.org/10.1080/1461670X.2014.885269

Reuters. "Drug Hitmen Kidnap Four Mexican Journalist: Report." July 28, 2010. https://www.reuters.com/article/us-mexico-drugs-idUSTRE66R5VC20100729.

Rey, Germán. "Colombia: Cuatro décadas de violencia." *Infoamérica*, no. 10 (2016): 27–37.

Reyna García, Víctor Hugo. "Journalists as Mobility Agents: Labor Mobilities, Individualized Identities, and Emerging Organizational Forms." *Journalism* 24, no. 2 (2021).

Reyna García, Víctor Hugo. "Más allá de la violencia: La incertidumbre laboral en el periodismo mexicano." *Sur le journalisme, About journalism, Sobre jornalismo* 7, no. 1 (2018): 98–113.

BIBLIOGRAPHY

Robinson, Piers, Peter Goddard, Katy Parry, and Craig Murray. *Pockets of Resistance: British News Media, War, and Theory in the 2003 Invasion of Iraq.* Manchester: Manchester University Press, 2010.

Rodelo, Frida, Mireya Márquez, Grisel Salazar, Celia del Palacio, Martín Echeverría, Armando Gutiérrez, Karles Antonio, Julieta Brambila, Josefina Buxadé, Rubén González, Sallie Hughes, and José Luis Lemini. "Periodistas en México: Encuesta de sus perfiles demográficos, laborales y profesionales." *Global Media Journal México* 20, no. 39 (2023): 110–59. https://doi.org/10.29105/gmjmx20.39-512.

Rodelo, Frida Viridiana. "Periodismo en entornos violentos: el caso de los periodistas de Culiacán, Sinaloa." *Comunicación y sociedad*, no. 12 (2009): 101–18.

Roudakova, Natalia. "Journalism as 'Prostitution': Understanding Russia's Reactions to Anna Politkovskaya's Murder." *Political Communication* 26, no. 4 (2009): 412–29.

Roudakova, Natalia. "Media—Political Clientelism: Lessons from Anthropology." *Media, Culture & Society* 30, no. 1 (2008): 41–59.

Ruiz Parra, Emiliano. "Goyo: En la boca del lobo." *Cosecha roja*, February 7, 2015. https://cosecharoja.org/goyo-en-la-boca-del-lobo/.

Sack, Robert David. *Human Territoriality: Its Theory and History.* Cambridge: Cambridge University Press, 1986.

Salazar Rebolledo, María Grisel. "Aliados estratégicos y los límites de la censura: El poder de las leyes para silenciar a la prensa." *Revista Mexicana de Ciencias Políticas y Sociales* 64, no. 235 (2018): 495–522. http://www.scielo.org.mx/pdf/rmcps/v64n235/0185-1918-rmcps-64-235-495.pdf.

Salazar Rebolledo, María Grisel. "¿Cooptar o reprimir? Intervenciones autoritarias sobre la prensa local mexicana." *América Latina Hoy: Revista de Ciencias Sociales* 84 (2020): 117–36.

Salazar Rebolledo, María Grisel. "Ejercer el periodismo en entornos violentos: Análisis empírico de las zonas de silencio en México." *Perfiles Latinoamericanos* 29, no. 58 (2021). dx.doi.org/10.18504/pl2958-001-2021.

Salazar Rebolledo, María Grisel. *Más allá de la violencia.* Mexico City: CIDE, 2022.

Salazar Rebolledo, María Grisel. "Strategic Allies and the Survival of Critical Media Under Repressive Conditions: An Empirical Analysis of Local Mexican Press." *International Journal of Press/Politics* 24, no. 3 (2019): 341–62.

Saldaña, Magdalena, and Rachel R. Mourão. "Reporting in Latin America: Issues and Perspectives on Investigative Journalism in the Region." *International Journal of Press/Politics* 23, no. 3 (2018): 299–323.

Salmerón Castro, Fernando I. "Caciques: Una revisión teórica sobre el control político local." *Revista Mexicana de Ciencias Políticas y Sociales* 30, nos. 117–18 (1984): 107–41.

Sambrook, Richard, ed. *Global Teamwork: The Rise of Collaboration in Investigative Journalism.* Oxford: Reuters Institute for the Study of Journalism, 2018.

Santiago Hernández, Violeta Alejandra. "Análisis del impacto de la violencia en la situación económica y el ejercicio de la libertad de expresión en un grupo de periodistas veracruzanos." *Anuario de Investigación CONEICC* 1, no. 27 (2020): 22–37.

BIBLIOGRAPHY

Santiago Hernández, Violeta Alejandra. "Periodismo resiliente: El ideal del rol social para ejercer el periodismo en contexto de violencia macrocriminal en México." In *Ecossistema jornalístico*, ed. Liliane Ito e Rita Paulino, 277–98. Lisbon: Ria Editorial, 2021.

Schedler, Andreas. "The Collapse of Solidarity in Criminal Civil War: Citizen Indifference Towards the Victims of Organized Violence in Mexico." Paper presented at the American Political Science Association 2014 Annual Meeting, Washington, DC, September 2014.

Schedler, Andreas. "The Criminal Community of Victims and Perpetrators: Cognitive Foundations of Citizen Detachment from Organized Violence in Mexico." *Human Rights Quarterly* 38, no. 4 (2016): 1038–69.

Schedler, Andreas. "The Criminal Subversion of Mexican Democracy." *Journal of Democracy* 25, no. 1 (2014): 5–18.

Schedler, Andreas. *En la niebla de la Guerra: Los ciudadanos ante la violencia criminal organizada*. Mexico City: CIDE, 2018.

Schedler, Andreas. "The Menu of Manipulation." *Journal of Democracy* 13, no. 2 (2002): 36–50.

Schedler, Andreas, Larry Jay Diamond, and Marc F. Plattner, eds. The Self-Restraining State: Power and Accountability in New Democracies. Boulder, CO: Lynne Rienner Publishers, 1999.

Scherer García, Julio. *Vivir*. Mexico City: Grijalbo, 2012.

Schudson, Michael. "Autonomy from What?" In *Bourdieu and the Journalistic Field*, ed. Rodney Benson and Erik Neveu, 214–23. Cambridge: Polity Press, 2005.

Segura, María Soledad, and Silvio Waisbord. *Media Movements: Civil Society and Media Policy Reform in Latin America*. London: Zed Books, 2016.

Slavtcheva-Petkova, Vera. *Russia's Liberal Media*. New York: Routledge, 2018.

Slavtcheva-Petkova, Vera, Jyotika Ramaprasad, Nina Springer, Sallie Hughes, Thomas Hanitzsch, Basyouni Hamada, Abit Hoxha, and Nina Steindl. "Conceptualizing Journalists' Safety Around the Globe." *Digital Journalism* 11, no. 7 (2023): 1211–29.

Smith, Benjamin T. *The Dope: The Real History of the Mexican Drug Trade*. New York: W. W. Norton, 2021.

Smith, Benjamin T. *The Mexican Press and Civil Society, 1940–1976: Stories from the Newsroom, Stories from the Street*. University of North Carolina Press, 2018.

Smith, Benjamin T. "The Paradoxes of the Public Sphere: Journalism, Gender, and Corruption in Mexico, 1940–70." *Journal of Social History* 52, no. 4 (2019): 1330–54.

Snow, David A. "Grievances, Individual and Mobilizing." In *The Wiley-Blackwell Encyclopedia of Social and Political Movements*, ed. David A. Snow et al. Hoboken, NJ: Wiley, 2013.

Snyder, Richard, and Angélica Durán Martínez. "Drugs, Violence, and State-Sponsored Protection Rackets in Mexico and Colombia." *Colombia Internacional*, no. 70 (2009): 61–91.

Sosa, Luz del Carmen. "Nadie investiga el asesinato de fotógrafo de *El Diario*." *El Diario*, September 16, 2012. https://diario.mx/Local/2012-09-16_ac5b8680/nadie-investiga-el-asesinato—de-fotografo-de-el-diario/.

Stanig, Piero. "Regulation of Speech and Media Coverage of Corruption: An Empirical Analysis of the Mexican Press." *American Journal of Political Science* 59, no. 1 (2015): 175–93. https://doi.org/10.1111/ajps.12110.

BIBLIOGRAPHY

Tarrow, Sidney. "Cycles of Collective Action: Between Moments of Madness and the Repertoire of Contention." *Social Science History* 17, no. 2 (1993): 281–307.

Tarrow, Sidney. *Power in Movement: Social Movements and Contentious Politics.* Cambridge: Cambridge University Press, 2012.

Trejo, Guillermo, and Sandra Ley. *Votes, Drugs, and Violence: The Political Logic of Criminal Wars in Mexico.* Cambridge: Cambridge University Press, 2020.

Trujillo Báez, Norma. "El crimen de Regina Martínez: El teatro de la justicia." Instituto Prensa y Sociedad. https://impunidad.ipys.org/pages/historias/regina-martinez.html.

Trujillo Báez, Norma. "Felipe Calderón y Fidel Herrera ocultaron la violación a Ernestina Ascencio: Perito." *Pie de Página*, February 25, 2020. https://piedepagina.mx/felipe-calderon-y-fidel-herrera-ocultaron-la-violacion-a-ernestina-ascencio-perito/.

Trujillo Báez, Norma. "La geografía de los desaparecidos en Veracruz." *Pie de Página*, June 13, 2019. https://piedepagina.mx/la-geografia-de-los-desaparecidos-en-veracruz/.

Trujillo Báez, Norma. "El sexenio en el que los periodistas repetíamos: 'Nos van a matar.'" *DesInformémonos*, June 2, 2021. https://desinformemonos.org/el-sexenio-en-el-que-los-periodistas-repetiamos-nos-van-a-matar/.

Turati, Marcela. *Fuego cruzado: Las víctimas atrapadas en la guerra del narco.* Mexico City: Grijalbo, 2011.

Urbániková, Marína, and Lenka Haniková. "Coping with the Murder: The Impact of Ján Kuciak's Assassination on Slovak Investigative Journalists." *Journalism Practice* 16, no. 9 (2022): 1927–47.

Valdés Castellanos, Guillermo. *Historia del narcotráfico en México.* Mexico City: Aguilar, 2013.

Valdez Cárdenas, Javier. *Narcoperiodismo: La prensa en medio del crimen y la denuncia.* Madrid: Aguilar, 2016.

Van der Haak, Bregtje, Michael Parks, and Manuel Castells. "The Future of Journalism: Networked Journalism." *International Journal of Communication* 6, no. 16 (2012): 2923–38.

Vandevoordt, Robin. "Covering the Syrian Conflict: How Middle East Reporters Deal with Challenging Situations." *Media, War & Conflict* 9, no. 3 (2016): 306–24.

Vandevoordt, Robin. "Why Journalists Covered Syria the Way They Did: On the Role of Economic, Social, and Cultural Capital." Journalism 18, no. 5 (2017): 609–25.

Varela, Micaela. "El exalcalde de Chihuahua Hugo Schultz, condenado a ocho años de prisión por ayudar a los asesinos de Miroslava Breach." *El País*, June 16, 2021. https://elpais.com/mexico/2021-06-16/el-exalcalde-de-chihuahua-hugo-schultz-condenado-a-ocho-anos-de-prision-por-ayudar-a-los-asesinos-de-miroslava-breach.html.

Vázquez, Juan. "Así te espía el gobierno en internet." Artículo 19, July 23, 2015. https://articulo19.org/asi-te-espia-el-gobierno-en-internet/.

Vázquez, Juan. "Ataques contra medios con explosivos o armas de fuego." Artículo 19, August 4, 2015. https://articulo19.org/ataques-contra-medios-con-explosivos-o-armas-de-fuego/.

Vázquez, Juan. "Lanzan Granada a Instalaciones de Periódico en Coahuila." Artículo 19, July 21, 2011. https://articulo19.org/lanzan-granada-a-instalaciones-de-periodico-en-coahuila/.

BIBLIOGRAPHY

Verza, María. "¿Cómo informar sobre un México corrupto, violento, en guerra? *Ríodoce* da pasos de resistencia." *Sociedad Interamericana de Prensa*, August 4, 2017. https://www.sipiapa.org/notas/1211623-como-informar-un-mexico-corrupto-violento-guerra.

Villamil, Jenaro. "Filtran versión de que asesinato de Regina Martínez fue 'pasional.'" *Proceso*, June 23, 2012. https://www.proceso.com.mx/nacional/2012/6/23/filtran-version-de-que-asesinato-de-regina-martinez-fue-pasional-104649.html.

Voltmer, Katrin. *The Media in Transitional Democracies*. Hoboken, NJ: Wiley, 2013.

Voltmer, Katrin, and Herman Wasserman. "Journalistic Norms Between Universality and Domestication: Journalists' Interpretations of Press Freedom in Six New Democracies." *Global Media and Communication* 10, no. 2 (2014): 177–92. https://doi.org/10.1177/1742766514540073.

Waisbord, Silvio. "Antipress Violence and the Crisis of the State." *Harvard International Journal of Press/Politics* 7, no. 3 (2002): 90–109.

Waisbord, Silvio. "Between Support and Confrontation: Civic Society, Media Reform, and Populism in Latin America." *Communication, Culture & Critique* 4, no. 1 (2011): 97–117.

Waisbord, Silvio. "Center for Media at Risk Launch Symposium, Panel 4: Journalism." Annenberg School for Communication Annenberg School for Communication, May 23, 2018. Video, 2:12:15. https://www.youtube.com/watch?v=TsnVBVMijVY&t=2878s.

Waisbord, Silvio. "Democratic Journalism and 'Statelessness.'" *Political Communication* 24, no. 2 (2007): 115–29.

Waisbord, Silvio. "Mob Censorship: Online Harassment of US Journalists in Times of Digital Hate and Populism." *Digital Journalism* 8, no. 8 (2020): 1030–46.

Waisbord, Silvio. "The Vulnerabilities of Journalism." *Journalism* 20, no. 1 (2019): 210–13.

Waisbord, Silvio. *Watchdog Journalism in South America: News, Accountability, and Democracy*. New York, Columbia University Press, 2000.

World Justice Project. "Cuánta Tortura: Prevalencia de violencia ilegal en el proceso penal mexicano 2006–2016." 2019. https://worldjusticeproject.mx/wp-content/uploads/2019/11/GIZ-Reporte_Cuánta-Tortura.pdf.

Yousuf, Mohammad, and Maureen Taylor. "Helping Syrians Tell Their Story to the World: Training Syrian Citizen Journalists Through Connective Journalism." *Journalism Practice* 11, nos. 2–3 (2017): 302–18.

Zelizer, Barbie. "Terms of Choice: Uncertainty, Journalism, and Crisis." *Journal of Communication* 65, no. 5 (2015): 888–908.

Zepeda, Mayra. "Atacan instalaciones de Grupo Reforma y El Mañana." *Animal Político*, July 11, 2012. https://www.animalpolitico.com/2012/07/atacan-instalaciones-de-grupo-reforma-y-el-manana/.

Zepeda Gil, Raúl. "Violencia en Tierra Caliente: Desigualdad, desarrollo y escolaridad en la guerra contra el narcotráfico." *Estudios sociológicos* 36, no. 106 (2018): 125–59.

Zuckermann, Leo. "Los nuevos virreyes." *Proceso*, April 28, 2004.

INDEX

Acapulco, Guerrero, 87, 156
agency, 221; and field theory, 23, 120, 153; paradox of embedded agency, 22
Agenda de Periodistas, 56, 150, 176, 178, 194; and its meeting in Mexico City, 151, 152, 155
Aguayo, Sergio, 34, 35, 69, 75, 99
Allende, Coahuila, 103, 116
Angel of Independence monument, 4; social protests at, 150, 174
Animal Político (Mexico), 150, 171
Argentina, 195
Artículo 19, 4, 7, 65, 74–76, 89, 95, 98, 99, 107, 122, 191, 204, 205, 207, 209, 223

Baja California (state), 45, 89. *See also* Tijuana
Baja California Sur (state), 46, 205
Barrón, Eliseo, 53, 54, 57, 65, 178
Bjørnskov, Christian, 36

Boko Haram, 197
Bourdieu, Pierre, 22, 24; and the field of journalism, 17
Brazil, 199, 200, 202
Breach, Miroslava, 65, 150, 210, 261n109
Bukele, Nayib, 199

Cacho, Lydia, 82
caciques, 35, 39, 91, 92, 95, 109, 137, 189, 191
Calderón, Felipe, 7, 43, 45, 46, 175
Canché, Pedro, 83
Caparrós, Martín, 129
capital, as defined by Bourdieu, 23. *See also* cultural capital; organizational capital; social capital; symbolic capital
Cartel de Sinaloa, 42, 54, 105, 107, 173
Cartel del Golfo, 43, 102
Castellanos, Francisco, 31, 94, 126
Castells, Manuel, 153
cautious journalism, 16, 17, 25, 27, 119, 131, 144, 161, 181, 198

INDEX

censorship, 9, 10, 12, 27, 37, 66, 93, 101, 102, 106, 115, 121, 162, 195, 196, 204, 206, 207; censors, 10, 91, 92, 103, 111, 188, 207, 249n16; criminal censorship, 193; environmental censorship, 94; mob censorship, 63, 95; self-censorship, 47, 66, 93–95, 140, 147, 156, 191–93, 202

Chamorro Cardenal, Joaquín, 203

Chiapas (state), 67, 89, 109, 182

Chihuahua (state), 42, 45, 57, 65, 88, 89, 132, 150, 182. *See also* Ciudad Juárez

Chile, 196, 201

China, 17, 196, 197

Ciudad Juárez, Chihuahua, 9, 15, 18, 20, 42, 44, 104, 106, 107, 124, 129, 145, 173, 174, 178, 182, 183, 190

Ciudad Victoria, Tamaulipas, 102, 105, 106, 134, 145, 146, 171

civic-minded journalism, 16, 17, 36, 132, 171, 182; civic-minded journalists, 3, 6, 9, 165; as Mexican style, 21, 34; and resilient newsmakers, 25, 27

Coahuila (state), 51, 57, 89, 99, 115, 116, 131, 146, 171, 178, 182. *See also* Allende; La Laguna; Piedras Negras

Coatzacoalcos, Veracruz, 1–6

collective strategies for autonomous safety, 122, 140, 143, 197; collective monitoring, 144, 145; collective news agenda, 144, 146; collective reporting and publishing, 145, 146; news sharing, 147, 148

collective strategies of resistance, 155, 177, 197; collective professionalization, 181, 182; emergency responders, 181, 183; lobbying, 175, 181, 185, 186; social protest, 173, 174–76, 181, 184, 185

Colombia, 65, 110, 135, 174, 198, 199, 201, 202, 211

Comisión Nacional de Derechos Humanos, 77, 223

Committee to Protect Journalists, 103, 170

control strategies used by governors, 40

Cortez, Edgar, 67, 71, 74

Costa Rica, 199

COVID-19, 8, 158, 204, 205, 263n25

critical journalism, 40, 69, 132, 165, 188, 195, 203; concept of, 16; critical Chinese and Russian journalists, 197; critical journalists, 10, 16, 26, 181, 182, 192, 195, 196, 212; practicing critical journalism, 9, 13, 34, 39, 94, 209

critical news startups, 23, 48, 140, 142–44, 166, 193; *La Marea*, 141, 142, 144; *Voz Alterna*, 141, 142, 144, 178, 186

critical press, 8, 34, 36, 98, 187, 188, 195, 201, 212

cronistas, 4, 19, 115, 129, 145

Cuba, 199

Culiacán, Sinaloa, 91, 97, 98, 102, 104, 119, 124, 135, 149, 169, 224, 234

cultural capital, 23, 26, 85, 86, 118, 122, 156, 158, 161

Davidson, Sarah, 16, 154, 159, 252n9

Der Spiegel (Germany), 200

Duarte, Javier, 1, 125, 161, 162

Durango (state), 45, 54, 65, 89, 131, 139. *See also* Gómez Palacio

democracy: electoral, 34, 35, 187; insecure, 13, 32, 120; unsafe, 33, 36, 187

Ecatepec, Estado de México, 145

Ecuador, 199

Efecto Coyuyo (Venezuela), 199

Egypt, 196

El Diario de Juárez (Chihuahua), 9, 15, 22, 41, 42, 47, 95, 107, 124, 128, 132, 136, 138, 142, 166

El Faro (El Salvador), 199

El Imparcial (Oaxaca), 161, 184, 210

El Informador (Jalisco), 126, 135

El Mañana (Tamaulipas), 105, 171

INDEX

El Norte (Nuevo León), 105, 171
El País (Spain), 165
El Salvador, 196
El Siglo de Torreón (Coahuila), 105, 130, 131–34, 138, 139, 146, 166, 167, 194
El Universal (Mexico), 125, 140, 173
electoral authoritarianism, 31, 32, 34, 36, 48, 56, 94, 96, 99, 249n16
Encinas, Alejandro, 210
Espejo (Sinaloa), 24, 128, 142
Espinoza, Rubén, 65, 75, 141, 157, 178
Estado de México (state), 51, 101, 109, 146, 177. *See also* Ecatepec
Excélsior (Mexico), 171
Expreso (Tamaulipas), 105, 170, 171

Fiscalía Especial para la Atención de Delitos Cometidos contra la Libertad de Expresión (FEADLE), 69, 70, 74–78, 210, 211
Flores, Balbina, 33–35, 75
Foucault, Michel, 153
Fox, Vicente, 39, 45
France, 23, 142
Freedom House, 71, 122, 174
Freytag, Andreas, 36
Fuentes, Carlos, 153

Garza, Javier, 89, 130, 131–34, 139, 146, 167
Gatopardo (Mexico), 130
Gibson, Edward, 39
Gobierno Espía, 99; and malware Pegasus, 100, 208
Gómez Palacio, Durango, 173
González de Bustamante, Celeste, 79, 181, 193, 264n1
Grillo, Ioan, 42, 83, 127, 145, 253n35
Grupo Prensa Oaxaca, 177, 178, 182, 184, 186
Guadalajara, Jalisco, 101, 104, 145, 146, 184
Guardian, The, 165, 200

Guerrero (state), 45, 66, 83, 87–89, 100, 109, 126, 156, 157, 185, 207. *See also* Acapulco; La Montaña
Guerrero, Eduardo, 206

Hermosillo, Sonora, 75
Hernández López, Julio, 37, 38, 56, 106, 164
Hernández, Anabel, 51
Hughes, Sallie, 13, 18, 21, 37, 40, 62, 93, 155, 159, 252n9, 264n1; civic-minded journalism defined by, 16; civic-oriented newsrooms defined by, 192

Instituto Nacional de Estadística y Geografía, 83, 206
International Consortium of Investigative Journalists, 201
interviews, with newsmakers, 9, 190, 191, 193
Iraq, 198; invasion of, 65; occupation of, 121

Jalisco (state), 44, 51, 68, 88, 126, 135. *See also* Guadalajara
Jiménez Mota, Alfredo, 75, 178, 210
Joint Operation Chihuahua, 42, 44
journalists: belong to sexual or gender minorities, 62, 82, 83, 188; bill that protects journalists, 165, 186; and civic allies, 24, 85, 87, 118, 177, 181, 184, 185, 225; displaced journalists, 73, 157, 160, 163; groups of renegade journalists, 14; journalistic vocation, 8, 26, 143, 159, 160, 203, 212; most violent year for, 205; professional values of, 26, 34, 48, 55, 154, 158, 159, 193, 194, 198, 203, 212, 213; and resistance movements, 176–81, 183, 184; in situations of stress, 66, 137, 154, 158, 159, 168, 193, 202; social recognition of, 155, 160; total number of murdered journalists in Mexico, 7; war correspondents, 6, 21, 66, 183; women journalists, 81, 82, 188, 173, 200, 203, 204, 246n73

INDEX

journalism: business model of, 14, 34, 40, 49, 143; the field of, 5, 6, 10, 19, 20, 25, 31, 32, 57, 80, 83, 118, 164, 187, 203; future of, 193; Mexican journalism, 16, 47, 48, 53, 54, 93, 96, 130, 149, 175, 177, 196; narco-politics as a topic of, 54, 84, 101, 119, 125, 128, 162, 163; and objectivity, 156, 164, 172; present-day journalism, 203

Jiménez de la Cruz, Gregorio, 1–6, 12, 19, 20, 53, 174, 178; "El Pantera" pseudonym of, 2; #QueremosGoyoVivo hashtag for, 3; #LoQueremosVivo hashtag for, 3; #DóndeEstáGoyo hashtag for, 3

Kaldor, Mary, 42
Kenya, 198

La Jornada (Mexico), 84, 125, 137, 149, 171, 205, 223–25
La Laguna, Coahuila, 105
La Montaña, Guerrero, 84, 87
Lara Klahr, Marco, 64, 86
Lebanon, 196
Libya, 198
López Obrador, Andrés Manuel, 70; daily morning press conferences of, 96, 207
Los queremos vivos, 173–76, 261n109

macho culture, 81, 83
Márquez, Mireya, 18, 40, 166, 172, 264n1
Martínez, Regina, 79, 81, 102, 135, 147, 161, 162, 178, 234; and Cartel Project, 165; Regina Square, 164
Matamoros, Tamaulipas, 102, 124, 171
Mazatlán, Sinaloa, 48, 100
Mecanismo de Protección para Personas Defensoras de Derechos Humanos y Periodistas, 69, 70–74, 78, 90, 95, 157, 158, 175, 205, 208, 209
Medellín de Bravo, Veracruz, 76
Mejía Lechuga, Jesús, 65

Mérida Initiative, 7
Mexican army, 43, 107, 208
México bronco, 6
Mexico City, 1, 3, 4, 13, 58, 72, 74, 76, 79, 80–90, 98, 133, 137, 148, 150, 151, 156, 157, 161, 164, 169, 172, 173, 184, 185, 190, 204, 205, 234
Mexico Drug War, 7, 175
Michoacán (state), 13, 45, 46, 55, 66, 84, 89, 94, 102, 109, 137, 168, 178, 180, 186. *See* Morelia; Nueva Italia; Tierra Caliente
Milenio (México), 130, 147, 225; in Guadalajara, 146; as national television broadcasters, 139; in Torreón, 54
Moreira, Humberto, 99
Morelia, Michoacán, 31, 50, 57, 85, 101, 104, 110, 161, 224
Monterrey, Nuevo León, 18, 51, 61, 62, 77, 90, 100, 105, 115, 116
Movimiento de Regeneración Nacional, 101

Nayarit (state), 45, 205
Nerone, John, 11, 12, 63, 88, 92–94, 104, 105, 189
New York Times, 130, 200, 208
Nicaragua, 199
Noroeste (Sinaloa), 125, 132, 138, 140, 160, 166, 167, 169, 170, 172
Norway, 198
Novak, Rosemary, 16, 154, 159, 197, 252n9
Novaya Gazeta (Russia), 198
Nueva Italia, Michoacán, 106
Nuevo Laredo, Tamaulipas, 66, 102, 105, 123, 124, 134, 171
Nuevo León (state), 45, 51, 61, 72, 77, 89, 168, 171, 182, 184. *See also* Monterrey

Oaxaca (state), 17, 57, 65, 88, 89, 100, 109, 127, 128, 130, 159, 160, 161, 169, 179
organizational capital, 24, 85, 118, 130, 161, 164, 237n48

INDEX

organizational strategies for autonomous safety, 121, 135; anonymous publication, 137, 138; organizational training, 134, 135; management monitoring as an, 136; strategic news frames, 138, 139
organizational strategies of resistance, 155; emergency assistance and support, 168–72; precautionary measures, 165–67
Osorno, Diego Enrique, 6, 9, 20, 129, 130, 150
Osorno, Guillermo, 56, 150, 151, 186

Página 3 (Oaxaca), 128, 142, 256n2
Panama Papers, 201
Partido Revolucionario Institucional (PRI) 32, 45, 96, 101, 110, 161, 188; authoritarian regime of, 9; *priismo* and, 37
Pastrana, Daniela, 2, 3, 53, 173, 175, 179, 180, 181, 183
Pax Mafiosa, 42
Peña Nieto, Enrique, 45, 234; La Casa Blanca of, 193,
Periodistas de a Pie, 3, 53, 122, 141, 172, 173–76, 180–83
personal strategies for autonomous safety, 121, 123; discursive literary practices, 125, 129, 130; extreme vetting, 125, 127, 128, 138; logistical foresight, 125, 127, 129, 197; strategic self-censorship, 117, 125, 132, 138, 197, 252n9
personal strategies of resistance, 155; learning precautionary actions, 160, 161; meaningful resistance, 158–60
Peru, 196, 199, 201
Piccato, Pablo, 19
Piedras Negras, Coahuila, 116
Prensa, no disparen, 4–6, 12, 20, 21, 24, 174, 176
Proceso (Mexico), 19, 24, 39, 74, 79, 90, 132, 135, 137, 138, 147, 161, 162, 164, 165, 172
Puebla (state), 46, 89

Puerto Rico, 196, 199
Putin, Vladimir, 197, 198
Putnam, Robert, 180

Quintana Roo (state), 46, 73, 83, 89, 205

Ramos, Antonio, 84–86
Red de Periodistas de Juárez, 16, 20, 56, 175, 178, 180, 182, 183
Red de Periodistas Noroeste, 117, 118, 179, 182
Reforma (Mexico), 3, 45, 55, 132, 133, 136, 137, 168, 169, 173
Relly, Jeannine, 80, 181, 193, 264n1
Repnikova, María, 17, 196, 197
Reporters Without Borders, 4, 7, 33, 74, 75, 205
Resiliencia, 16, 195
Reynosa, Tamaulipas, 102, 124
Ríodoce (Sinaloa), 91, 124, 125, 128, 135, 138, 149, 172
Rodelo, Frida Viridiana, 17, 264n1
Rodríguez, Armando, 15, 173, 178
Rodríguez Castañeda, Rafael, 39, 79, 162
Ruiz Parra, Emiliano, 2, 4, 5, 20, 129
Russia, 17, 65, 81, 196, 197, 198

Salazar, Grisel, 24, 40, 41, 193; study of repression of the press in Latin America, 101
Santiago, Luis Carlos, 15, 178
Schedler, Andreas, 32, 42, 57, 58, 68, 153
Scherer, Julio, 32, 42, 57, 58, 161, 162, 164
Seattle, 142
Secretaría de Gobernación, 70–74, 95, 157, 174, 175, 205, 210, 211
Secretaría de la Defensa Nacional, 117
Segura, María Soledad, 24, 176, 185
self-defense groups, 7, 35, 46, 92, 95, 97, 109–11, 169, 189
Sinaloa (state), 17, 24, 45, 55, 89, 125, 140, 150, 152, 160, 166, 167, 169, 178. *See also* Culiacán; Mazatlán

INDEX

Smith, Benjamin, 12, 94, 99, 248n16
social capital, 24, 27, 85, 86, 111, 118, 122, 140, 154, 156, 164, 172, 178, 180, 200, 212, 213
Sociedad Interamericana de Prensa, 4, 52
Sonora (state), 166, 210. *See also* Hermosillo
Sudan, 198
symbolic capital, 23, 24, 118, 142, 147, 164
Syria, 23, 65, 119, 196

Tamaulipas (state), 45, 51, 57, 66, 72, 88, 89, 103, 115, 116, 124, 127, 134, 146, 147, 159, 166, 171, 180, 182, 205. *See* Ciudad Victoria; Matamoros; Nuevo Laredo; Reynosa; Tampico
Tampico, Tamaulipas, 104, 105, 171
Televisa, 49, 139, 171
Tierra Caliente, Michoacán, 84, 85, 87, 137
Tijuana, Baja California, 65, 132, 138, 174, 198
Trujillo, Norma, 125, 141, 142

Ukraine, 198
United States, 23, 89, 98, 127, 131, 133, 152, 180, 187, 197; arms from, 43; army, 200; cocaine market in, 43; diplomatic cables from the government of, 117; drug market in, 195; global chains linked to, 87; history of violence against the press in, 12, 88, 93; New Journalism in, 20; trials of drug traffickers in, 118; U.S. Agency for International Development, 69, 71, 117, 122. *See also* Seattle; Washington, DC

Valdez, Javier, 9, 91, 129, 135, 149–52, 155, 178, 210, 261n109, 264n1
Venezuela, 199
Veracruz (state), 4, 45, 52, 53, 57, 66, 67, 74, 81, 88, 89, 107, 116, 140, 141, 142, 155, 159, 166, 178, 182–84, 186, 205. *See also* Coatzacoalcos; Medellín de Bravo; Villa Allende; Xalapa (capital)
Villa Allende, Veracruz, 1–3
Voces Irritilas, 178, 182

Waisbord, Silvio, 12, 24, 67, 95, 176, 185, 194
Walsh, Rodolfo, 195, 196
Washington, DC, 133
Washington Post, 165
Wikileaks, 117, 200
World Press Freedom Index, 205
Worlds of Journalism Mexico poll, 203, 205, 208, 211, 263n25

Xalapa, Veracruz, 3, 79, 104, 161, 174

Yucatán (state), 46, 89, 205

Zavaleta, Noé, 147, 164
Zelizer, Barbie, 14
Zeta (Tijuana), 132, 138, 198
Zetas, Los, 51, 116, 117, 131; and the Cartel del Golfo 43, 102; crónica about, 130; and the Cartel de Sinaloa, 54, 105

www.ingramcontent.com/pod-product-compliance
Lightning Source LLC
Jackson TN
JSHW081257070125
76712JS00002B/7